Essential French Gra

Teach Yourself®

Essential French Grammar

Robin Adamson

European Languages and Studies
University of Western Australia

and

Brigitte Edelston

Communication and Language Studies
University of Dundee

For UK order enquiries: please contact Bookpoint Ltd,
130 Milton Park, Abingdon, Oxon OX14 4SB.
Telephone: +44 (0) 1235 827720. *Fax:* +44 (0) 1235 400454.
Lines are open 09.00–17.00, Monday to Saturday, with a 24-hour
message answering service. Details about our titles and how to
order are available at www.teachyourself.com

For USA order enquiries: please contact McGraw-Hill Customer
Services, PO Box 545, Blacklick, OH 43004-0545, USA.
Telephone: 1-800-722-4726. *Fax:* 1-614-755-5645.

For Canada order enquiries: please contact McGraw-Hill
Ryerson Ltd, 300 Water St, Whitby, Ontario L1N 9B6, Canada.
Telephone: 905 430 5000. *Fax:* 905 430 5020.

Long renowned as the authoritative source for self-guided learning –
with more than 50 million copies sold worldwide – the
Teach Yourself series includes over 500 titles in the fields of
languages, crafts, hobbies, business, computing and education.

British Library Cataloguing in Publication Data: a catalogue record
for this title is available from the British Library.

Library of Congress Catalog Card Number: on file.

First published in UK 1998 by Hodder Education, part of Hachette
UK, 338 Euston Road, London NW1 3BH, as *Teach Yourself
French Grammar*.

First published in US 1998 by The McGraw-Hill Companies, Inc.

This edition published 2010.

The *Teach Yourself* name is a registered trade mark of
Hodder Headline.

Copyright © 1998, 2003, 2010 Robin Adamson and
Brigitte Edelston

Typeset by MPS Limited, A Macmillan Company.

Printed in Great Britain for Hodder Education, an Hachette
UK Company, 338 Euston Road, London NW1 3BH.

The publisher has used its best endeavours to ensure that the URLs
for external websites referred to in this book are correct and active
at the time of going to press. However, the publisher and the
author have no responsibility for the websites and can make no
guarantee that a site will remain live or that the content will remain
relevant, decent or appropriate.

Hachette UK's policy is to use papers that are natural, renewable
and recyclable products and made from wood grown in sustainable
forests. The logging and manufacturing processes are expected to
conform to the environmental regulations of the country of origin.

Impression number   10 9 8 7 6 5 4 3 2 1
Year   2014 2013 2012 2011 2010

Contents

Abbreviations

masc./m.	masculine
fem./f.	feminine
sing.	singular
plu./pl.	plural
infinit./inf.	infinitive
past.part/pp	past participle
pt.p	present participle
Q	question
A	answer

Credits

Front cover: © Oxford Illustrators

Back cover and pack: © Jakub Semeniuk/iStockphoto.com, © Royalty-Free/Corbis, © agencyby/iStockphoto.com, © Andy Cook/iStockphoto.com, © Christopher Ewing/iStockphoto.com, © zebicho – Fotolia.com, © Geoffrey Holman/iStockphoto.com, © Photodisc/Getty Images, © James C. Pruitt/iStockphoto.com, © Mohamed Saber – Fotolia.com

Pack: © Stockbyte/Getty Images

Meet the authors

Robin fell in love early with French and has lived and studied in France and taught at all levels, but mainly in universities. She was the foundation Director of the Centre for Applied Language Studies at the University of Dundee, creating the innovative programme of communicative language teaching and setting up exchanges with French universities so that she could spend as much time in France as possible.

Brigitte comes from St Amand in the north of France. After studying English, she began to teach French to English speakers in Scotland, specializing in communicative methodologies and in comparisons between the two languages. She has taught French to students at many levels and done postgraduate work in teaching languages to adults. She is now the Convener of Languages at the University of Dundee.

We have enjoyed teaching French together for nearly 20 years. We are convinced that the best approach to learning a foreign language is to have two teachers – one who speaks your own language and a native speaker. Our students – undergraduates, school pupils, primary school teachers and postgraduates – have always appreciated our double act and we hope you will too.

And our Franco-Scottish background explains why the story that underpins our grammar involves a visit from a Scottish family to their son's future in-laws in St Amand. It was a pleasure preparing this book for you and we hope you'll enjoy following the story and learning **Essential French grammar** with us.

Only got a minute?

French is, after English, the world's second most popular language with foreign learners. Because it is the modern language that has had most influence on English, English speakers start with a definite advantage.

French is: a romance language; spoken on all five continents; spoken in over 50 countries; an official language of many international agencies, including the United Nations and the European Union; the language of fashion, wine and food; the language of international trade and diplomacy.

Most French words come from Latin, and many of them later came from French into English so they will be familiar to you. The grammar also has similarities to English and other Indo-European languages in terms of: word order; sentence construction; verb tenses.

Luckily for you, you won't need to learn many new grammatical concepts, but you will have to add some details to the English grammar you already know. For example:

- All French nouns have gender (masculine or feminine) and number (singular or plural).
- Everything in a sentence that relates to each noun – articles, adjectives, verbs – must show the gender (grammatical agreement) and number (number agreement) of the noun.
- French has nine subject pronouns and six verb forms that agree with them.
- French has three past tenses doing different jobs from the English past tenses. It does not have the continuous tenses (verbs with a word ending in *-ing*, for example: *I am reading*) which are so common in English.
- French uses the subjunctive much more than English.

In this book, we'll guide you through all the French grammar you need, so that by the end you'll have mastered the essential aspects of the language and be able to use it with confidence.

5 Only got five minutes?

French is the world's second most popular language with foreign learners. It is a romance language, spoken on all five continents and in over 50 countries. It is an official language of many international agencies, of the United Nations and of course of the European Union. French is the language of fashion, wine and food, and of international trade and diplomacy. If you want to speak and write French with pleasure and confidence beyond the tourist level, you will need a secure knowledge of the grammar.

This book will show you that grammar can be enjoyable as well as useful. It will take you through the structures you need to move your accuracy, fluency and confidence in both spoken and written French to a new and exciting level.

Because French is the modern language that has had most influence on English, English speakers start with definite advantages in vocabulary and grammar. You will find more about this on our web pages at www.teachyourself.com and on http://french.about.com/. Pronunciation, however, can be a problem, so you will need to work on it using recordings and the Internet and through contact with native speakers. In this book about French grammar, we have limited the vocabulary so that you will find the grammatical examples easier to understand, and we have not attempted to cover the details of pronunciation.

Most French words come from Latin, and many of them later came from French into English so they will be familiar to you (for example *abdication, abdomen, lieutenant, limitation, lingerie, magazine, mannequin, referendum, refuge*). Spelling can cause difficulties though, particularly learning to use essential accents (for example **étudiant, problème, français, pâté, naïve**).

An important feature for English speakers learning French is **agreement** – an essential and reassuring aspect of French grammar. All French nouns have masculine or feminine gender, even though this may not seem logical: for example **le château** (*the castle*), **la maison** (*the house*). They also have number (singular or plural). Everything in a sentence that relates to each noun – articles, adjectives, verbs – will usually show the noun's gender (gender agreement: **le beau château, la belle maison**) and its number (number agreement: **deux beaux châteaux, trois belles maisons**). Once you've mastered the agreement patterns, you'll wonder how English does without them.

Pronouns need to be fitted into a web of agreements too. When you're learning French verbs, you will have to adjust to the idea of nine subject pronouns and make sure that every verb changes to agree with them, usually by changing the ending: for example **je chante** (*I sing*), **vous chantez** (*you sing*).

French **verbs** also have endings that change for each subject depending on the tense, for example **je chante/nous chantons** (*I/we sing*), **je chantais/vous chantiez** (*I/you used to sing*), **je chanterai/ils chanteront** (*I/they shall/will sing*). Regular verbs may end in **-er, -ir** or **-re** and they follow three predictable patterns. But many verbs, especially the most common, are irregular and each one has to be learned! French has three past tenses doing different jobs from the English past tenses, and it does not have the compound continuous tenses (verbs with a word ending in *-ing*, for example *I am reading*) which are so common in English. It uses the subjunctive much more than English.

Adjectives in French are a key element in mastering the language. Apart from adjusting them to their noun by following the pattern of agreements, you may find their place in the sentence is different in French (**le château français, la ville anglaise**).

Once you have learned to use – and love – all these features of the grammar, you can be confident that you can enjoy using the rich expressive resources of French in any situation.

10 Only got ten minutes?

Because French is the world's second most popular language (after English) with foreign learners, there is a mass of information available to help you in the early stages. This book is for the next step: it will give you all the essential grammar you need to move your accuracy, fluency and confidence in both spoken and written French to a new level. For other aspects of learning French, you will need to supplement the book with our web pages (www.teachyourself.com), other French language websites (for example http://french.about.com/), books, recordings and computer programs.

As a romance language, French is closely connected to other European languages such as Spanish and Italian. It is spoken on all five continents and in over 50 countries and is an official language of many international agencies: the European Union and the Council of Europe, the United Nations, the OECD, the Red Cross, the Olympic Games, UNESCO and NATO. French can open new horizons for you. It is considered to be the language of culture, art, music, literature, fashion, wine and food, and of international trade and diplomacy. If you want to speak and write French with pleasure and confidence in areas like these, a secure knowledge of the grammar is essential. The grammar in this book is presented in an enjoyable way to help you reach the high level you are aiming for.

We recommend that you start a notebook when you begin this course – either set it up on your computer or buy one specially as your trusty learning companion. At various points in the book, we will suggest what you need to make a note of, and gradually you will have ideas of your own about how to create your personal grammar support system.

Vocabulary

As a speaker of English, you will already have realized that you have a head start in recognizing and understanding French words. Because of their shared history, particularly their derivation from Latin, English and French have many words in common and the basic features of grammar are not radically different. However, there are challenging differences in pronunciation and spelling and you will have to work on these as well as on the grammar in this book. Because we are concentrating on grammar in this book, we have limited the vocabulary to the context of the storyline. You will need to do extra work on new vocabulary in the areas you are interested in – reading French on-screen or from books and newspapers and making lists in your notebook as you go.

Make alphabetical, subject and gender lists of French words that are familiar to you and keep adding to your lists as your French improves. You will notice that some areas of English vocabulary are very close to French: for example food (**le menu, le restaurant, le café, la casserole, le dîner, le champagne**) and fashion (**la mode, la robe, la blouse, le mannequin, le bouton, le costume, la cravate, l'uniforme**). Be sure to check the spelling and find out if the meaning is the same in both languages. Another list of false friends (for example **la casserole, le costume**) might be helpful.

Pronunciation

Mastering where to put the emphasis in words, and learning to pronounce nasal sounds and other vowels, will certainly repay the effort. You can get help with pronunciation from other books in this series, from the Internet, from French films on DVD and by meeting and talking to native speakers.

Spelling

The accents, which seem very fiddly to English speakers, are vitally important, especially for pronunciation. They are possibly the biggest spelling problem for English speakers. Knowing this, you may want to start by preparing a section of your notebook where you note accented words as you meet them. From your lists work out:

▶ which accents are most frequent
▶ which letters are most often accented.

Two practical tips:

▶ Practise writing accented words, adding the accents as you go, rather than reaching the end of the word and then going back to add them.
▶ You will need to find out how your word-processing program produces accents, adding the accents as you type.

Grammar

French grammar has many similarities to English – this makes the differences all the more tricky and important. Here are a few of the more interesting points of French grammar that this book will help you to use with confidence.

AGREEMENT

One of the reassuring characteristics of French is the network of agreements that holds sentences together:

▶ All French nouns have masculine or feminine gender, even though this may not seem logical: for example **le livre** (*the book*), **la bibliothèque** (*the library*). When you learn a noun, be sure to learn its gender at the same time.

▶ Other words in the sentence that relate to each noun show this relationship by taking the noun's gender (gender agreement: **ce livre français est intéressant; la grande bibliothèque ouvre à 11 heures**) and its number – singular or plural (number agreement: **les livres nouveaux sont arrivés; les bibliothèques universitaires ouvrent à neuf heures**).

When you get used to this comforting network, you'll wonder why English doesn't do the same thing!

PRONOUNS

▶ French uses many types of pronoun – subject, object, relative, possessive – and they also fit into the web of agreements binding the parts of a sentence together.
▶ You'll have to learn to use nine different subject pronouns – instead of seven in English – and change the verb to agree with them. Usually you do this by changing the ending: **je lis; vous lisez; nous lisons**.
▶ Object pronouns (**ils le lisent**) can also play a role in developing the web of agreements. As you will see, they follow strict rules of word order.

VERBS

▶ The infinitives of French verbs show by their endings (**-er, -ir, -re**) which of three predictable patterns they follow. You'll need some more lists to help you learn the endings for each type of infinitive.
▶ Like English, French has many irregular verbs and they are often the most frequently used. Learning how to use them is one of the pleasures of French grammar. Lists in your notebook will help here too.
▶ The endings of French verbs not only reflect the subject (subject agreement) but also show the verb tense (time agreement): **j'étudie le français** (*I study French*), **j'étudiais le français** (*I used to study French*), **j'étudierai le français** (*I shall study French*).

▶ The French past tenses (perfect, imperfect, past historic) do different jobs from the English past tenses and they work together in a different way.

▶ French does not have the continuous tenses so typical of English (*I am studying, I was studying*), so you have to get used to using other tenses to express this idea.

▶ Some French verb tenses are composed of only one word: **il écrit en français** (*he writes in French*), **il écrivait en français** (*he used to write in French*), **il écrira en français** (*he will write in French*). These are called simple tenses, but they are harder to learn than the compound (two- or three-word) tenses based on the two auxiliary verbs **avoir** and **être**: **il a écrit un roman** (*he wrote a novel*), **il avait écrit des poèmes** (*he had written some poems*).

▶ Most French verbs make statements and belong to the indicative mood. Another mood is the interrogative, used for questions. The subjunctive mood is one of the delights of learning French. It is much more frequent in French than in English and allows you to express fine shades of meaning, doubt and uncertainty.

▶ Some French verbs, like verbs in English, are always followed by the same preposition. But, because of differences between English and French, you have to learn the preposition when you learn the verb:

▷ The meaning may be different: **réussir <u>à</u>** (*to succeed in*), **se contenter <u>de</u>** (*to be satisfied with*).

▷ A French verb may need a preposition when the English one doesn't: **avoir besoin <u>de</u>** (*to need*), **téléphoner <u>à</u> quelqu'un** (*to phone someone*), **demander <u>à</u> quelqu'un** (*to ask someone*).

▷ Or an English verb may need a preposition when the French one doesn't: **chercher** (*to look <u>for</u>*), **écouter** (*to listen <u>to</u>*), **regarder** (*to look <u>at</u>*).

More lists for your notebook! But you will gradually come to enjoy using this tightly controlled and highly expressive verb system.

ADJECTIVES

▶ Adjectives automatically take the gender and number of the noun they go with: **un livre français, une amie française, des livres italiens, des amies allemandes**.

▶ Most adjectives follow the noun they qualify: **un garçon écossais, une ville industrielle**.

▶ But a few adjectives, including some very frequent ones, come before the noun: **une petite ville en Écosse, un long voyage**.

Again, your lists will come in handy.

These are some of the essential features of French grammar you will find in this book. They will help you enjoy using French with confidence.

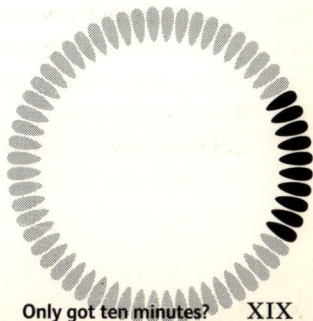

Introduction

How to use this book

Essential French Grammar is divided into 18 units and each one will help you to use French for specific things like talking about yourself, asking about people, describing people and so on. You'll see in the Contents that each unit is based on a theme connected with the story of the Lemaires and the Dicksons, ranging from the family to banking. All the examples come from the story and all are in modern French. You won't find obscure or old-world examples in this book. Every time you read an example, you'll know it fits into the story so it will be easier and quicker for you to understand and you'll be able to concentrate on the grammar.

We know you're all at different stages, so, although the book starts with the basics and goes on to the more complex grammar, we've organized it so that you can begin wherever you like. If there's a particular point you need, you can use the **Index** and the **Contents** and go straight to it. If terminology is a problem, the **Glossary** is there to take the strain. Just need to work on those irregular verbs? The **Verb tables** have all the details.

The book will work for you because it's a partnership between you and us. You decide what you need – and we help you to decide. Then we show you how to get to where you want to be.

All the units follow the same pattern. They start by showing you the theme of the unit and what you will learn in it. Then there are six carefully interrelated sections. Each unit begins with **Getting started**. This lets you check if you're ready for that unit. Then we show you how the grammar works in real life (**Say it in French**) so that you're already prepared for what you find in the grammar section (**The main points**). **The story** will show you how much you've learned. Different sorts of language activities (in **A quick check**) make sure you've learned the grammar – and there's a **Key** at the back of the book. If you're hooked and want to know more, go on to **The next stage**. There are **Insight** boxes throughout the units to make learning easier and at the end of each unit you'll find **Ten Things to Remember** to help you recap. You'll never feel lost because we've given you cross-references to other units wherever we think they'll help.

You'll soon get more confident and then it's a good idea to cover up the English on the right-hand side of the page, and just look at the French. Your notebook is an essential tool. Use it where we suggest it and make it your own, unique record of learning French grammar.

Storyline

The storyline runs through the whole book, with a new chapter in each unit. You'll meet the same people and follow some of their activities in a momentous year. All the examples in the book fit into the context of this important year in the lives of the Lemaires and the Dicksons. You'll get to know the characters and see how their lives change – and we hope that learning French grammar may also change yours!

The Lemaire family live in Saint-Amand-les-Eaux in the north of France, and the Scottish family, the Dicksons, live in Dundee in Scotland. Georges and Isabelle Lemaire have two children, Stéphanie, aged 20, and Nicolas, 17. Stéphanie is on a six-month work experience placement with an oil company in Aberdeen as part of the last year of her commerce degree (*le D.U.T.*). Nicolas is in his seventh year of secondary school, studying sciences. Stéphanie met Mark Dickson, a research engineer in the same oil company, at the beginning of her stay in Aberdeen. They are planning to become engaged at the end of the summer.

Mark has one sister, Sandy, 20, who is in her second year of university, studying English and French. Their younger brother, Andrew, is in his final year at school. Stéphanie and Mark go to St Amand at the beginning of May and the Lemaires meet Mark for the first time. Mark's parents – Alison and Patrick Dickson – are hoping to spend a few days with Stéphanie's parents in July and have enrolled to learn French at evening classes in preparation for the big event.

How are Alison Dickson, a history and geography teacher, and Patrick, manager of a supermarket, going to communicate with the Lemaires? Georges Lemaire, a highly skilled plumber, and Isabelle, a busy housewife actively involved in voluntary work with the Catholic church, speak no English. Will the date of the engagement be decided during the Dicksons' stay? Read on!

We hope you enjoy discovering French grammar while getting to know the Lemaire and the Dickson families. You can contact us through our web pages at www.teachyourself.com if you'd like to let us know how you get on.

1

Greetings and introductions

In this unit you will learn
- *To introduce yourself/someone else*
- *Numbers to 100*
- *To greet people*
- *To talk about yourself/someone else*
- *To ask questions about someone (age, address, nationality, occupation, family circumstances)*

Topic
- *Meeting people*

Grammar
▶ Subject pronouns: **je** (*I*), **tu** (*you*), **il** (*he*), **elle** (*she*), **on** (*one/we/they*), **nous** (*we*), **vous** (*you*), **ils/elles** (*they*)
▶ Verbs: present tense of **avoir** (*to have*), **être** (*to be*)
▶ -er verbs: regular **habiter** (*to live*); irregular **aller** (*to go*)
▶ A reflexive verb: **s'appeler** (*to be called*)
▶ Using **tu** or **vous**?
▶ Asking questions
▶ The negative forms: **ne … pas/n'… pas** (*not*)
▶ Stressed pronouns: **moi, toi, lui/elle, nous, vous, eux/elles**
▶ Gender

The next stage
▶ Expressions with **avoir** and **être**
▶ Changes in spelling of -er verbs
▶ Questions: inversion of verb and subject pronoun
▶ Gender rules and exceptions

Getting started

So that you can say a little about yourself in French, it is important to learn some key verbs, such as **avoir** *to have*, **être** *to be*, **habiter** *to live*, **s'appeler** *to be called* and the subject pronouns (i.e. **je** *I*, **tu** *you*, **il** *he*, etc.). With a few numbers and a little vocabulary you are well on your way.

Say it in French

1 INTRODUCING YOURSELF/SOMEONE ELSE

Bonjour, **je m'appelle** Georges Lemaire.
Hello, my name is Georges Lemaire.
J'ai 46 ans.
I'm 46 years old.
J'habite St-Amand-les-Eaux.
I live in St-Amand-les-Eaux.
Je suis Georges.
I'm Georges.
Je vous **présente** ma famille.
This is my family.

2 NUMBERS TO 100

Here is a list of numbers to 100. Learn them at your own pace and refer to the list frequently.

Note that after 60, the French count in 20s: 70 is **soixante-dix**, 80 is **quatre-vingt**s and 90 is **quatre-vingt-dix**.

0 zéro	10 dix	20 vingt
1 un	11 onze	21 vingt et un
2 deux	12 douze	22 vingt-deux
3 trois	13 treize	23 vingt-trois
4 quatre	14 quatorze	24 vingt-quatre
5 cinq	15 quinze	25 vingt-cinq
6 six	16 seize	26 vingt-six
7 sept	17 dix-sept	27 vingt-sept

| 8 huit | 18 dix-huit | 28 vingt-huit |
| 9 neuf | 19 dix-neuf | 29 vingt-neuf |

30 trente	40 quarante	50 cinquante	60 soixante
31 trente et un	41 quarante et un	51 cinquante et un	61 soixante et un
32 trente-deux ...	42 quarante-deux ...	52 cinquante-deux ...	62 soixante-deux ...

70 soixante-dix	80 quatre-vingts	90 quatre-vingt-dix
71 soixante et onze	81 quatre-vingt-un	91 quatre-vingt-onze
72 soixante-douze	82 quatre-vingt-deux	92 quatre-vingt-douze
73 soixante-treize	83 quatre-vingt-trois ...	93 quatre-vingt-treize ...
74 soixante-quatorze		
75 soixante-quinze		100 cent
76 soixante-seize		
77 soixante-dix-sept		
78 soixante-dix-huit		
79 soixante-dix-neuf		

Insight

In Switzerland and Belgium, instead of saying **soixante-dix, soixante et onze, soixante-douze, soixante-treize**, etc., they say **septante: septante et un, septante-deux, septante-trois** ...

And they say **nonante** instead of **quatre-vingt-dix: nonante et un, nonante-deux, nonante-trois**, etc.

3 GREETING PEOPLE

Stéphanie présente son petit ami Mark à la famille Lemaire.
(Stéphanie introduces her boyfriend Mark to the Lemaire family.)

Stéphanie	Mark, je te **présente** mon père et ma mère.	*Mark, this is my father and my mother.*
Mark	Enchanté.	*Pleased to meet you.*
Stéphanie	Je vous **présente** Mark, mon copain.	*This is my friend Mark.*

Isabelle Georges	Ravis de faire votre connaissance.	*Delighted to make your acquaintance.*
Georges	Comment **allez-vous**?	*How do you do?*
Mark	Bien, merci.	*I'm well, thank you.*
Stéphanie	Voici mon frère, Nicolas.	*This is my brother Nicolas.*
Mark	Salut, ça **va**?	*Hi, how are you?*
Nicolas	Ça **va** bien, merci. Et toi?	*Fine, thank you. What about you?*
	Comment **tu vas**?	*How's it going?*

4 TALKING ABOUT YOURSELF/SOMEONE ELSE

Voici ma femme Isabelle:	*This is my wife Isabelle:*
Elle a 43 (quarante-trois) ans.	*She's 43.*
Moi, **j'ai** 46 (quarante-six) ans.	*(Myself) As for me, I'm 46 years old.*
Nous avons deux enfants.	*We have two children.*
Ils s'appellent Stéphanie et Nicolas.	*They're called Stéphanie and Nicolas.*
Stéphanie **a** 20 (vingt) ans et Nicolas **a** 17 (dix-sept) ans.	*Stéphanie is 20 and Nicolas is 17.*

5 ASKING QUESTIONS ABOUT SOMEONE

Georges	**Vous habitez** Aberdeen aussi?	*Do you live in Aberdeen too?*
Mark	Oui, **je suis** ingénieur dans une compagnie pétrolière.	*Yes, I'm an engineer in an oil company.*
Isabelle	Est-ce que **vos parents habitent** Aberdeen?	*Do your parents live in Aberdeen?*
Mark	Non, **ils** n'**habitent** pas Aberdeen. **Ils habitent** Dundee.	*No, they don't live in Aberdeen. They live in Dundee.*
Isabelle	**Êtes-vous** né en Écosse?	*Were you born in Scotland?*
Mark	Oui, à Dundee.	*Yes, in Dundee.*
Georges	**Vous aimez** Aberdeen?	*Do you like Aberdeen?*
Mark	Oui, beaucoup.	*Yes, very much.*

Insight

Although **j'habite Aberdeen** is more commonly used, it is possible to say **j'habite à Aberdeen**.

The main points

1 SUBJECT PRONOUNS

The subject pronouns and matching verbs are shown in **bold** type in **Say it in French** above. Here they are in full:

1st person singular	**je** (j' in front of vowel/ vowel sound)	I
2nd	**tu**	you
3rd	**il/elle/on**	he/she/it/one
1st person plural	**nous**	we
2nd	**vous**	you
3rd	**ils/elles**	they

2 *VERBS* AVOIR *AND* ÊTRE

Look for the different forms of **être** and **avoir** and the matching nouns or subject pronouns in the examples in **Say it in French** 1 and 4.

avoir *to have*
j'**ai**
tu **as**
il/elle/on **a**
nous **avons**
vous **avez**
ils/elles **ont**

être *to be*
je **suis**
tu **es**
il/elle/on **est**
nous **sommes**
vous **êtes**
ils/elles **sont**

M. Lemaire (=il) **est** plombier.
Mme Lemaire (=elle) **est** femme au foyer.
Elle **a** 43 ans.
Ils **ont** deux enfants.

Mr Lemaire (=he) is a plumber.
Mrs Lemaire (=she) is a housewife.
She is 43.
They have two children.

Remember that in French you use the verb **avoir** to say your age.

Nicolas **a** dix-sept ans.
J'**ai** 46 ans.

Nicolas is 17.
I am 46.

3 *VERBS ENDING IN* -ER

80% of French verbs end in **-er** and most of them are regular.

Regular verbs such as *habiter* **to live**
To use **-er** verbs you just: take the **-er** off the infinitive, this gives you the *stem*; add the endings.

For example:

habiter: take the **-er** off to get the stem (**habit-**); add the endings (see the following table); match them to the subjects. Because the **h**

at the beginning of **habiter** is not pronounced, the first sound is
a and so the **e** on **je** is dropped.

Pronoun	Stem	Ending
j'	habit-	**E**
tu	habit-	**ES**
il/elle/on	habit-	**E**
nous	habit-	**ONS**
vous	habit-	**EZ**
ils/elles	habit-	**ENT**

HABITER

j'habit**E** Londres	*I live in London*
tu habit**ES** Paris	*you live in Paris*
il/elle habit**E** Marseille	*he/she lives in Marseilles*
nous habit**ONS** Édimbourg	*we live in Edinburgh*
vous habit**EZ** Cardiff	*you live in Cardiff*
ils/elles habit**ENT** Lille	*they live in Lille*
Les Lemaire habit**ent** St-Amand-les-Eaux dans le nord de la France.	*The Lemaires live in St-Amand-les-Eaux in the north of France.*

Useful verbs such as **aimer** *to like*, **détester** *to hate*, **donner** *to give*,
quitter *to leave*, follow the same pattern. Here are some more
regular **-er** verbs. Compile your own list now in your notebook and
keep adding to it as you learn.

List of regular **-er** verbs

aider	*to help*	**désirer**	*to wish*
aimer	*to like*	**détester**	*to hate*
chercher	*to look for*	**discuter**	*to discuss*
commander	*to order*	**écouter**	*to listen to*
danser	*to dance*	**emprunter**	*to borrow*
déjeuner	*to have breakfast*	**étudier**	*to study*
		expliquer	*to explain*
demander	*to ask*	**fermer**	*to close*

fumer	*to smoke*	**monter**	*to go up*
gagner	*to win*	**oublier**	*to forget*
jouer	*to play*	**parler**	*to talk*
laisser	*to leave*	**porter**	*to carry*
louer	*to rent/hire*	**raconter**	*to tell*
marcher	*to walk*	**remercier**	*to thank*

Insight

Students often make the mistake of saying **j'étude**. But the **i** remains part of the stem (**étudier → étudi-**) so you should say: j'**étudie, nous étudions,** etc.

Études is a noun:

Je fais des études en chimie. *I am studying chemistry.*
(literally 'I am doing studies in chemistry.')

▶ The stems of some -**er** verbs change their spelling with some subjects:

appeler *to call*
préférer *to prefer*

These verbs are given in full at the end of the **Verb tables**.

ALLER

There is one key -**er** verb in **Say it in French 3** that is irregular. **Aller,** *to go* does not follow the pattern given above for **habiter.** It is used in expressions such as:

Ça va?	*How is it going?*
Comment **allez**-vous?	*How do you do?/How are you?*
je **vais** très bien	*I'm very well*
tu **vas** à Dundee	*you are going to Dundee*
il/elle/on **va** au travail	*he/she/one goes (or we go) to work*
nous **allons** à l'arrêt de bus	*we're going to the bus stop*
vous **allez** à St Amand	*you're going to St Amand*
ils/elles **vont** en France	*they're going to France*

8

4 A REFLEXIVE VERB

s'appeler	je **m'**appelle Stéphanie	*I'm called Stéphanie*
	tu **t'**appelles Mark?	*you're called Mark?*
	il/elle/on **s'**appelle Dickson	*he/she is called Dickson,*
		we're called Dickson
	nous **nous** appelons Lemaire	*we're called Lemaire*
	vous **vous** appelez Alison?	*you're called Alison?*
	ils/elles **s'**appellent Dupont	*they're called Dupont*

In French you say *I call myself, we call ourselves, …* This type of verb is called **reflexive**. You will find out more about reflexive verbs in Unit 3 **The main points 2 and 3.**

Stéphanie a un frère.	*Stéphanie has a brother.*
Il **s'appelle** Nicolas.	*He is called Nicolas.*
Ils **s'appellent** Lemaire.	*They're called Lemaire.*

Insight

▶ French is a language that flows, and words are joined up in meaningful phrases to facilitate pronunciation. Pronunciation can affect grammar rules and spelling.

▶ In words like the following, the final **e** or **a** is elided and replaced by an apostrophe when followed by a vowel or vowel sound:

| **je** (*I*) | **te** ((*to*) *you*) | **me** ((*to*) *me*) |
| **se** ((*to*) *oneself, one another*) | **le** (*the, him, it*) | **la** (*the, her*) |

For example:

je + **ai** becomes **j'ai**

je + **me** + **appelle** becomes **je m'appelle** (pronounced [jemapel]).

▶ Generally speaking, the final letters of words are not pronounced. Exceptions are the final letter of nouns ending in **r** (**le bar**), **b** (**le pub**), **c** (**le bic**), **l** (**le fil**) and **f** (**la nef**).

(Contd)

▶ Some final letters in numbers are pronounced when the numbers are used on their own, e.g. **huit**, **six** [siss]. But if the number precedes a noun, the final letter is not pronounced, e.g. **dix personnes** [diperson], **six croissants** [sikrwasã].

▶ In front of a vowel, an **s** is pronounced as [z], e.g. **dix amis** is pronounced [dizami], **nous avons** is pronounced [nouzavõ].

▶ For additional information on pronunciation, visit our web pages at www.teachyourself.com.

5 USING TU OR VOUS

Did you notice, in **Say it in French 3**, that Nicolas says **Comment tu vas?** when talking to Mark. He uses **tu**, the informal, friendly form, as opposed to: **Comment allez-vous?** which is a formal way of speaking to *one* person. Georges says: **Comment allez-vous?** He addresses Mark more formally because they do not know one another.

Here are some guidelines on when to use the formal **vous** and the informal **tu**:

TU for
▶ friends
▶ family
▶ children
▶ students
▶ teenagers
▶ animals

VOUS for
▶ adults meeting someone for the first time
▶ someone you don't know well
▶ someone with whom you do not have a friendly/personal relationship, i.e. unless your doctor or a shop assistant was a personal friend of yours, you would always say **vous**
▶ people you want to show respect to: a superior/somebody in authority, an employee, in-laws, etc.

6 ASKING QUESTIONS

As you can see from **Asking questions about someone** in **Say it in French 5,** there are three ways of asking questions:

▶ You can make a statement and let your voice rise:

Ça va? (↑)
Vous habitez Aberdeen? (↑)

This way of asking questions is only used in spoken French or reported speech.

▶ You can add **est-ce-que** at the beginning of your sentence:

Est-ce que vos parents habitent Aberdeen?

▶ You can change the order of the verb and the subject pronoun:

Êtes-vous né en Écosse?

When you do this with an **-er** verb and the pronoun **il/elle/on**, if the verb ends in a vowel, you insert **-t-**:

Aime**-t**-il Dundee?   *Does he like Dundee?*
Joue**-t**-elle au football?   *Does she play football?*

These three ways of asking questions can also be used with question words, *when? how?* etc. See Unit 2 **The main points 8**.

7 THE NEGATIVE FORMS: NE … PAS/N' … PAS

Compare these two sentences:

J'habite Aberdeen.   *I live in Aberdeen.*
Je **n'**habite **pas** Dundee.   *I do not live in Dundee.*

To say that you 'do *not* do something'/'are not', you use **ne … pas**. **Ne** comes after the subject. **Pas** comes after the verb.

Les Lemaire **ne** sont **pas** écossais.   *The Lemaires are not Scottish.*

Ne, like **je**, drops the **e** and becomes **n'** in front of a vowel or vowel sound:

Stéphanie **n'**habite **pas** Lille.	*Stéphanie does not live in Lille.*
Mark **n'**aime **pas** Londres.	*Mark doesn't like London.*

8 *STRESSED PRONOUNS:* MOI, TOI, LUI/ELLE

Stressed pronouns are useful if you want to find out something about someone.

▶ If you are speaking to one person, you say:

et *toi*? (informal register), or et **vous?** (formal register)

J'aime ma famille. **Et toi?**	*I love my family. What about you?*
Je n'aime pas le football. **Et vous?**	*I don't like football. Do you?*

▶ If you are speaking to several people, you say:

et vous?

Nous aimons beaucoup l'Angleterre. **Et vous?**	*We like England very much. Do you?*

▶ If you want to know what other people think, you say:

et **elle?** (feminine singular); et **lui?** (masculine singular)
et **elles?** (feminine plural); et **eux?** (masculine plural)

Sandy va bien maintenant. **Et lui?**	*Sandy is fine now. What about him?*
Tous les garçons sont ici. **Et elle?**	*All the boys are here. What about her?*
Nous allons en France. **Et eux?**	*We're going to France. How about them?*

Here is a complete list of stressed pronouns and the subjects they correspond to:

moi	*me*	*corresponds to*	**je**
toi	*you*	→	**tu**
lui	*him*	→	**il**
elle	*her*	→	**elle**
soi	*oneself*	→	**on**
nous	*us*	→	**nous**
vous	*you*	→	**vous**
eux	*them*	→	**ils**
elles	*them*	→	**elles**

These pronouns can also be used to add emphasis to the subject:

Moi, je m'appelle Georges.　　*(Myself/As for me), I'm called Georges.*

They can be used after **et** (*and*) and after prepositions such as **après** (*after*), **avant** (*before*), etc. See Unit 6 **The main points** 3.

Moi, je vais bien. **Et toi?**　　*I am well. What about you?*
Après **vous.**/Après **toi.**　　*After you.*

9 GENDER

Subjects:

▶ to say *she* in French, you use **elle**
▶ to talk about several girls or women (*they*), you use **elles**
▶ to say *he* you use **il**
▶ to talk about more than one man or a mixed group (*they*), you use **ils**

Stressed pronouns:

▶ to say *and her*, you use **elle**: et *elle*
▶ to say *and them* (feminine group), you use **elles**: et *elles*

- ▶ to say *and him*, you use **lui**: et *lui*
- ▶ to say *and them* (masculine or mixed group), you use **eux**: et *eux*

However, not only people have gender in French. All nouns, objects, ideas, fruit and vegetables – *everything* has gender. For example **une table** (*a table*) is feminine → **elle**. **Une voiture** (*a car*) is also feminine. As you progress through the book, you will discover that gender is extremely important in French because it affects verb and adjective endings, pronouns, etc.

Insight

In your notebook, keep separate lists of masculine and feminine nouns, and add to them as you learn more nouns.

Here is a list to help you separate French nouns into the two groups:

Masculine	Feminine
▶ days of the week	▶ most words ending in **-e**
▶ male members of the family	▶ female members of the family
▶ vegetables and countries not ending in **-e**	▶ vegetables and countries ending in **-e**
▶ nouns ending in **-isme**, **-asme**, **-age**, **-ège**, **-ème**, **-ède**	▶ words ending with a double consonant + **-e** (**une allumette** *a match*)
	▶ nouns ending in **-tion**, **-sion**

Insight

Gender is very important in French, because adjectives and past participles agree with the noun in gender (feminine or masculine) and number (plural or singular). For more information, visit our web pages at www.teachyourself.com.

The story

In this passage, look for **verbs**, **subject pronouns** and **verb endings**.

Nicolas	Moi, j'ai 17 ans. Et toi? Quel âge as-tu?	*(Me/myself) I'm 17. And you? How old are you?*
Mark	J'ai 24 ans. Tu es lycéen?	*I'm 24. Are you a student?*
Nicolas	Oui, je suis en première, section S. Et toi, tu travailles?	*Yes, I'm in 6th year science stream. And how about you, do you work?*
Mark	Oui, je suis ingénieur dans une compagnie pétrolière à Aberdeen. Est-ce que tu aimes l'école?	*Yes, I'm an engineer with an oil company in Aberdeen. Do you like school?*
Nicolas	Non, pas du tout. Je n'aime pas les profs, surtout mon prof d'anglais … Toi et moi, nous partageons la même chambre. On monte? Je t'aide à porter tes valises. D'accord?	*No, not at all. I don't like the teachers, especially my English teacher … You and I are sharing the same room. Shall we go up? I'll help you carry your suitcases. All right?*
Mark	Oui, merci.	*Yes, thank you.*
Nicolas	Comment s'appellent tes parents?	*What are your parents called?*
Mark	Ils s'appellent Patrick et Alison.	*They're called Patrick and Alison.*
Nicolas	Tu as des frères et des sœurs?	*Do you have brothers and sisters?*
Mark	Oui, j'ai un frère et une sœur. Mon frère s'appelle Andrew et ma sœur s'appelle Sandy.	*Yes, I have a brother and a sister. My brother's called Andrew and my sister's called Sandy.*
Nicolas	Est-ce que tes parents travaillent?	*Do your parents work?*
Mark	Ma mère est professeur d'histoire-géographie. Mon père est directeur de supermarché.	*My mother is a history and geography teacher. My father is the manager of a supermarket.*

A quick check

Voici la famille Dickson

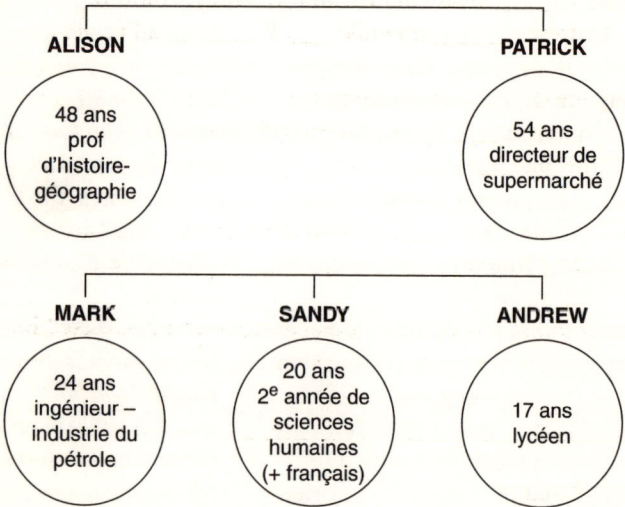

ALISON

48 ans
prof
d'histoire-
géographie

PATRICK

54 ans
directeur de
supermarché

MARK

24 ans
ingénieur –
industrie du
pétrole

SANDY

20 ans
2e année de
sciences
humaines
(+ français)

ANDREW

17 ans
lycéen

1 Introduce the Dickson family in French by filling in the gaps:

   a Je vous _____ Alison. Elle _____ 48 ans.
   b Elle _____ professeur d'histoire-géographie.
   c Voici Patrick. _____ _____ 54 ans.
   d Il _____ _____.
   e Ils _____ trois enfants: Mark, Sandy, Andrew.
   f Andrew _____ travaille ___. Il _____ à l'école.

2 Complete the following questions:

   a Comment _____ les parents de Mark?
   b Quel âge _____ Sandy?
   c _____ Sandy travaille?
   d Les Dickson _____ -ils (à) Aberdeen?
   e Et Stéphanie? _____ - ___ - ___ (à) Dundee?

3 Answer in French the questions you have just completed in 2 above.

The next stage

1 *EXPRESSIONS* WITH AVOIR *AND* ÊTRE

Avoir is sometimes used in French where **être** (*to be*) is used in English:

J'ai 20 ans.	*I am 20 years old.*
J'ai faim.	*I am hungry.*
J'ai froid.	*I am cold.*
J'ai chaud.	*I am hot.*

Avoir and **être** are also used as auxiliary verbs in some past tenses: the perfect (see Unit 13 **The main points 2, 3**), the pluperfect (see Unit 15 **The main points 1**) and the perfect subjunctive (see Unit 17 **The main points 5**).

2 CHANGES IN SPELLING -ER VERBS

Some -er verbs have a change in spelling in some tenses. See list at the end of the **Verb tables**.

a Verbs ending in **-yer**

envoyer *to send*	
j'**envoie**	nous **envoyons**
tu **envoies**	vous **envoyez**
il/elle/on **envoie**	ils/elles **envoient**

b Verbs ending in **-ger**
Verbs such as **manger** *to eat*, **nager** *to swim*, **plonger** *to dive* add an -e in the first person plural (**nous** form) to retain the same pronunciation (a soft **g**) as in the infinitive:

nous mangeons, nous nageons, nous plongeons, ...

c Verbs ending in **-cer**
Verbs such as **commencer** (*to begin*) have a cedilla on the **c** in the first person plural (**nous** form) to retain the soft **c** sound of the infinitive:

nous commençons

d Verbs ending in **-ter/-ler**
Verbs such as **jeter** or **appeler** double the **t** or **l**, except for the **nous** and **vous** forms:

jeter *to throw*	
je **jette**	nous **jetons**
tu **jettes**	vous **jetez**
il/elle/on **jette**	ils/elles **jettent**

épeler *to spell*	
j'**épelle**	nous **épelons**
tu **épelles**	vous **épelez**
il/elle/on **épelle**	ils/elles **épellent**

or add a grave accent:

acheter to buy	
j'**achète**	nous **achetons**
tu **achètes**	vous **achetez**
il/elle/on **achète**	ils/elles **achètent**

3 QUESTIONS: INVERSION OF VERB AND SUBJECT PRONOUN

As-**tu** faim? *Are you hungry?*
Ont-ils des frères et des sœurs? *Do they have brothers and sisters?*

It is only possible to invert a verb and a pronoun. If a noun such as **Mark** or **la sœur de Mark** is used, you use a matching pronoun after the verb while retaining the noun:

Mark, a-**t**-il faim? *Is Mark hungry?*
La sœur de Mark (Sandy) *Does Mark's sister (Sandy) like*
 aime-**t**-elle Dundee? *Dundee?*
Alison, joue-**t**-elle au tennis? *Does Alison play tennis?*

4 GENDER RULES AND EXCEPTIONS

The guidelines given in **The main points 9** are useful suggestions which you should bear in mind, but do not be surprised if you encounter words which break the rules:

▶ Most words ending in **-age**, for example, are masculine except:

   la cage (*the cage*), **la nage** (*swimming*), **l'image** (*image, picture*), **la page** (*page*), **la plage** (*the beach*), **la rage** (*rabies*).

▶ Most words ending in **-tion** are feminine, but there are exceptions such as **le bastion** (*stronghold*).

▶ Although most animals, like humans, have both a masculine and a feminine form, there are some animals which are always feminine in gender: **la girafe** (*giraffe*), **l'autruche** (*ostrich*), **la perruche** (*budgie*).

▶ Some professions remain masculine and do not have a feminine form:

le professeur (*teacher*)	Il est professeur. Elle est professeur.
l'auteur (*author*)	Il est auteur. Elle est auteur.
le juge (*judge*)	Il est juge. Elle est juge.
le chauffeur (*driver*)	Il est chauffeur. Elle est chauffeur.

▶ Some words have a different meaning depending on whether they are masculine or feminine:

le livre (*book*)	**la livre** (*pound*)
le mort (*dead man*)	**la mort** (*death*)
le physique (*physique*)	**la physique** (*physics*)
le poste (*post/job*)	**la poste** (*post office*)

TEN THINGS TO REMEMBER

1 The subject pronoun **je** becomes **j'** in front of vowels and vowel sounds: **j'aime, j'habite**.

2 This elision of the **e** and use of the apostrophe also applies to words such as **me** (*me, myself*), **te** (*you, yourself*), **se** (*oneself, one another*), **ne** (the first part of negatives **ne … pas** (*not*), **ne … jamais** (*never*), etc.), **de** (*of*), **le/la** (*the*).

3 The French use two words to form the negative: **ne … pas, ne … jamais** (Unit 4 **The main points** 5).

4 Learn the present tense endings that go with the subject pronouns (**je, tu, il**, etc.) for **-er** verbs. They represent 80% of all French verbs. You will meet the endings for other verb endings (**-ir, -re, -oir**) in subsequent chapters.

5 In all present tense verbs and in most other tenses, the ending **-ons** always goes with **nous**, and **-ez** with **vous**.

6 The reflexive pronouns used when you conjugate the verb **s'appeler** are used with all reflexive verbs: **je m'appelle, tu t'appelles, il/elle/on s'appelle, nous nous appelons, vous vous appelez, ils s'appellent**. There are many reflexive verbs in French.

7 Get used to manipulating the three ways of asking questions. If you always use the statement with your voice raised, it can lead to problems of understanding when you are in France.

8 French doesn't like vowel clashes and therefore pronunciation can affect structures. If you choose to ask a question by inverting an **-er** verb with the pronouns **il/elle/on**, you need to add **-t-: Aime-t-il? Prépare-t-il le dîner? Mange-t-on des escargots en France?**

9 Note the changes in spelling in various parts of **-er** verbs as a result of pronunciation (Unit 1 **The next stage** 2).

10 You cannot invert a verb and a noun or a person's name. You need to use the structure 'noun + comma + verb + pronoun': **Ton cousin Jacques, fait-il du sport?**

2

Likes and dislikes

In this unit you will learn
* *To express preferences*
* *To ask about likes, dislikes and hobbies*
* *Question words*
* *Days and dates*

Topics
* *Hobbies*
* *Sport*

Grammar
▶ Definite articles **le, la, l'**, **les** (*the*) and indefinite articles **un, une, des** (*a, an*)
▶ Articles with nouns in the plural
▶ Contracted articles: definite articles after *at/with/to* (**au, aux**) and after *of/from* (**du, des**)
▶ Partitive articles: **du, de la, de l', des** (*some/any*)
▶ Demonstrative adjectives: **ce/cet**, **cette**, **ces** (*this, that, these, those*)
▶ Possessive adjectives: **mon/ma/mes** (*my*)
▶ The verb **faire** (*to do*) in the present tense
▶ Question words: **comment?**, **qui?**, **quand?** (*how?, who?, when?*)

The next stage
▶ Partitive articles after negatives
▶ Irregular plurals
▶ More about demonstratives
▶ More about possessive adjectives
▶ When to use **faire** and **jouer**

Getting started

As you saw in Unit 1 **The main points 2,** the article in French is omitted after **être** before a profession. You say:

Il est professeur.   *He is a teacher.*

This is an exception to the ground rule, as articles are usually used in French:

Mark aime **le** football.   *Mark likes football.*
Nicolas a **des** amis sur Internet.   *Nicolas has friends on the Internet.*

1 In this unit you will learn when to use the definite articles **le, la, les** and when to use the indefinite articles **un, une, des:**

Georges regarde **un** match de   *Georges is watching a football*
  football à **la** télévision.   *match on the television.*
Il adore **le** football.   *He loves football.*

2 You will find out more about the plural of nouns and the use of definite and indefinite articles in French with plural nouns. In some cases you will see they are used in French when they would not be used in English:

Nicolas aime **les** ordinateurs. *Nicolas likes computers.*
Nicolas rencontre **des** amis ce soir. *Nicolas is meeting friends this evening.*

3 You will learn to say *any/some* in French:

Avez-vous **des** passe-temps?   *Do you have any hobbies?*
J'ai **des** amis français.   *I have some French friends.*

4 You will also learn how definite articles contract with the prepositions **à** (*at/with/to*) and **de** (*of/from*):

Nicolas va **au** cinéma.   *Nicolas goes to the cinema.*
Nicolas joue **du** piano.   *Nicolas plays the piano.*

5 An article can be replaced by a demonstrative adjective (**ce/cet, cette, ces**) if you want to refer specifically to one or more things. In the following examples, the demonstrative adjective singles out a particular video, a specific picture or specific ideas:

Nicolas préfère **cette** vidéo.   *Nicolas prefers this video.*
Stéphanie adore **ce** tableau de   *Stéphanie likes this painting by*
  Monet.   *Monet very much.*
Aimez-vous **ces** idées d'avant-   *Do you like these avant-garde*
  garde?   *ideas?*

6 A noun can also be preceded by a possessive adjective (**mon/ma/ mes**), which indicates possession or refers to family members, etc.:

Leur père, Georges, a des trophées   *Their father, Georges, has*
  de chasse.   *hunting trophies.*
Stéphanie admire **sa** mère car elle   *Stéphanie admires her mother*
  fait du travail bénévole.   *because she does voluntary work.*

7 The verb **faire** is very useful when you are talking about your hobbies/activities. In this unit, you will learn to use it in the present tense:

Mark **fait** du football et du rugby.   *Mark plays football and rugby.*

8 You have already met (Unit 1) the question words **quel?** (*what?*) in **Quel âge as-tu?** (*How old are you?*) and **comment?** (*how?*) in **Comment allez-vous?** (*How are you?*). In this unit, you will meet more question words: **où?** (*where?*), **quand?** (*when?*), etc.:

Quand est-ce que Mark joue   *When does Mark play rugby?*
  au rugby?
Où joue-t-il au rugby?   *Where does he play rugby?*

Look carefully at all the structures in the following examples before moving on to **The main points**.

Say it in French

1 DISCUSSING HOBBIES, LIKES AND DISLIKES

Georges adore **le** football.	*Georges adores football.*
Moi, je préfère **la** broderie et **le** canevas.	*Myself, I prefer embroidery and cross-stitch.*
Nicolas déteste **le** sport. Il préfère les ordinateurs.	*Nicolas hates sport. He prefers computers.*

Mark joue **au** squash. Il fait du ski et **de la** plongée sous-marine.	*Mark plays squash. He skis and dives.*
Nicolas adore **la** cuisine d'Isabelle, surtout **sa** purée Parmentier.	*Nicolas loves Isabelle's cooking especially her Parmentier purée.*

2 ASKING ABOUT HOBBIES, LIKES AND DISLIKES, PLACES

Qu'est-ce que tu fais comme loisirs?	*What do you do in your spare time?*

Qu'est-ce que tu aimes?	*What do you like?*
Quel plat préfères-tu?	*What is your favourite dish?*
Que détestes-tu?	*What do you hate?*
Quand jouez-vous au squash?	*When do you play squash?*
Qui joue avec vous?	*Who plays with you?*
Où se trouve Aberdeen?	*Where is Aberdeen?*
Comment allez-vous au travail?	*How do you go to work?*

3 DAYS AND DATES

Mark joue au squash **le lundi** et **le mardi**.	*Mark plays squash on Mondays and Tuesdays.*
Il joue au rugby **le samedi** ou le **dimanche** après-midi.	*He plays rugby on Saturday or Sunday afternoons.*
Est-ce que tu joues au rugby **samedi**?	*Are you playing rugby this Saturday?*
Georges est né **le 26 novembre 1964**.	*Georges was born on 26 November 1964.*
Stéphanie est née **le 1er janvier**.	*Stéphanie was born on 1 January.*
Mark est né **le 3 septembre**.	*Mark was born on 3 September.*

The main points

1 DEFINITE AND INDEFINITE ARTICLES

Articles are different in French according to the **gender** of the noun (Unit 1 **The main points** 9) and the **number** of the noun (singular or plural).

	definite article: the	indefinite article: a, an
masc. sing.	**le, l'** (in front of a vowel)	**un**
fem. sing.	**la, l'** (in front of a vowel)	**une**
masc. fem. plural	**les**	**des**

Definite article

The definite article is used in French even when you are talking about something in general terms. In English, you talk and write about *football/swimming*, etc., but French uses the definite article **le/la** in front of the noun (depending on its gender): **le football** (*football*), **la natation** (*swimming*). See **Say it in French 1**.

Aimez-vous **le** football?	*Do you like football?*
Stéphanie aime **le** chant.	*Stéphanie likes singing.*
Georges regarde **le** football sur Canal +.	*Georges watches football on Canal plus.*
Georges regarde **le** match Paris-Nice.	*Georges is watching the Paris-Nice match. (a specific match)*

Indefinite article

The indefinite article also changes according to the gender of the noun. You use **un** in front of a masculine noun and **une** in front of a feminine noun:

Mark habite **un** appartement à Aberdeen.	*Mark lives in a flat in Aberdeen.*
Nicolas va à la vidéothèque et emprunte **une** vidéo.	*Nicolas goes to the video library and borrows a video.*
Georges regarde **un** match de football à la télévision.	*Georges is watching a football match on the television. (not specific)*

2 ARTICLES WITH NOUNS IN THE PLURAL

French normally adds an -s to nouns to show that they are plural. Plural articles also have the ending -s. The plural of **le/la** (*the*) is **les**, and the plural of **un/une** (*a/an*) is **des**.

In English, plural nouns are most often used without an article, while in French an article is used.

Il y a souvent **des** matchs de football sur Canal +.	*There are often football games on Canal plus.*

Nicolas adore **les** plats comme **les** frites et **les** pizzas.

Nicolas adores dishes such as chips and pizzas.

3 CONTRACTED ARTICLES

The definite articles **le, les** contract with **de** (*of/from*) and **à** (*at/with/to*) to become **du/des** and **au/aux**.

Insight

You will need to keep referring to this section. Contracted articles are used often and can be surprising as there are no equivalents in English.

Here is a pattern to help you:

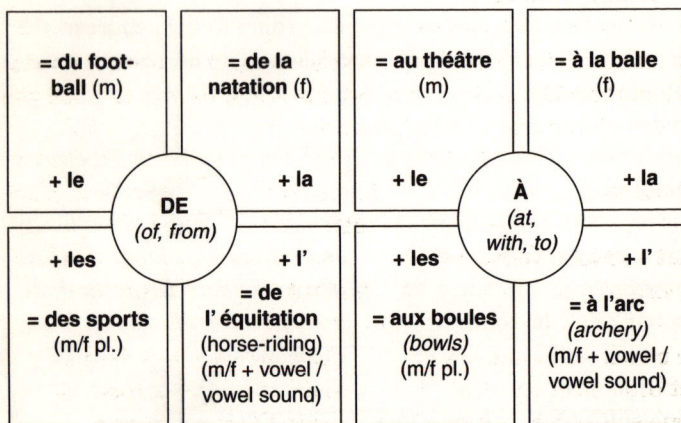

DE (of, from)		À (at, with, to)	
+ le = **du football** (m)	**+ la** = **de la natation** (f)	**+ le** = **au théâtre** (m)	**+ la** = **à la balle** (f)
+ les = **des sports** (m/f pl.)	**+ l'** = **de l' équitation** (horse-riding) (m/f + vowel / vowel sound)	**+ les** = **aux boules** (*bowls*) (m/f pl.)	**+ l'** = **à l'arc** (*archery*) (m/f + vowel / vowel sound)

Mark joue **au** squash.	*Mark plays squash.*
Georges fait **du** ball-trap.	*Georges does clay-pigeon shooting.*
Nicolas va souvent **au** cinéma.	*Nicolas often goes to the cinema.*
Il aime jouer **aux** échecs.	*He likes to play chess.*
Isabelle reste **à la** maison ou va **au** centre d'accueil du presbytère.	*Isabelle stays at home or goes to the drop-in centre at the presbytery.*
Alison joue **du** piano.	*Alison plays the piano.*

Aimer can be followed directly by an infinitive (e.g. **jouer**).

4 PARTITIVE ARTICLES: SOME, ANY

If you want to talk about a quantity or use *some* or *any*, you use **de** with the definite article. This is called the **partitive article**. As you saw in 3 above, there is a contraction with **le** and **les** and you say:

J'ai **du** temps libre. (**de** combines with **le** to become **du**)
J'ai **des** problèmes. (**de** combines with **les** to become **des**)

More about these in Unit 4 **The main points 2.**

5 DEMONSTRATIVE ADJECTIVES: THIS, THAT, THESE, THOSE

These also change according to the gender and number of nouns. Look at the following grid and examples and refer to it when you find demonstratives in other situations.

masc. sing.	fem. sing.	masc. fem. plural
ce	**cette**	**ces**
cet + vowel/vowel sound		
this/that	*this/that*	*these*

Ce match est formidable.	This match is wonderful.
Cet ordinateur est bien.	This computer is good.
Cette émission est intéressante.	This TV programme is interesting.
J'aime bien ces tableaux.	I really like these paintings.

6 POSSESSIVE ADJECTIVES: MON, MA, MES

In French, it is important to remember that possessive adjectives agree in number and gender with *what is possessed* and not with the person who owns it (More about this in Unit 7 **The main points 1**). The gender of the person who owns something is totally irrelevant in French and does not affect the choice of possessive adjective.

Nicolas taquine **sa** sœur (fem.) et
 Stéphanie n'aime pas toujours
 son frère (masc.).

Nicolas teases his sister and
 Stéphanie doesn't always
 like her brother.

Here is a complete grid:

masc. sing.	fem. sing.	masc. fem. plural	
mon	ma mon + vowel	mes	my
ton	ta ton + vowel	tes	your
son	sa son + vowel	ses	his/her/its
notre	notre	nos	our
votre	votre	vos	your
leur	leur	leurs	their

7 THE VERB FAIRE

Faire is very useful for talking about your leisure activities. See **Say it in French 1** and **The main points 3**. It is an irregular verb:

faire	je **fais** le ménage	*I do the housework*
	tu **fais** du sport	*you play sport*
	il/elle/on **fait** du football	*he/she plays football*
	nous **faisons** des promenades	*we go for walks*
	vous **faites** du travail bénévole	*you do voluntary work*
	ils/elles **font** du ski	*they go skiing*
	Mark **fait** du football, du ski et de la plongée sous-marine.	*Mark plays football and goes skiing and diving.*

The present tense in French is also used where in English you would use the form *is + ing*: Mark **fait** du football. (*Mark is playing football.*) The present tense can also be used in speech to talk about future actions, which are indicated by time expressions, e.g. **demain** (*tomorrow*), **l'année prochaine** (*next year*). See the future tense in Unit 11 **Getting started 1, 2** and **The main points 1, 2**.

Demain, il **fait** de la plongée.   *He is diving tomorrow.*

8 QUESTION WORDS

The three ways of asking questions that were given in Unit 1 **The main points 6** can also be used with question words:

Quel âge tu as?	*How old are you?*
Quel âge est-ce que tu as?	*How old are you?*
Quel âge as-tu?	*What age are you?*
J'ai 24 ans.	*I'm 24.*

....

Insight

Quel? is an adjective and it changes to match the gender and number of the noun it accompanies. Don't forget to check your agreements when you write.

....

Quels sports (masc. plural) tu fais?	*What sports do you play?*
Quelle est votre date (fem. sing.) de naissance?	*What is your date of birth?*
Quelles activités (fem. plural) est-ce que tu fais?	*Which activities do you do?*

Other question words:

Comment?	Comment s'appellent-ils?	*(How) What are they called?*
Qui?	Qui joue avec moi?	*Who is playing with me?*
Que?, qu'?	Qu'est-ce que tu fais?	*What are you doing?*
Où?	Où habitez-vous?	*Where do you live?*
Pourquoi?	Pourquoi dites-vous ça?	*Why do you say that?*
Quand?	Quand faites-vous du sport?	*When do you play sport?*
	Quand allez-vous en vacances?	*When do you go on holiday?*
Combien/ combien de?	Combien de temps est-ce que Mark reste en France?	*How long is Mark staying in France?*

In spoken French, the question word can be placed at the end of the sentence:

▶ **Vous faites du sport quand?**
▶ **Vous faites du sport avec qui?**
▶ **Vous habitez où?**

Quand tends to be used at the end of the sentence when speaking.

9 MORE DAYS AND DATES

Here are the names of other days and months so that you can say what the date is and answer some of the questions above:

Aujourd'hui, c'est le *Today is Monday,*
lundi 2 (deux) février. *2nd February.*
le …

lundi (*Monday*)	1ᵉʳ janvier (*January*)	5 mai	9 septembre
mardi (*Tuesday*)	2 février (*February*)	6 juin	10 octobre
mercredi (*Wednesday*)	3 mars (*March*)	7 juillet	11 novembre
jeudi (*Thursday*)	4 avril (*April*), etc.	8 août	12 décembre
vendredi (*Friday*)			
samedi (*Saturday*)			
dimanche (*Sunday*)			

In French, days and months do not have a capital letter.

You only use an ordinal number – **le premier** (*the first*) – for the first of the month. After that, say **le deux, le trois, le quatre**, etc. when you say the date.

Note the difference between:

Qu'est-ce que tu fais **lundi**?	*What are you doing on Monday?*
Qu'est-ce que tu fais **ce lundi**?	*What are you doing this Monday?*

and

Qu'est-ce que tu fais **le lundi**?   *What do you do on Mondays?*
                                      (every Monday)

You also use **le** when talking about a specific day followed by
a date:

Qu'est-ce que tu fais **le lundi**   *What will you be doing on*
  20 mars?   *Monday, 20th March?*

The story

Look for the different articles and question forms in the dialogue
below.

Stéphanie	Mark, Nicolas! Le dîner est prêt.	*Mark, Nicolas! Dinner is ready.*
Nicolas	Nous arrivons.	*We're coming.*
Isabelle	Georges, on mange. Qu'est-ce que tu fais?	*Georges we are eating. What are you doing?*
Georges	Je regarde un match de foot.	*I'm watching a football match.*

(Isabelle to Mark)

Isabelle	Georges adore le football. Moi, je préfère la cuisine et la couture. Est-ce que vous jouez au football?	*Georges adores football. Myself, I prefer cooking and sewing. Do you play football?*
Mark	Oui, je joue au football et aussi au rugby.	*Yes I play football and rugby too.*
Stéphanie	Il joue aussi au squash, au golf et il fait de la plongée sous-marine.	*He also plays squash, golf and goes diving.*
Nicolas	Maman, qu'est-ce qu'on mange?	*Mum, what are we having?*
Isabelle	Nicolas n'aime pas le sport. Il préfère son ordinateur et son estomac. N'est-ce pas, Nicolas?	*Nicolas doesn't like sport. He prefers his computer and his stomach. Isn't that right, Nicolas?*
Stéphanie	Qu'est-ce que tu fais ce soir?	*What are you doing this evening?*
Nicolas	Je vais au cinéma puis à la pizzeria.	*I am going to the cinema and then to the pizzeria.*
Isabelle	Quand rentres-tu? Pas trop tard, j'espère.	*When are you coming home? Not too late, I hope.*

A quick check

Mark montre des photos de sa famille. Georges et Isabelle posent des questions.
Mark is showing pictures of his family. Georges and Isabelle are asking questions. As they don't know one another well, they are using **vous**.

1 Complete the following questions and answers, using question words, articles and possessive adjectives. (One word per gap)

   a _____'est-ce que _____ maman fait comme passe-temps?

b Elle aime ___ randonnées en montagne, ___ photographie et faire ___ ski.

c Et _____ père? _____ sports fait-il?

d Il joue ___ golf.

e ___ est-ce qu'il joue au golf? (where)

f ___ est sur ___ photo?

g C'est ___ frère Andrew et ici c'est ___ sœur Sandy.

h ___'est-ce qu'elle fait dans ___ vie?

i Elle est étudiante. Elle fait ___ études de sciences humaines et de français.

2 One way of asking questions with interrogative words is suggested in the following sentences. Write out the other two ways.

Comment est-ce que tu t'appelles?
Où habites-tu?
Tu joues au rugby quand?

3 Give your date of birth and the date today.

The next stage

1 *PARTITIVE ARTICLES AFTER NEGATIVES*

After negatives or after expressions of quantity (Unit 4 **The main points** 3) the partitive article – **du, de la, de l', des** – becomes simply **de** or **d'**:

Nicolas n'a **pas d'**argent.　　　*Nicolas doesn't have any money.*
　　　　　　　　　　　　　　　Nicolas has no money.

Il a **beaucoup de** temps libre.　*He's got a lot of free time.*

2 IRREGULAR PLURALS

Most plurals are indicated by -s. However, there are nouns which have irregular plurals. Here are some that form the plural with -x:

▶ Most nouns in -eau/-eu:

le bateau	les bateaux	*boats*
le gâteau	les gâteaux	*cakes*
le cheveu	les cheveux	*hair*
le jeu	les jeux	*games*

▶ Some nouns in -al:

| *le cheval* | *les chevaux* | *horses* |
| *le journal* | *les journaux* | *newspapers* |

▶ Nouns in -ou add an -s, except: **hibou** *(owl)*, **joujou** *(toy)*, **caillou** *(stone)*, **chou** *(cabbage)*, **genou** *(knee)*, **pou** *(louse)*, which add -x:

| le hibou | les hiboux |
| le pou | les poux |

3 MORE ABOUT DEMONSTRATIVES

To be more specific in pinpointing something, you can use a demonstrative adjective and add -ci or -là (*here* or *there*) after the noun. A hyphen is used between the noun and -ci and -là:

| Cette raquette-**ci** | *This particular racket* |
| Ce ballon-**là** | *That ball there* |

4 MORE ABOUT POSSESSIVE ADJECTIVES

The possessive adjectives **mon, ton, son** are used before a vowel, even if the noun is feminine. This can seem surprising, but it is to make the pronunciation easier:

| **Mon/ton/son** amie | *My/your/his/her girlfriend* |
| **Mon/ton/son** ordinateur | *My/your/his/her/its computer* |

5 *WHEN TO USE* FAIRE *AND* JOUER

(See **Say it in French 1, The main points 3**). With **jouer** (*to play*), you use **à** for sports **et de** with musical instruments:

| Il **joue au** rugby. | *He plays rugby.* |
| Vous **jouez du** piano. | *You play the piano.* |

Jouer à can be replaced by **faire de**:

| Il **fait du** rugby. | *He plays rugby.* |

Faire can also be used for activities other than sports:

Nicolas **fait du** dessin assisté par ordinateur.	*Nicolas does computer-aided design.*
Isabelle **fait de la** couture.	*Isabelle sews.*
J'aime **faire des** promenades.	*I like to go for walks.*

TEN THINGS TO REMEMBER

1 Articles may seem simple but they need very careful consideration: **Je voudrais un dessert** (*I would like a dessert*), **Je voudrais du dessert** (*I would like some dessert*), **Je voudrais le dessert** (*I would like the dessert* – i.e. the one on the menu, or instead of the cheese). **Je mange le bœuf** could mean you are eating the whole animal! You should say: **Je mange du bœuf**.

2 You never find **à** or **de** used with the articles **le** or **les**. They are always combined: **à + le → au; à + les → aux; de + le → du; de + les → des**.

3 The demonstrative adjective (**ce, cette, ces**) agrees in gender and number with the noun it precedes. **Ce** is used with a masculine noun but becomes **cet** in front of a masculine noun beginning with a vowel or vowel sound: **cet ami**.

4 Possessive adjectives also agree with the noun in gender and number, and not with the possessor as in English: **sa sœur** (*his/her sister*), **son frère** (*his/her brother*).

5 In front of a feminine noun beginning with a vowel or vowel sound, use the masculine form of the possessive adjective (**mon, ton, son**) to make pronunciation easier: **mon amie, son invitation**.

6 Make sure you learn all the key irregular verbs. As in most languages, including English, they are vital for speaking and writing.

7 Unlike English, French does not use a preposition (*in, on*) in front of a day: **lundi, le lundi** (*on Monday, on Mondays*).

8 If you want to say *in the morning, in the afternoon*, etc., you say **le matin, l'après-midi**. You cannot use **dans** (*in*) with times of the day. However, you can say **pendant/durant la journée** (*during the day*).

9 **Lundi** refers to this coming Monday; **le lundi** means every Monday.

10 After expressions of quantity (**beaucoup de, un kilo de**) and negative verbs, the partitive articles **du, de la, de l'** and **des** become **de** unless you are speaking about specific groups or things: **beaucoup <u>d</u>'amis** (*lots of friends*), **un kilo <u>de</u> pommes de terre** (*a kilo of potatoes*), **pas <u>d</u>'argent** (*no money*), **jamais <u>de</u> patience** (*never any patience*).

3

Describing people, things and routines

In this unit you will learn
- *To describe people: their age, their size, their appearance, their clothes*
- *To describe things*
- *To talk about regular activities*
- *To tell the time*

Topic
- *Routines*

Grammar
- ▶ Adjectives
- ▶ Reflexive verbs
- ▶ Questions with reflexive verbs
- ▶ More numbers (from 100 onwards, saying *1st*, *2nd*, *3rd* ...,
  saying you are in your twenties, etc.)

The next stage
- ▶ More about adjectives – position of adjectives
- ▶ Adjectives with adverbs
- ▶ Present participles: the *-ing* form of verbs

Getting started

As you saw in Unit 2 **The main points 1–6,** the gender and number of nouns affect other words in the sentence, such as articles, interrogative adjectives **quel?, quels?, quelle?, quelles?** and demonstrative adjectives **ce/cet, cette, ces.**

1 In Unit 3, you will see that adjectives also agree in gender and number with the nouns they relate to. This means that their endings change, unlike in English where they remain the same:

Mark est **grand**.	*Mark is tall.*
Sandy est **grande**.	*Sandy is tall.*

In English, most adjectives come before the noun. In French, they usually come after the noun:

Mark a les cheveux **noirs**.   *Mark has black hair.*

– except for a few short adjectives, which you will also meet in this unit:

Andrew et son copain ont de   *Andrew and his mate have great*
  belles bicyclettes.   *bicycles.*

You will see that some adjectives can have different meanings according to whether they come before or after the noun:

Patrick aime avoir une voiture   *Patrick likes to have a clean*
  propre et bien entretenue.   *and well-maintained car.*
Andrew voudrait sa **propre** voiture. *Andrew would like his own car.*

2 You have already met the reflexive verb **s'appeler** in Unit 1 **The main points 4.** Reflexive verbs use the extra pronoun **se** which changes according to the subject (**je, tu, il** ...):

Quand **vous** réveillez-vous?   *When do you wake up?*
À quelle heure **te** couches-tu? *(At) what time do you go to bed?*

The extra pronoun (reflexive pronoun) can mean *myself, yourself, yourselves*, etc.:

Je **me** lave.   *I wash (myself)*

– but it can also mean *one another, each other*:

Nous **nous** parlons souvent.   *We often talk to each other.*
Quand Stéphanie et Nicolas **se** *When Stéphanie and Nicolas*
  disputent, ils ne **se** parlent plus.   *argue, they do not speak*
                                   (to each other)

3 In this unit, you will also meet numbers from 100 onwards and learn to say the approximate age of someone (e.g. in his late twenties/thirties).

Say it in French

Read the following examples, identify all the **adjectives** and look carefully at their position and their **agreement** with the nouns they refer to.

1 DESCRIBING PEOPLE

Mark est un **beau** garçon **bronzé**.

Il mesure 1,82 m.

Il a les yeux **bleus** et les cheveux **noirs**.

Il est **musclé** car il est très **sportif**.

Son père a les cheveux **gris** et les yeux **bleus**.

Sa mère Alison a les cheveux **brun clair** et elle a les yeux **gris-vert**.

Elle mesure 1,57 m. Elle est **mince** et très **élégante**. Elle a la quarantaine.

Sandy est **brune**. Elle est très **jolie**.

Elle travaille comme modèle pour un magazine de mode.

Andrew a les cheveux **noirs bouclés**.

Il a l'air très **coquin**.

Il mesure 1,70 m et il est **bronzé**.

Mark is a good-looking boy with a tan.

He is 1.82 m tall.

He has blue eyes and black hair.

He has good muscles because he is very keen on sport.

His father has grey hair and blue eyes.

His mum Alison has light-brown hair and greyish green eyes.

She is 1.57 m tall. She is slim and very smart. She is in her forties.

Sandy is dark. She is very pretty.

She works as a model for a fashion magazine.

Andrew has curly black hair.

He looks very cheeky.

He is 1.70 m tall and is suntanned.

2 DESCRIBING PEOPLE'S CLOTHING

Alison porte une **jolie** jupe **bleue,** un **beau** chemisier **blanc** et des chaussures **assorties**.

C'est une jupe **longue, classique,** taille 40.

Patrick porte un **vieux** survêtement, car il fait du jardinage.

Alison is wearing a pretty blue skirt, a nice white blouse and matching shoes.

It is a long skirt, in a classical style, size 12.

Patrick is wearing an old tracksuit, because he is gardening.

3 TALKING ABOUT DAILY ACTIVITIES

Andrew est souvent à l'extérieur.	*Andrew is often outdoors.*
Il **se lève** très tôt pour distribuer les journaux en vélo.	*He gets up very early to deliver newspapers on his bike.*
Il **se douche** en vitesse.	*He has a quick shower.*
Il **s'habille** rapidement et il déjeune.	*He gets dressed quickly and has breakfast.*
Il **se dépêche** de distribuer les journaux, car il **se rend** à l'école à 8 h 30.	*He delivers the papers quickly because he goes to school at 8.30.*
Le soir, il **s'amuse** avec ses amis.	*In the evenings he enjoys himself with his friends.*

4 DESCRIBING THINGS/PLACES

Il **se déplace** en vélo.	*He goes around on his bike.*
Son vélo est un VTT **bleu** et **blanc** avec 22 vitesses.	*His bike is a blue and white mountain bike with 22 gears.*
Il travaille pour un **petit** magasin **populaire** vendant des journaux près de chez lui.	*He works for a small popular shop selling newspapers near his house.*
Il n'a pas le temps de ranger sa chambre. Elle est mal **rangée**.	*He doesn't have time to tidy up his bedroom. It is untidy.*
Alison porte de **jolies** boucles d'oreille **rondes**.	*Alison is wearing pretty round earrings.*
Ce sont des boucles d'oreille en or, très **chic**.	*They are very smart gold earrings.*

5 TELLING THE TIME

Je me réveille **à sept heures** du matin et je me couche **à onze heures** du soir.

I get up at seven in the morning and go to bed at eleven in the evening.

Andrew se lève **à six heures et demie** pour distribuer les journaux.

Andrew gets up at half past six to deliver papers.

Ses cours commencent à **8 h 45** et finissent à **15 h 55**.

His lessons start at a quarter to nine and finish at five to four.

Il sort avec des amis et rentre à **23 h 15**.

He goes out with friends and comes home at a quarter past eleven.

The main points

1 *ADJECTIVES*

Être + adjective

To describe a person or a thing, the verb **être** can be used to link the noun and the adjective that relates to it:

Mark est très **sportif**. *Mark is very keen on sport.*
La chambre d'Andrew est mal **rangée**. *Andrew's bedroom is untidy.*

If there is more than one adjective after **être**, they are separated by **et** (*and*), **ou** (*or*), **mais** (*but*) or by a comma:

Patrick est **grand** et **fort**. *Patrick is big and strong.*
Le vélo est **bleu, blanc** et **rouge**. *The bike is blue, white and red.*

Most adjectives end: in any letter if they are masculine singular
in **-s** if they are masculine plural
in **-e** if they are feminine singular
in **-es** if they are feminine plural

Mark est intelligent.	*Mark is intelligent.*
Patrick, Mark et Andrew sont sportifs.	*Patrick, Mark and Andrew are keen on sport.*
Alison est élégante et bien habillée.	*Alison is elegant and well dressed.*
Sa bicyclette est bleue et blanche.	*His bike is blue and white.*
Ses chaussures sont assorties à sa robe.	*Her shoes match her dress.*

As you can see from these examples and **Say it in French 1**, after the verb **être** adjectives agree in gender and number with the subject.

Noun + adjective
Most adjectives follow the noun:

| Mark a les yeux **bleus**. | *Mark has blue eyes.* |
| Il a les cheveux **noirs**. | *He has black hair.* |

These adjectives also agree in number and gender with the noun they qualify:

Patrick porte un survêtement **usagé** (masc. sing.).	*Patrick wears a worn tracksuit.*
Alison porte une jupe **bleue** (fem. sing.), une veste **bleue** (fem. sing.) et des chaussures **assorties** (fem. pl.).	*Alison is wearing a blue skirt, a blue jacket and matching shoes.*
Andrew a les cheveux **bouclés** (masc. pl.).	*Andrew has curly hair.*

Change of spelling
Some adjectives change their endings when they qualify a feminine noun.

▶ Adjectives ending in **-eau**

masc. sing.	fem. sing.	masc. plural	fem. plural	
beau	**belle**	**beaux**	**belles**	*beautiful*
un **beau** garçon	une **belle** fille	de **beaux** garçons	de **belles** filles	
nouveau	**nouvelle**	**nouveaux**	**nouvelles**	*new/recent*
un **nouveau** film	une **nouvelle** amie	de **nouveaux** films	de **nouvelles** amies	

See **The main points, Noun + adjective** for the position of **beau** and **nouveau**.

▶ Adjectives ending in **-euf**:

masc. sing.	fem. sing.	masc. plural	fem. plural	
neuf	**neuve**	**neufs**	**neuves**	*new, not old*
un vélo **neuf**	une robe **neuve**	des vêtements **neufs**	des robes **neuves**	
veuf	**veuve**	**veufs**	**veuves**	*widowed*
un homme **veuf**	une femme **veuve**	des hommes **veufs**	des femmes **veuves**	

▶ Adjectives ending in **-eur**

masc. sing.	fem. sing.	masc. plural	fem. plural	
menteur	**menteuse**	**menteurs**	**menteuses**	*lying*
il est **menteur**	elle est **menteuse**	ils sont **menteurs**	elles sont **menteuses**	
rieur	**rieuse**	**rieurs**	**rieuses**	*cheerful*
il est **rieur**	elle est **rieuse**	ils sont **rieurs**	elles sont **rieuses**	

Many adjectives ending in **-teur** have **-trice** in the feminine:

masc. sing.	fem. sing.	masc. plural	fem. plural	
innovateur	**innovatrice**	**innovateurs**	**innovatrices**	*innovative*
un projet	une idée	ils sont	elles sont	
innovateur	**innovatrice**	**innovateurs**	**innovatrices**	

Adjectives ending in -l, -n, -s double the consonant and add -e:

masc. sing.	fem. sing.	masc. plural	fem. plural	
bas	**basse**	**bas**	**basses**	*low*
cruel	**cruelle**	**cruels**	**cruelles**	*cruel*
gentil	**gentille**	**gentils**	**gentilles**	*nice, kind*
gros	**grosse**	**gros**	**grosses**	*fat*
mignon	**mignonne**	**mignons**	**mignonnes**	*cute*
pareil	**pareille**	**pareils**	**pareilles**	*same*

Nicolas a une **grosse** chatte.	*Nicolas has a big (female) cat.*
Elle est **gentille**, plutôt **mignonne**, mais **cruelle** avec les oiseaux.	*She is nice, rather cute, but cruel with birds.*
Ces deux jupes sont **pareilles**.	*These two skirts are alike.*

▶ Adjectives ending in -t either double the -t:

masc. sing.	fem. sing.	masc. plural	fem. plural	
coquet	**coquette**	**coquets**	**coquettes**	*smart*

Alison est très **coquette**.	*Alison is very particular about her appearance.*

or add a grave accent è and an e (→ **ète**):

masc. sing.	fem. sing.	masc. plural	fem. plural	
complet	**complète**	**complets**	**complètes**	*complete/full*

Cette auberge de jeunesse est **complète**. *This youth hostel is full.*

▶ Adjectives ending in **-er** also add a grave accent and an **-e** in the feminine:

masc. sing.	fem. sing.	masc. plural	fem. plural	
cher	chère	chers	chères	*dear, expensive*
dernier	dernière	derniers	dernières	*last*

Chères amies ...   *Dear (female) friends ...*
L'année **dernière**, je ...   *Last year I ...*

▶ Adjectives ending in **-ic** become **-ique**:

masc. sing.	fem. sing.	masc. plural	fem. plural	
public	publique	publics	publiques	*public*

▶ Some adjectives are highly irregular:

masc. sing.	fem. sing.	masc. plural	fem. plural	
blanc	blanche	blancs	blanches	*white*
favori	favorite	favoris	favorites	*favourite*
frais	fraîche	frais	fraîches	*fresh*
franc	franche	francs	franches	*frank, straight*
vieux	vieille	vieux	vieilles	*old*
vieil + vowel				

Nicolas regarde son émission **favorite**.   *Nicolas is watching his favourite programme.*

Adjective + noun
Some adjectives come before the noun. See **Say it in French 2**. These are usually short common adjectives, such as **beau, bon, grand**, etc.

Here is a list of adjectives that usually come *before the noun*:

autre	*other*	**long**	*long*
***beau (bel)**	*handsome*	**mauvais**	*bad*
bon	*good*	***nouveau (nouvel)**	*new*
chaque	*each*	**petit**	*small*
grand	*big/tall*	**tel**	*such*
gros	*big/fat*	**vaste**	*vast*
haut	*high*	***vieux (vieil)**	*old*
jeune	*young*	**vilain**	*naughty*
joli	*pretty*		

*When the masculine adjectives **beau, nouveau, vieux** come before a singular noun beginning with a vowel or a vowel sound, they change their endings to become **bel, nouvel** and **vieil**:

Patrick est un très **bel** homme.	*Patrick is a very handsome man.*
Andrew va acheter un **nouvel** album.	*Andrew's going to buy a new album.*
Ce n'est pas un **vieil** homme.	*He is not an old man.*

Most of the adjectives in the box above are one-syllable adjectives. They agree in number and gender with the noun they relate to:

Patrick porte aussi de **vieilles** baskets.	*Patrick is also wearing old trainers.*
Patrick porte un **vieux** survêtement.	*Patrick is wearing an old tracksuit.*
Andrew a la grippe. Il a **mauvaise** mine.	*Andrew's got the flu. He looks poorly.*

Colour adjectives, although short, come after the noun:

Alison porte une jupe **bleue**.	*Alison is wearing a blue skirt.*
Patrick porte un survêtement **gris**.	*Patrick is wearing a grey tracksuit.*

Exceptions to the rules on agreement of adjectives
Some adjectives remain unchanged:

▶ adjectives derived from fruit and nuts:

Nouns	Adjectives	Examples
un marron/des marrons (*wild chestnut*)	**marron**	des yeux **marron**
une noisette/des noisettes (*hazelnut*)	**noisette**	des yeux **noisette**
une orange/des oranges (*orange*)	**orange**	des boules **orange**

▶ **chic** – des boucles d'oreille très **chic**
▶ hyphenated adjectives with two colours do not change their spelling:

Elle a les yeux **gris-vert**.   *She has greyish-green eyes.*

▶ when there are two adjectives, a colour and an adjective that refers to it, neither of them agrees:

Il a les yeux **bleu clair**.   *He has light-blue eyes.*
Les nuages sont **gris foncé**.   *The clouds are dark grey.*

Look at the difference between the spelling of the adjectives in the following examples:

Elle a les cheveux **bruns** et **foncés**.   *She has dark-brown hair.*
Elle a les yeux **brun foncé**.   *She has dark-brown eyes.*

2 REFLEXIVE VERBS

Reflexive verbs (where the subject and the object are the same person) are easily noticeable in French as they have an extra pronoun: **se** in front of the infinitive, which changes form to match the subject of the verb (See Unit 1 **The main points 4**).

They mean that:

▶ the subject is doing something to himself/herself (*myself, yourself, himself/herself/oneself*, etc.):

Andrew **se** lève tôt, il **se** douche, il **s'habille** et **se** dépêche.	*Andrew gets up early, has a shower (showers), gets dressed and hurries up.*

As you can see from these examples and **The main points 3**, the object of a reflexive verb is not always expressed in English. The formula *to get dressed* is more usual in English than *to dress oneself*.

In French, the subject performs the action on him/herself, i.e. *Andrew gets himself up, showers himself*, etc.

▶ the subject and another person or other persons (also subject of the verb) are doing something to one another:

Stéphanie et Nicolas **se disputent** souvent, mais ils **s'aiment** quand même.	*Stéphanie and Nicolas often quarrel, but they like each other all the same.*

The idea of interaction (*each other/one another*) is not always explicit in English:

Mark et Stéphanie **se rencontrent** toujours après le travail.	*Mark and Stéphanie always meet after work.*

3 QUESTIONS WITH REFLEXIVE VERBS

When asking questions with reflexive verbs using inversion, remember that the reflexive (object) pronoun does not move. It always remains before the verb:

Comment **t'appelles-tu**?/Comment est-ce que tu **t'appelles**?/Comment **vous** appelez-vous?	*What are you called?/ What's your name?*
Vous promenez-vous à la campagne?	*Do you walk in the country?*
Vous entendez-vous bien?	*Do you get on well?*

4 MORE NUMBERS

Asking/telling the time

| Quelle heure est-il? | *What time is it?* |

For the 12-hour clock system you simply add the expression in bold below to indicate *a quarter past, half past, a quarter to* …:

Il est une heure.	*It's one o'clock.*
Il est une heure **et quart**.	*It's a quarter past one.*
Il est une heure **et demie**.	*It's half past one.*
Il est deux heures **moins le quart**.	*It's a quarter to two.*
Il est midi.	*It's noon.*
Il est minuit.	*It's midnight.*

This 12-hour system does not show whether it is in the morning or in the afternoon. If it is not obvious from the context, you add the time of day, just as in English:

Il est une heure **du matin**.	*It's one o'clock in the morning.*
Il est une heure **de l'après-midi**.	*It's one o'clock in the afternoon.*
Il est onze heures **du soir**.	*It's eleven o'clock at night/in the evening.*

The 24-hour system is used more formally in business timetables, schedules, etc. In this system, you do not use **et quart, et demie, moins le quart**, but simply the number of minutes: **quinze, trente, quarante-cinq**:

| Il est 23 h 00 (vingt-trois heures). | *It's 23.00.* |
| Il est 23 h 15 (vingt-trois heures quinze). | *It's 23.15.* |

Il est 23 h 30 (vingt-trois heures trente).   *It's 23.30.*
Il est 23 h 45 (vingt-trois heures quarante-cinq).   *It's 23.45.*

The word **heures** cannot be omitted.

Ordinal numbers
▶ To speak about *first*, *the first*, you say:

le premier/la première, les premiers, les premières.

le deuxième	le neuvième
le troisième	le dixième
le quatrième	le vingtième
le cinquième	le vingt et unième
le sixième	le vingt-deuxième
le septième	le vingt-troisième ...
le huitième	

These numbers agree with the person or noun referred to:

Mark se lève **le premier**.   *Mark gets up first.*
Stéphanie quitte le travail **la**   *Stéphanie leaves work first.*
  première.

▶ To say *second*, *third*, *fourth* ..., again put the definite article
le/la/les first, and then add **-ième/s** to the number:

Nicolas est le **deuxième** de   *Nicolas is second in his*
  sa classe en maths.   *class in maths.*
Georges regarde souvent **la**   *Georges often watches*
cinquième.   *Channel 5*

▶ **le second/la seconde** can replace **le deuxième/la deuxième**
when talking about ranks/classes:

C'est **la seconde** fois qu'il   *It's the second time that he*
  gagne.   *has won.*
Il voyage en **seconde** classe.   *He travels second class.*
En **second** lieu ...   *Secondly ...*

To say that someone is in their twenties, thirties, etc.
You remove the -e from the number and add **-aine**. These numbers are always feminine:

Isabelle a **la quarantaine**.
Alison a aussi **la quarantaine**,
  mais Patrick a une petite
cinquantaine.

Isabelle is in her forties.
Alison is also in her forties, but
  Patrick is in his early fifties.

To count after 100

100	cent, cent un, cent deux, cent trois …
200	deux cents, deux cent un, deux cent deux, deux cent trois …
300	trois cents, trois cent un, trois cent deux …
370	trois cent soixante-dix, trois cent soixante et onze …
1 000	mille, mille un, mille deux …
2 000	deux mille, deux mille un, deux mille deux …
10 000	dix mille …
10 280	dix mille deux cent quatre-vingts …
10 372	dix mille trois cent soixante-douze …
1 000 000	**un** million …
2 000 000	deux millions, deux millions un …
2 120 000	deux millions cent vingt mille …
1 000 000 000	**un** milliard …
1 000 000 115	**un** milliard cent quinze …

Insight

Vingt and **cent** are spelled with an **-s** when they are not followed by other numbers:

▶ **quatre-vingts** *but* **quatre-vingt-deux**
▶ **deux cents** *but* **deux cent deux**.

Mille never adds an **-s**.

With numbers after 1,000, a full stop or a space is used in French, whereas a comma is used in English:

1.000 or 1 000 mille

1,000 *a thousand*

2.331 or 2 331 deux mille trois cent trente et un

2,331 *two thousand three hundred and thirty-one*

The words **million** and **milliard** take **de** when they are followed by a noun:

Il y a plus de 56.000.000 **de** gens en France. (cinquante-six millions)

There are over 56,000,000 people in France.

The story

When reading this dialogue, look for **expressions of time, reflexive verbs** and **adjectives**.

Mark et Stéphanie parlent d'Aberdeen et de leur appartement.

Mark and Stéphanie are talking about Aberdeen and their flat.

Mark	Je me lève vers sept heures. Je me douche et je m'habille. Stéphanie se réveille un peu plus tard. Nous quittons l'appartement vers huit heures.	*I get up about seven o'clock. I have a shower and get dressed. Stéphanie wakes up a little later. We leave the flat about eight o'clock.*
Stéphanie	Nous partageons l'appartement mais Mark est souvent absent. Il se rend sur la plate-forme pétrolière pour plusieurs semaines. Je m'occupe donc de l'appartement.	*We share the flat but Mark is often away. He goes to the oil rig for several weeks. So I look after the flat.*
Isabelle	Il est joli?	*Is it pretty?*
Stéphanie	Oui, c'est un petit appartement situé dans le centre-ville. Il est bien décoré, clair, bien chauffé et très confortable. Les voisins sont très sympathiques.	*Yes, it is a small flat situated in the town centre. It is well decorated, well lit, well heated and very comfortable. The neighbours are very friendly.*
Mark	Stéphanie et moi, nous nous rencontrons souvent pour le déjeuner. Nous rentrons ensemble le soir.	*We often meet for lunch, Stéphanie and I. We go home together in the evening.*

A quick check

La famille Lemaire

1 a Complete the sentences given below, using the information provided on Georges and Isabelle and the adjectives in brackets.

| **Georges** (blond) (grand) yeux (bleu) cheveux (bouclé) 1,92 m 46 ans | **Isabelle** cheveux (brun) (mi-long) (mince) (joli) yeux (marron) 43 ans | **Stéphanie** (joli) yeux (bleu) cheveux (blond) (bouclé) (mince) |

George est un homme _____.
Il mesure _____.
Il est _____. Il ___ les cheveux _____ et les yeux _____.
Isabelle a les _____ _____, _____.
Elle est _____ et _____.
Elle a les _____ _____.
Ils ont la _____ (in their forties).

| **Nicolas** cheveux (blond) yeux (noisette) (grand) (mince) 1,90 m |

b Write a few sentences to describe Stéphanie and Nicolas.

2 Say and write the following figures/times in French (in words).
231 456
245 985
3 500 765
6.15, 3.45, 3.05 (using the 12-hour system)
13.55, 22.35, 23.45 (using the 24-hour system)

The next stage

1 MORE ABOUT ADJECTIVES

Adjectives following a verb
As you saw in **The main points 1**, adjectives can follow the verb
être, and they agree with the subject:

Il est **fatigué**.   *He is tired.*

They can also follow other verbs and qualify the subject:

▶ verbs of state, such as **sembler** (*to look*), **paraître/apparaître**
(*to appear*):

    Il semble **épuisé**.   *He seems exhausted.*
    Elle paraît **charmante**. *She looks charming.*

▶ verbs of action, such as **rentrer** (*to come back*), **sortir** (*to go out*):

    Ils rentrent **fatigués** le soir. *They get home tired in the evening.*

When a noun is qualified by two adjectives, they can be placed
after the noun and are linked by **et** (*and*), **mais** (*but*) or **ou** (*or*):

Cette voiture paraît ancienne   *This car looks old but/and well*
  mais/et bien entretenue.   *kept.*

Position of adjectives
▶ Some adjectives can have a different meaning according to
their position *before* or *after* the noun:

    Georges est un homme **grand**.   *George is a tall man.*
    Le Général de Gaulle est un   *General de Gaulle is a*
      grand homme de l'histoire   *great man in French*
      française.   *history.*
    Ce n'est pas la **même** idée.   *It is not the same idea.*
    L'idée **même** m'amuse.   *The very idea amuses me.*

| Isabelle rencontre souvent des gens **pauvres**. | *Isabelle often meets poor people.* |
| L'entreprise caritative fait beaucoup pour ces **pauvres** gens. | *The charity does a lot for these unfortunate people.* |

Here is a list of adjectives which have a different meaning depending on their position:

ancien + noun = former	une **ancienne** élève	*a former pupil (female)*
noun + **ancien** = old	un village **ancien**	*an old village*
certain + noun = certain	un **certain** « je ne sais quoi »	*a certain 'je ne sais quoi'*
noun + **certain** = sure	un fait **certain**	*a sure fact*
cher + noun = dear	chers amis	*dear friends*
noun + **cher** = expensive	une voiture **chère**	*an expensive car*
même + noun = same	C'est la **même** chose.	*It's the same thing.*
noun + **même** = itself	C'est cette personne **même**.	*It's the very same person.*
propre + noun = own	Son **propre** ordinateur.	*His own computer.*
noun + **propre** = clean	Il a un appartement **propre**.	*He has a clean flat.*

▶ If several adjectives which usually go before the noun are used, such as **joli, nouveau,** only one adjective goes before the noun and the other adjectives go after the noun:

| Alison porte une **jolie** jupe nouvelle. | *Alison is wearing a pretty new skirt.* |

Other adjectives may follow the second adjective, provided a comma or a link word such as **et** (*and*), **mais** (*but*), **ou** (*or*) is used:

| Andrew a un **beau** VTT **propre** et **neuf.** | *Andrew has a nice clean new mountain bike.* |

60

Patrick porte un **vieux** survêtement **foncé**, légèrement **usé**.   *Patrick is wearing an old dark tracksuit, slightly worn.*

▶ A few adjectives can be joined to other adjectives: **demi-/mi-/ semi-** (*half*) (+ hyphen). They do not agree when they are joined to another adjective.

The main adjective agrees with the noun it relates to:

Isabelle a les cheveux **mi**-longs.   *Isabelle has longish hair.*
Elle aime le lait **demi**-écrémé.   *She likes semi-skimmed milk.*
C'est une région **semi**-autonome.   *It's a semi-autonomous region.*

▶ Some noun + adjective combinations are so common that they act as a single noun. In this case, the adjective agrees with the noun:

Les **grands**-parents   *Grandparents*
Il faut faire attention aux **ronds**-points.   *One must be careful at roundabouts.*

T**el/telle/tels/telles** (such)
These adjectives can be used with or without an indefinite article. In each case, the meaning is slightly different:

Une **telle** personne   *Such a person*
Telle personne   *A certain person*

Adjectives ending in '-ic' in English
These adjectives often end in **-ique** (fem./masc.) in French:

Noun	Adjective
l'ecclésiastique	ecclésiastique(s)
l'économie	économique(s)
l'élastique	élastique(s)
public is an exception:	
le public	public/publique/publics/publiques

2 ADJECTIVES WITH ADVERBS

Adjectives can have an adverb before them (Unit 6 **The main
points, Position of adverbs**), such as **très** (*very*), **trop** (*too much*),
complètement (*completely*), etc. if they come after the verb **être** or
another verb:

Ils sont **trop fatigués**.	*They are too tired.*
Ils rentrent **complètement** épuisés.	*They come back completely exhausted.*

Adjectives which go before the noun can also be preceded by **trop**
(*too*), **très** (*very*):

Isabelle est une **très petite** femme.   *Isabelle is a very small woman.*

If an adjective which usually goes before the noun is modified
by an adverb – except **très** (*very*) and occasionally **trop** (*too*) – it
comes after the noun:

Isabelle est une femme **vraiment petite**.	*Isabelle is a really small woman.*

3 PRESENT PARTICIPLES: THE '-ING' FORM

(See **Verb tables**.) For most verbs, you just take off the **-ons** from
the second person plural (**nous** form) of the present tense and add
-ant, for example:

descendre *to go down*	nous descendons	descend-	+ ant **descendant**
partir *to leave*	nous partons	part-	+ ant **partant**
précéder *to precede*	nous précédons	précéd-	+ ant **précédant**

There are three exceptions to this ground rule:

avoir	nous avons	**ayant**
être	nous sommes	**étant**
savoir	nous savons	**sachant**

Present participles are **verbs,** always ending in **-ant.** They do not agree in number or gender with the subject: Le magasin **vendant** des journaux … (see **Say it in French 4**).

Andrew et Mark **étant** jeunes, beaux et forts, ils sont très populaires avec les filles.	*Being young, handsome and strong, Andrew and Mark are very popular with girls.*
L'horloge **s'étant** arrêtée, je ne connais pas l'heure exacte.	*The clock having stopped, I do not know the exact time.*

Many adjectives in French also end in **-ant** but they agree in gender and number with the noun they relate to:

Cette émission est intéress**ante.**	*This programme is interesting.*
Les acteurs sont très amus**ants.**	*The actors are very funny*

If you are using a French word ending in **-ant,** it is important to check to see if it is an adjective or a verb.

TEN THINGS TO REMEMBER

1 Reflexive pronouns come before the verb they are attached to and cannot be separated from it by **ne** (the first part of the negative). Put the **ne** part of the negative after the subject: **Il ne se lève pas tôt.** (*He doesn't get up early.*)

2 Reflexive pronouns are much more common in French than in English. When you learn a reflexive verb, remember that the reflexive pronoun must always be used in French: **Ils se disputent** (*They argue*), **Ils se lèvent** (*They get up*).

3 Adjectives in French mainly come after the noun. This is not easy for English speakers.

4 Adjectives are part of the web of agreements in French sentences, and they agree in gender and number with their noun. This means it is essential to learn the gender of a noun when you first meet it.

5 A few adjectives of colour (like **marron, orange, bleu-vert, bleu clair**) are invariable, i.e. they do not agree with the noun.

6 **Demi** and **semi** do not agree when they come before the noun: **une demi-heure** (see Unit 4 **The next stage 2**).

7 A few short, commonly used adjectives such as **petit** (*small*), **grand** (*big*), **nouveau** (*new*) and **vieux** (*old*) come before the noun, just as they do in English.

8 Ordinal numbers (**le premier, le deuxième,** etc.) always come before the noun.

9 Colour adjectives always come after the noun: **le chat noir**.

10 Some short adjectives such as **ancien, grand, même** and **propre** can give the sentence a different meaning, depending on whether they come after or before the noun.

4

Making requests

In this unit you will learn
- *To say what you want or need*
- *To ask what/where/how much something is*
- *To ask what/which one someone would like*
- *Quantities and sizes*

Topic
- *Shopping*

Grammar
▶ Verbs and expressions to say what you want or need: **je voudrais** (*I'd like*), **avoir besoin de** (*to need*)
▶ Partitive articles **du, de la, de l', des** (*some, any*)
▶ Expressions of quantity and size
▶ Question adjectives and pronouns: *what/which, which one(s)*
▶ More negatives: **ne ... plus** (*no longer/no more*), **ne ... jamais** (*never*)

The next stage
▶ More about articles
▶ More expressions of quantity
▶ More about using articles after negatives
▶ **Ne ... personne, personne ne** (*nobody*), **rien ne, ne ... rien** (*nothing*)
▶ **Avoir besoin de** (*to need*) in the negative
▶ **La plupart de** (*most of*)

Getting started

Look back at Unit 1 **The main points** 3 for verbs which can express what you want/desire, such as **aimer, désirer** + noun or + infinitive:

Nous **aimons** la France.	*We like France.*
Nicolas **désire** sortir.	*Nicolas wants to go out.*

1 In this unit, you will meet other verbs and expressions to express needs, likes and dislikes:

Nicolas **voudrait** acheter un DVD.	*Nicolas would like to buy a DVD.*
Nicolas **a besoin de** nouveaux CD.	*Nicolas needs some new CDs.*

2 You will also learn to use more partitive articles **du, de la, de l', des** (*some, any*). See Unit 2 **The main points** 4.

Mark voudrait acheter **des** cadeaux pour sa famille.	*Mark would like to buy some presents for his family.*

3 You will meet expressions of quantity:

Mark voudrait acheter **deux boîtes de** chocolats pour des amis et **une bouteille de** bon vin pour son père.	*Mark would like to buy two boxes of chocolates for some friends and a bottle of good wine for his father.*

4 To ask what sort of thing someone wants or does, you can use interrogative adjectives **quel(s)**, **quelle(s)** (which/what), which agree with the noun they accompany. See Unit 2 **The main points 8**. Also look back at Unit 1 **The main points 6**, if you have problems with asking questions.

Quelle sorte voulez-vous?	*What type do you want?*
Qu'est-ce que vous désirez?	*What do you want?*
	(What would you like?)

In this unit you will meet interrogative pronouns **lequel?**, **laquelle?** (*which one(s)*)?, which replace the noun they refer to and help you to ask more specific questions:

Lequel (masc. sing.) voulez-vous?	*Which one do you want?*
Lequel préférez-vous?	*Which one do you prefer?*

5 You have already used the negative **ne … pas** (not). See Unit 1 **The main points 7**. In this unit you will meet other useful negatives such as **ne … plus** (no longer, no more):

Mark **n'**aime **pas** faire les courses.	*Mark does not like shopping.*
Mark **n'**a **plus** beaucoup de temps pour faire ses achats.	*Mark doesn't have a lot of time to do his shopping any more.*

Say it in French

1 SAYING WHAT YOU NEED OR WANT

Stéphanie, je **voudrais** acheter des cadeaux pour mon père, ma mère, Andrew et Sandy.	*Stéphanie, I would like to buy presents for my father, my mother, Andrew and Sandy.*
Je **voudrais** une bonne bouteille de vin pour mon père.	*I'd like a good bottle of wine for my father.*

Je **désire** acheter un St Émilion ou un bourgogne.	*I want to buy a St Émilion or a wine from Burgundy.*
Je **voudrais** acheter un CD ou un T-shirt pour Andrew.	*I'd like to buy a CD or a T-shirt for Andrew.*
Pour Maman, **j'aimerais** acheter du parfum à l'aéroport.	*For mum I'd like to buy some perfume at the airport.*
J'ai aussi **besoin de** lames à rasoir pour moi.	*I also need some razor blades for myself.*

2 ASKING WHAT/WHICH ONE SOMEONE WOULD LIKE

Quel parfum voudrais-tu acheter?	*Which perfume would you like to buy?*
Lequel préfères-tu?	*Which one do you prefer?*
Une eau de toilette est aussi très bien.	*An eau de toilette is also quite good.*
Laquelle préfères-tu?	*Which one do you prefer?*
Il y a de jolis T-shirts.	*There are some nice T-shirts.*
Lesquels préfères-tu?	*Which ones do you prefer?*

3 FINDING OUT WHERE TO GET THINGS AND PRICES

Qu'est-ce que vous avez comme vins?	*What wines do you have?*
Où est-ce qu'il y a un marchand de vins?	*Where is there a wine store?*
Combien coûte ce vin?	*How much does this wine cost?*
Ça fait combien en tout?	*How much is it all together?*
C'est combien?	*How much is it?*

4 QUANTITIES AND SIZES

Je désire **une bouteille de** vin.	*I want a bottle of wine.*
Je voudrais **deux boîtes de** chocolats.	*I'd like two boxes of chocolates.*

Pour sa mère, Stéphanie a **une liste de** courses. Elle voudrait: **1 kilo de** pommes de terre, **une demi-livre de** beurre, **500 g de** pâté, **deux litres de** vin rouge, **deux briques de** lait, **un paquet de** sucre.

Stéphanie has a shopping list for her mother. She would like: 1 kg of potatoes, half a pound of butter, 500 g of pâté, two litres of red wine, two cartons of milk, a packet of sugar.

Je voudrais un T-shirt **demi-patron** ou **patron**.

I'd like a medium size or large size T-shirt.

Je ne veux **plus rien**, merci.

I don't need anything else, thank you.

The main points

1 VERBS AND EXPRESSIONS TO SAY WHAT YOU WANT OR NEED

Désirer and **vouloir**

The verb **désirer** can be followed by a noun:

Je **désire du jambon** fumé.   *I want/I'd like some smoked ham.*

It can also be followed by an infinitive:

Je **désire faire** des achats.   *I want/I'd like to do some shopping.*

The verb **désirer** is used in French to say what you want and also to ask what someone wants: **Que désirez-vous?** However, it is not the most commonly used expression to say what you would like. The most polite way is to use the conditional of **vouloir** (*to want*). See Unit 8 **The main points** 1, **Vouloir** and Unit 18 **The main points** 3.

The conditional of vouloir:	
je **voudrais**	nous **voudrions**
tu **voudrais**	vous **voudriez**
il/elle/on **voudrait**	ils/elles **voudraient**

Using **vouloir** in the present tense to say what you want: **Je veux un café au lait** (*I want a white coffee*) could be too abrupt. See Unit 8 **The main points 1, Vouloir.**

Je voudrais un café et deux croissants.	*I'd like a coffee and two croissants.*
Mark **voudrait** acheter un St Émilion pour son père.	*Mark would like to buy a St Émilion for his father.*
Nous **voudrions** regarder les T-shirts.	*We'd like to look at the T-shirts.*

Avoir besoin de to need

Mark **a besoin de** beaucoup d'argent pour acheter ses cadeaux.	*Mark needs a lot of money to buy his presents.*

2 PARTITIVE ARTICLES: SOME, ANY

See grid, Unit 2 **The main points 3.**

Partitive articles follow the same contraction rule as **de** + definite article:

le combines with **de** to make **du**
les combines with **de** to make **des**

Here is a complete list of partitive articles:

masc. sing.	fem. sing.	masc. plural	fem. plural
du	**de la**	**des**	**des**
de l'+ vowel	**de l'**+ vowel		
du fromage (some cheese)	**de la margarine** (some margarine)	**des croissants** (some croissants)	**des baguettes** (some baguettes)
de l'ail (some garlic)	**de l'aspirine** (some aspirin)		

Mark voudrait **du** vin rouge.	*Mark would like some red wine.*
Il voudrait aussi acheter **des** fleurs pour Isabelle.	*He would also like to buy some flowers for Isabelle.*
Stéphanie achète **du** beurre, **du** pâté, **de** l'ail, **de la** limonade, **de** l'huile, **des** pommes de terre ... pour sa mère.	*Stéphanie buys some butter, pâté, garlic, lemonade, oil, potatoes ... for her mother.*

As you can see from these examples, articles in a list are repeated in French, even if they have the same gender and number.

3 EXPRESSIONS OF QUANTITY AND SIZE

The partitive article becomes **de**, not only after a negative
(Unit 2 **The next stage** 1), but also after expressions of quantity.

Je voudrais **un peu de** fromage.	*I would like a little cheese.*
Nous voudrions **un morceau de** brie, **un paquet de** café moulu et **une boîte de** choucroute garnie.	*We would like a piece of Brie, a packet of ground coffee and a tin of sauerkraut with meat.*

Non-specific quantities and sizes

assez de	*enough of*
beaucoup de	*a lot of*
moins de	*less*
plus de	*more*
une boîte de	*a box/tin of*
un bouquet de	*a bunch of*
une brique de	*a carton of (milk, juice)*
une carafe de	*a carafe of*
une cuillerée de	*a spoonful of*
un morceau de	*a piece of*
un pack de	*several cartons/bottles of*
un paquet de	*a packet of*
une plaque de	*a bar of*
une plaquette de	*a bar of*
un pichet de	*a jugful/carafe of*

une pincée de	*a pinch of*
une portion de	*a portion/helping of*
une tasse de	*a cup of*
une tranche de	*a slice of*
un verre de	*a glass of*

Pour faire une mousse au chocolat, Isabelle a besoin de **500 g de** chocolat, de six œufs et de **200 cl de** crème fraîche.	*To make a chocolate mousse, Isabelle needs 500 g of chocolate, six eggs and 200 cl of fresh cream.*

Precise quantities

un litre de	*(100 cl) a litre of*
une bouteille de	*(75 cl) a bottle of*
100 grammes de	*100 g of*
1 kg de	*one kilo of*
une livre de	*one pound of*
une demi-livre de	*half a pound of*

4 QUESTION ADJECTIVES AND PRONOUNS

Interrogative adjectives
Interrogative **adjectives**, Unit 2 **The main points 8**, are shown in the following grid. As you can see, they are followed by a noun, and they agree with it in number and gender:

masc. sing.	fem. sing.	masc. plural	fem. plural
quel	**quelle**	**quels**	**quelles**
quel parfum?	**quelle** crème?	**quels** T-shirts?	**quelles** pommes?
(Which perfume?)	*(Which cream?)*	*(Which T-shirts?)*	*(Which apples?)*

Interrogative pronouns
Interrogative **pronouns** replace the noun. They are formed with the definite article **le/la/les + quel/le/s**. They agree with the noun they replace in gender and number: *le*quel, *la*quelle, etc.:

masc. sing.	fem. sing.	masc. plural	fem. plural
lequel	**laquelle**	**lesquels**	**lesquelles**
Lequel	**Laquelle**	**Lesquels**	**Lesquelles**
voulez-vous?	désirez-vous?	prenez-vous?	désirez-vous?
(Which one do you want?)	*(Which one do you want?)*	*(Which ones are you taking?)*	*(Which ones do you want?)*

More examples with interrogative pronouns:

Je voudrais un T-shirt.	*I'd like a T-shirt.*
Lequel désirez-vous?	*Which one would you like?*
Il y a deux sortes de crèmes hydratantes.	*There are two types of moisturizing lotion.*
Laquelle préfères-tu?	*Which one do you prefer?*
Ta mère aime les parfums français?	*Does your mum like French perfumes?*
Lesquels préfère-t-elle?	*Which ones does she prefer?*
Ces fleurs sont toutes très jolies.	*These flowers are all very pretty.*
Lesquelles préférez-vous?	*Which ones do you prefer?*

Insight

The interrogative pronouns **lequel, lesquels** and **lesquelles** combine with the preposition **à** to give **auquel, auxquels** and **auxquelles**. (See Unit 2 **The main points 3.**)

With the preposition **de**, they combine to become **duquel, desquels** and **desquelles**.

Desquelles (i.e. crèmes hydratantes, fem. pl.) **parlez-vous?**	*Which ones (lotions) are you talking about?*
Auxquels (i.e. T-shirts, masc. pl.) faites-vous référence?	*Which ones (T-shirts) are you referring to?*

5 MORE NEGATIVES

As you will remember, when you use the negative **ne ... pas**, the **ne** comes after the subject and the **pas** comes after the verb (See Unit 1 **The main points** 7). The same applies to other negatives.

Useful negatives:

ne ... plus	*no longer, not any of, no more of*
ne ... jamais	*no longer, never*
ne ... guère	*hardly*
ne ... point	*emphatic 'no'*
ne ... rien	*nothing*
ne ... que	*only*
ne ... personne	*nobody*
ne ... aucun(e)	*no, none*
ne ... ni ... ni	*neither ... nor*

Je **n'**ai **rien** à faire.	*I have nothing to do.*
Je suis au régime. **Je ne** mange **ni** gâteaux **ni** bonbons.	*I am on a diet. I eat neither cakes nor sweets.*
Je **ne** veux **qu'**un verre d'eau.	*I only want a glass of water.*
Je **n'**ai **aucune** idée au sujet d'un cadeau pour Sandy.	*I have no ideas about a present for Sandy.*
Il **n'**y a **personne** à la caisse.	*There is nobody on the till.*
Des ennuis, je **n'**en veux **point**.	*I do not want any worries.*

When negatives are used as expressions of quantity meaning *not/never ... any of*, they are followed by **de** without an article (see Unit 2 **The next stage** 1 and **The main points** 3 above).

Stéphanie ne boit **jamais de** whisky.	*Stéphanie never drinks whisky.*
Mark ne veut **plus de** fromage.	*Mark does not want any more cheese.*
Il n'achète **jamais de** roquefort.	*He never buys Roquefort.*
Je n'ai **pas de** monnaie.	*I haven't got any change.*
Je ne bois **plus de** vin rouge.	*I don't drink red wine any more.*

The story

Make a list of the **interrogative adjectives** and **interrogative pronouns** used in the dialogue. Identify the **nouns** which the interrogative pronouns replace.

Au supermarché *At the supermarket*

Stéphanie	On va au rayon de vêtements. Il y a beaucoup de vêtements en solde.	*Let's go to the clothes department. There are lots of clothes in the sale.*
Mark	D'accord.	*All right.*
Stéphanie	Ces T-shirts sont jolis. Lequel préfères-tu?	*These T-shirts are pretty. Which one do you prefer?*
Mark	Je préfère le bleu avec la vue de la Tour Eiffel.	*I prefer the blue one with the picture of the Eiffel Tower.*
Stéphanie	De quelle taille as-tu besoin?	*What size do you need?*
Mark	Je ne sais pas quelle taille. « Patron »? Qu'est-ce que ça veut dire?	*I don't know what size. What does 'patron' mean?*

Stéphanie	Ça veut dire *large*. Grand patron, c'est extra.	*It means large. 'Grand patron' is extra large.*
Mark	Je voudrais taille patron. Mon frère est grand pour son âge.	*I'd like the large size. My brother is big for his age.*
Stéphanie	Qu'est-ce que tu achètes pour Sandy?	*What are you buying for Sandy?*
Mark	Je n'ai aucune idée.	*I have no idea.*
Stéphanie	Peut-être des magazines français ou un roman?	*Perhaps French magazines or a novel?*
Mark	Lesquels à ton avis?	*Which ones, do you think?*
Stéphanie	*Marie-Claire, le Point, l'Express.*	Marie-Claire, le Point, l'Express.
Mark	Quel roman suggères-tu?	*Which novel do you suggest?*
Stéphanie	On va à la librairie. Ils ont plus de choix.	*We'll go to the bookshop. They have more choice.*
Mark	Laquelle? La librairie sur la place?	*Which one, the bookshop in the marketplace?*
Stéphanie	Oui, mais d'abord il faut passer à la caisse.	*Yes, but first of all we'll have to go to the till.*

A quick check

1 Rewrite the sentences below by putting the words in the right order. Add capital letters and hyphens wherever necessary.

a je un rouges kilo belles voudrais de pommes.

b taille vous acheter quelle désirez?

c je plus ne de veux viande merci

d nous ma acheter mère du voudrions parfum pour

e vous laquelle ces voudriez de robes?

2 **a** Add the appropriate articles in the following sentence:
Isabelle voudrait ___ pâté, ___ beurre, ___ fromage, ___ pommes de terre, ___ limonade, ___ croissants.

b Add an appropriate expression of quantity to the phrases below:

Stéphanie would like to cook for her mother. She needs …

Stéphanie a besoin de/d':

    ___ bouteille de bordeaux.
    ___ gros poulet.
    un ___ ___ oignons.
    500 _____ ___ champignons.
    une _____ ___ beurre.
    5 _____ ___ pommes de terre.

3 Your friend would like to buy the following items. Ask him/her which one s/he prefers.

Je voudrais:

une chemise
un pantalon
des bonbons
des cerises
du whisky

Laquelle préfères-tu?
_____ préfères-tu?
_____ préfères-tu?
_____ préfères-tu?
_____ préfères-tu?

The next stage

1 MORE ABOUT ARTICLES

All articles normally have to be repeated in a list in French.
See Unit 2 **Say it in French 1, 3** and Unit 4 **The main points 2**.

Voici les activités offertes: **les** randonnées en forêt, **le** golf, **la** natation …	*Here are the available activities: walks in the forest, golf, swimming …*

However, they are sometimes omitted in advertisements or in brochures:

Voici les nombreuses activités offertes par St Amand: randonnées en forêt, golf, natation, ball-trap, canoë-kayak …	*Here are the numerous activities available at St Amand: walks in the forest, golf, swimming, clay-pigeon shooting, canoeing …*

Insight

As gender is crucial in French, get into the good habit of always learning the correct article with every noun. Don't forget to keep adding to the lists of masculine and feminine nouns in your notebook.

2 MORE EXPRESSIONS OF QUANTITY

The adjective **demi/e-** (**une demi-livre** *half a pound*) can be used with many nouns to mean *half*. See also Unit 3 **The next stage 1**.

un **demi**-fromage	*half a cheese*
un **demi**-camembert	*half a Camembert*
une **demi**-heure	*half an hour*

When it comes **before** the noun, **demi-** is joined to it by a hyphen and it is invariable, whatever the gender of the noun. If **demi** follows the noun, it agrees with it in gender:

une heure et **demie**	*an hour and a half*
deux portions et **demie**	*two and a half portions*

3 USING ARTICLES AFTER NEGATIVES

Articles are not used after the negatives **ne … pas, ne … guère, ne … point, ne … jamais, ne … plus** when talking about quantities, or when the words *any/some* are used. See **The main points 5**.

In these cases you say: **pas** *de*, **guère** *de*, **point** *de*, **jamais** *de*, **plus d**e:

Elle **n'**a **pas** d'excuses.	*She doesn't have any excuses.*
Vous **n'**avez **guère de** patience.	*You have hardly any patience.*
Il **ne** mange **jamais de** poisson.	*He never eats fish (any fish).*
Je **n'**ai **plus** d'argent.	*I don't have any more money.*

However, if you want to refer to something specific, the definite article (examples 1 and 2, below) can be used and you can say:

Ils n'ont pas **le** chocolat, indiqué dans la recette, pour faire une bonne mousse au chocolat.	*They haven't got the chocolate mentioned in the recipe to make a good chocolate mousse.*
Je n'ai **plus le** vin que vous aimez tant.	*I haven't got any more of the wine you like so much.*

The indefinite article can also be used after a negative and you can say:

Il n'a **plus un** sou.	*He is penniless (doesn't have a penny).*
Il n'a **pas une** seule excuse.	*He doesn't have a single excuse.*

4 NE ... PERSONNE, PERSONNE NE *(NOBODY)*; NE ... RIEN, RIEN NE *(NOTHING)*

Personne can be the subject of the sentence. In that case, it comes before the **ne/n'**:

Personne ne sait pourquoi.   *Nobody knows why.*

When **rien** is the subject of the sentence, it also comes before the **ne/n'**:

Rien ne l'intéresse.   *Nothing interests him/her.*

5 AVOIR BESOIN DE ... *(TO NEED) IN THE NEGATIVE*

Note that the preposition **de** always follows **besoin** when it is used with a negative:

Je n'ai pas **besoin de** sel.   *I do not need any salt.*
Je n'ai **besoin de** rien.   *I don't need anything/need nothing.*
Il n'a **besoin de** personne.   *He doesn't need anybody.*

6 LA PLUPART DE *(MOST OF)*

After most expressions of quantity followed by **de**, e.g. **beaucoup de**, **un peu de** (**The main points 3**), the partitive article becomes **de**. After the expression **la plupart de** (*most of*), the partitive article is **du/de l'/de la/des**:

La plupart **des** gens   *Most of the people*
La plupart **du** temps   *Most of the time*

TEN THINGS TO REMEMBER

1 Note the difference between the negative sentence **Je n'ai pas d'argent** (*I don't have any money*) and the affirmative sentence **J'ai de l'argent** (*I have some money*). In the negative sentence, the article is omitted.

2 Expressions of quantity and size are not followed by articles: **un paquet de bonbons, beaucoup de vin, un peu de sel**.

3 Remember the expression **je voudrais** (*I would like*), which is a polite way of saying what you want.

4 **J'aimerais** is another way to say *I would like*. Both **je voudrais** and **j'aimerais** are in the conditional tense (Unit 18).

5 **La plupart de** (*most of*) and **la majorité de** (*the majority of*) are followed by an article, like the corresponding English expressions: **la plupart des gens** (*most of the people*, *most people*), **la majorité de la population** (*the majority of the population*).

6 As pointed out in Unit 1 (**The next stage 3**), you cannot ask a question by inverting a verb and a noun. If a noun is used, you have to restate it using a matching pronoun (noun + comma + verb + pronoun): **Le vin, coûte-t-il beaucoup?** (*Does the wine cost much?*) If you use a question word, however, the verb and noun can be inverted: **Combien coûte le vin?** (*How much does the wine cost?*)

7 But even when using a question word, you still cannot invert a proper name (the name of a person) and a verb (Unit 1 **Ten things to remember**). You need to use a pronoun to reinforce the name: **Combien de fois Jacques prend-il le train par semaine?** (*How many times a week does Jacques take the train?*) The only exception is when using **Comment: Comment va Jacques …?** (*How is Jacques going …?*)

8 In order to ask 'which one?' in French, you need to know the gender of the item you're referring to because **lequel** must agree with it: use **Lequel?** for a masculine noun and **Laquelle?** for a feminine noun. To say 'which ones?', use **Lesquels?** if the noun being replaced is masculine plural, and **Lesquelles?** if the noun is feminine plural.

9 When asking a question using **Lequel?**, etc., you can use any one of the three question forms: **Laquelle préfères-tu?**, **Laquelle est-ce que tu préfères?** or in spoken French **Tu préfères laquelle?**

10 The only negative expression which must agree with a feminine noun is **ne ... aucun** (because **aucun** is an adjective): **Je ne veux aucun problème** (*I don't want any problems*), **Je n'ai aucune idée** (*I have no idea*).

5

Saying what you prefer

In this unit you will learn
* **To ask and say what someone prefers**
* **To compare things, places, people**

Topic
* **Shopping**

Grammar
▶ Verbs in **-ir**, such as **choisir** (*to choose*), and verbs in **-re**, such as **vendre** (*to sell*)
▶ Demonstrative pronouns (*this/that/these/those*)
▶ More personal pronouns: direct object pronouns **me** (*me*), **te** (*you*), **le/la/les** (*him/her/them*) and the pronoun **en** (*some of it/of that*)
▶ Comparatives (*less/more*)

The next stage
▶ The irregular verb **prendre** (*to take*), and **re-** before verbs (meaning *again*)
▶ **C'est** or **il est/elle est?**
▶ **Plus de** (*more than*)
▶ The difference between **bon** (*good*) and **bien** (*well*), **meilleur** and **mieux** (*better*)

Getting started

1 You have already met regular and irregular verbs ending in -er. See Unit 1 **The main points** 3. In this unit, you will meet regular verbs ending in **-ir** such as **choisir** and in **-re** such as **vendre**:

Je **choisis** ce livre-ci.   *I choose this book.*
Le supermarché **vend** des vins   *The supermarket sells all qualities*
  de toutes qualités.   *of wine.*

2 Demonstrative adjectives **ce, cet, cette** (that, this), **ces** (these, those) were explained in Unit 2 **The main points** 5. To pinpoint something without repeating the noun, you need to use demonstrative pronouns:

Quel vin désirez-vous?   *Which wine would you like?*
Je voudrais **celui**-ci.   *I'd like this one.*
Celui-là coûte combien?   *How much does that one cost?*
Ceci est important.   *This is important.*

3 You already know how to say that you like or want something.

Je **voudrais** un nouveau logiciel.   *I'd like some new computer*
       software.
Je voudrais un café. Je **le** prends   *I'd like a coffee. I take it black*
  noir et sans sucre.   *and without sugar.*

To avoid repeating the noun, you use direct object pronouns, which, just as in English, are different from subject pronouns: *I* (subject), *me* (object), *he* (subject), *him* (object), etc.:

Il **la** voit tous les jours.   *He sees her every day.*
Je vais l'acheter demain.   *I am going to buy it tomorrow.*
  (le cadeau de mon père)   *(the present for my dad)*
Je **le** choisis car il est bien.   *I choose it because it's good.*
J'**en** voudrais un peu.   *I'd like a little (of it).*

4 In this unit you will learn how to compare things and to express an opinion.

Je préfère un vin **plus** doux.   *I prefer a sweeter wine.*
Je préfère les fruits **moins** amers. *I prefer less bitter fruit.*

Say it in French

1 *WHICH ONE DO YOU PREFER?*

Quel tableau préfères-tu?	*Which painting do you prefer?*
Celui-ci ou **celui-là**?	*This one or that one?*
Quelle carte choisis-tu?	*Which postcard do you choose?*
Je choisis **celle-ci**.	*I choose this one.*
Vous voulez **ceux-ci**? (ces chocolats)	*Do you want these? (these chocolates)*
Oui, je **les** prends.	*Yes, I'll have them.*
Lesquels voulez-vous?	*Which ones do you want?*
Je prends **ceux-ci**.	*I'll take these/those.*

2 *COMPARING THINGS, PLACES AND PEOPLE*

Je préfère les endroits **moins** fréquentés.	*I prefer places which are less crowded.*
Cet ordinateur est **plus** puissant **que celui-là**.	*This computer is more powerful that that one.*
Les livres sont **plus** chers à la librairie **qu'**au supermarché.	*Books are more expensive at the bookshop than at the supermarket.*
Mais, le choix est **plus** grand à la librairie.	*But there is a wider choice at the bookshop.*

The main points

1 *VERBS IN* -IR *AND* -RE

-ir verbs

For regular **-ir** verbs, you follow the same principle as for **-er** verbs. Take the **-ir** off the infinitive and add the following endings:

Pronoun	Stem	Ending
je	chois-	**IS**
tu	chois-	**IS**
il/elle/on	chois-	**IT**
nous	chois-	**ISSONS**
vous	chois-	**ISSEZ**
ils/elles	chois-	**ISSENT**

choisir

je chois**is** un livre	*I choose a book*
tu chois**is** un disque compact	*you choose a compact disc*
il/elle/on chois**it** un nouvel ordinateur	*he/she chooses, we choose a new computer*
nous chois**issons** du bon vin	*we choose good wine*
vous chois**issez** vos amis?	*do you choose your friends?*
ils/elles chois**issent** de nouveaux vêtements	*they are choosing new clothes*

Some regular **-ir** verbs

accomplir	*to accomplish*	**punir**	*to punish*
atterrir	*to land (of a plane)*	**rafraîchir**	*to refresh*
choisir	*to choose*	**ralentir**	*to slow down*
envahir	*to invade*	**réfléchir**	*to think of*
finir	*to finish*	**réussir**	*to succeed*
fournir	*to provide*	**rougir**	*to redden, blush*
grandir	*to grow up*	**salir**	*to dirty*
mûrir	*to ripen*	**vieillir**	*to grow old*

Mark **réfléchit** et **choisit** un joli vase pour les fleurs d'Isabelle.

Mark thinks and chooses a pretty vase for Isabelle's flowers.

Mark et Stéphanie **réussissent** à trouver la plupart des cadeaux.

Mark and Stéphanie manage to find most of the presents.

Mark adore manger des cerises, mais elles ne **mûrissent** et ne **rougissent** qu'en juin.

Mark loves to eat cherries but they only ripen and turn red in June.

Insight

Learners of French often wrongly abbreviate the **-ir** verb endings (**-issez, -issons, -issent**) to **-ez, -ons** and **-ent**. Don't forget the **-iss-**!

rougir (*to blush*): **vous rougissez** (*you are blushing*)

ralentir (*to slow down*): **Ils ralentissent aux feux**. (*They slow down at the traffic lights.*)

-re verbs

For regular **-re** verbs, take the **-re** off the infinitive to get the stem and add the following endings:

Pronoun	Stem	Ending
je	vend-	**S**
tu	vend-	**S**
il/elle/on	vend-	**-**
nous	vend-	**ONS**
vous	vend-	**EZ**
ils/elles	vend-	**ENT**

vendre

je vends mes vieux livres — *I sell my old books*

tu vends les tiens? — *do you sell yours?*

il/elle/on vend beaucoup de choses — *he/she sells, we sell a lot of things*

nous vendons des produits verts — *we sell 'green' products*

vous vendez quelque chose? — *do you sell anything?*

ils/elles vendent des vêtements — *they sell clothes*

Some regular -re verbs

correspondre	*to correspond*	**perdre**	*to lose*
défendre	*to defend*	**pondre**	*to lay (eggs)*
dépendre de	*to depend on*	**rendre**	*to give back*
descendre	*to go down*	**répondre**	*to answer*
entendre	*to hear*	**tondre**	*to mow*

St Amand est célèbre pour les carillonneurs. Tu **entends** les cloches de St Amand?

St Amand is famous for its bell-ringers. Can you hear the bells of St Amand?

Le vendredi, beaucoup de St Amandinois **se rendent** au marché pour acheter leurs fruits et légumes.

On Fridays many people in St Amand go to the market to buy their fruit and vegetables.

Les boulangeries **vendent** du bon pain.

The bakers sell good bread.

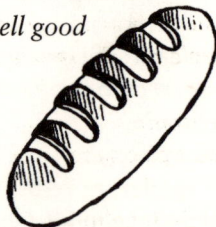

Stéphanie et Mark montent les 370 marches de l'Abbaye et **redescendent**.

Stéphanie and Mark go up the 370 steps of the Abbey and come down again.

2 DEMONSTRATIVE PRONOUNS

Ce + être + adjective

To say *it is*, *this is*, **ce** is used with **être** + adjective when you mention something you have already been speaking or writing about:

Ce n'est pas important. (… un problème)

This is not important. (… a problem)

C'est plutôt cher. (… le prix)

It is rather expensive. (… the price)

It can also be used with **être** and a following noun:

C'est un magasin bien achalandé.   *It is a well-stocked shop.*

Ci *(here),* **là** *(there)*
If you are referring to something specific, you add **ci** (*here*) and **là** (*there*) to **ce**: **ceci** (*this*); **cela** (*that*)

Ceci est à moi.   *This is mine.*
Cela est à lui.   *That's his.*

Ça – cela
ça (*this/that*) is an abbreviation of **cela**:

Je ne comprends pas ça.   *I don't understand that.*
Ça n'a pas d'importance.   *That doesn't matter.*

Ceci/cela
Ceci and **cela** refer to one object, one situation or something general.

Celui-ci, celui-là
If you are choosing between different objects, ideas or situations, you use the following demonstrative pronouns. They replace a noun and agree with it in gender and number:

masc. sing.	fem. sing.	masc. pl.	fem. pl.
celui-ci	**celle-ci**	**ceux-ci**	**celles-ci**
(this one)	*(this one)*	*(these ones)*	*(these ones)*
celui-là	**celle-là**	**ceux-là**	**celles-là**
(that one)	*(that one)*	*(those ones)*	*(those ones)*

See **Say it in French 1**.

J'ai besoin de piles pour mon   *I need some batteries for my*
  baladeur.   *personal stereo.*

Lesquelles choisissez-vous?	*Which ones will you choose?*
Celles-ci.	*These (ones).*
Celles-là ne sont pas de longue durée.	*Those (ones) are not long-life.*
Ces fleurs-ci sont jolies mais je prends **celles-là.**	*Those flowers are pretty but I'll take those.*

Celui de, celui qui/que

The following demonstrative pronouns:

celui (masc. sing.)/**celle** (fem. sing.) (*this, that*)
ceux (masc. pl.)/**celles** (fem. pl.) (*these, those*)

are used with:

de to indicate possession. See Unit 7 **The main points 3**.
que/qui (*that*). See Unit 11 **The main points 5**.

| Ce vélo, c'est **celui de** Nicolas. | *That bike is Nicolas'.* |
| **Celui que** je voudrais | *The one (that) I'd like* |

3 *MORE PERSONAL PRONOUNS*

Remember that, although these pronouns usually refer to people (personal), they can also refer to things: **il/le/la** (*it*); **ils/les** (*they*).

Direct object pronouns

Subject pronouns		Direct object pronouns	
je	*I*	**me**	*me*
tu	*you*	**te**	*you*
il/elle/on	*he/she/one*	**le/la**	*him/her/it*
nous	*we*	**nous**	*us*
vous	*you*	**vous**	*you*
ils/elles	*they*	**les**	*them*

Direct object pronouns come before the verb but after the subject in a statement:

Alors, tu **les** prends? (les fleurs)	*Well are you taking them? (the flowers)*
Mark adore Stéphanie. **Il la** regarde avec passion.	*Mark adores Stéphanie. He looks at her passionately.*
Mark donne une pâquerette à Stéphanie. Elle tire les pétales un à un et dit: « Je **t'**aime un peu, beaucoup, passionnément, à la folie, pas du tout. »	*Mark gives a daisy to Stéphanie. She pulls off the petals one by one and says: 'I love you a little, a lot, passionately, madly, not at all.'*
Et toi, est-ce que tu **m'**aimes?	*And you, do you love me?*
Stéphanie laisse tomber sa liste de courses. Mark **la** ramasse.	*Stéphanie drops her shopping list. Mark picks it up.*
Patrick aime sa voiture.	*Patrick likes his car.*
Il **la** lave tous les week-ends.	*He washes it every weekend.*
Patrick s'occupe du gazon.	*Patrick looks after the lawn.*
Il **le** tond tous les week-ends.	*He mows it every weekend.*

En (some of it, of that) as a personal pronoun

When you want to replace a noun by a pronoun, it is not always possible to use the direct object **le**, **la** when referring to things. For example, if you are talking about quantities – **du poisson** (*some fish*), **de l'argent** (*some money*) – you will need to use the pronoun **en** which means *some* (*of it/of that*).

Je **le** veux.	*I want it. (something specific, precise)*

but

J'**en** veux.	*I want some (of it).*
Combien **en** voulez-vous?	*How much (of it)/How many (of them) would you like?*
J'**en** voudrais deux, s'il vous plaît.	*I'd like two (of them), please.*

4 COMPARATIVES

There are three ways of comparing things or objects.

AUSSI ... QUE
To say that something or someone is *as ... as* something else, you use **aussi ... que**:

Mark est **aussi** intéressé par le sport **que** son frère.	*Mark is as interested in sport as his brother.*

MOINS ... QUE
To say that something or someone is *less ... than*, you use **moins ... que**:

Nicolas est beaucoup **moins** athlétique **qu'**Andrew.	*Nicolas is much less athletic than Andrew.*
Les parents de Stéphanie parlent **moins** vite **que** les gens dans la rue.	*Stéphanie's parents talk less quickly than people in the street.*
Le vin coûte **moins** cher en France **qu'**en Grande-Bretagne.	*Wine costs less in France than in Great Britain.*

PLUS ... QUE
To say that something or someone is *more ... than*, you use **plus ... que**:

Le vin de qualité supérieure coûte **plus** cher **que** le vin de table.	*Top quality wine costs more than table wine.*

Just as in English, the comparison doesn't have to be specific.
You can just say **aussi**, **plus**, **moins**, *without saying* **que** *(than)
(something else)*:

Il coûte **plus** cher.	*It costs more.*
C'est **aussi** intéressant.	*It is just as interesting.*

Two useful comparative adjectives
bon → becomes **meilleur/e/s** (*better*)
mauvais → becomes **pire/s** (*worse*)

Est-ce que le boudin blanc est
  meilleur que le haggis?
Stéphanie pense que c'est **meilleur**,
  mais que les andouillettes sont
  pires.

Is boudin blanc (white
  pudding) better than haggis?
Stéphanie thinks that it is
  nicer, but that chitterlings
  are worse.

There is one adverb which changes its form when it is used as a
comparative: **bien** becomes **mieux** (better)

Je vais **mieux**.   *I feel better.*

The story

When reading this dialogue, look particularly for **demonstrative
pronouns**, **direct object pronouns**, and -**ir** and -**re** verb endings.

Mark achète des cadeaux à la librairie.

Mark is buying presents at the bookshop.

Stéphanie	Voici le rayon des magazines. Lesquels choisis-tu?	*Here is the magazine section. Which ones are you choosing?*
Mark	Celui-ci a l'air intéressant.	*This one looks interesting.*
Stéphanie	Si tu préfères un magazine plus littéraire, il y a *l'Express, le Point, le Nouvel Observateur.*	*If you'd rather have a more literary magazine, there are* l'Express, le Point, le Nouvel Observateur.
Mark	Je prends *le Point.* Je voudrais aussi des journaux régionaux, mais j'attends la fin de la semaine.	*I'll take* le Point. *I'd also like some regional papers, but I'll wait till the end of the week.*
Stéphanie	Voici le rayon des livres de poche. Voici deux romans populaires. Celui-ci est plus passionnant que celui-là. C'est l'histoire d'un ménage à trois à Paris.	*Here is the paperback section. Here are two popular novels. This one is more exciting than that one. It's the story of a love triangle in Paris.*
Mark	Ce genre d'histoire te passionne. Moi, je préfère les livres de science fiction. C'est plus stimulant que les histoires d'amour.	*This type of story really appeals to you. As for me, I prefer science fiction. It is more stimulating than love stories.*
Stéphanie	Merci beaucoup, Mark!	*Thanks a lot, Mark!*
Mark	Sandy est aussi sentimentale que toi. Alors je prends celui-ci.	*Sandy is as sentimental as you. So I'll take this one.*
La vendeuse	Et avec ceci, monsieur?	*Something else, sir?*
Mark	C'est tout, merci, madame.	*That's all, thank you.*

Stéphanie	Il y a un marchand de cadeaux juste à côté. Ils vendent de jolies assiettes en porcelaine. Celle-ci montre la place et la station thermale. Celle-là montre l'Abbaye.	*There is a gift shop just next door. They sell gorgeous china plates. This one shows the square and the spa centre. That one shows the Abbey.*
Mark	Je préfère celle-ci. Elle est beaucoup plus fine que l'autre. Et elle coûte aussi moins cher. D'accord, je la prends pour ma voisine.	*I prefer this one. It's a lot finer than the other one. And it also costs less. OK, I'll take it for my neighbour.*
La vendeuse	Monsieur, vous désirez un emballage-cadeau?	*Would you like it gift-wrapped, sir?*
Mark	Oui, merci, madame.	*Yes, thank you.*
La vendeuse	Je l'emballe aussi dans du polystyrène pour la protéger.	*I'll also wrap it in some polystyrene to protect it.*
Mark	Je vous en remercie.	*Many thanks.*

A quick check

1 Write six pairs of sentences using a pronoun from the left-hand column and the word opposite it in the right-hand column. Use the verb **choisir** and the structure given in the example.

(Je) choisis (une assiette en porcelaine). Je prends (celle-ci).

a	je	une fleur
b	tu	un pot de confiture
c	il/elle/on	un stylo-plume
d	nous	un livre
e	vous	des brochures
f	ils/elles	des biscuits

2 a Add the appropriate endings to the verbs used in the following sentences:

À St Amand, nous entend_____ **les cloches de l'Abbaye** sonner tous les jours.
Ils entend_____ **leurs voisins** partir très tôt.
Quand Mark joue au rugby, il sal_____ **son maillot**.
Mark réfléch_____ et chois_____ **l'assiette en porcelaine** pour sa voisine.

b Replace the expressions in bold above with the corresponding **object pronoun.**

3 Using the notes in the box below, write two sentences, each one using a comparative.

Exemple: Il fait chaud – l'Afrique – le Pôle Nord
Il fait **plus** chaud en Afrique **qu'**au Pôle Nord.
Il fait **moins** chaud au Pôle Nord **qu'**en Afrique.

> Un hôtel quatre étoiles – luxueux – un hôtel deux étoiles
> La Tour Eiffel – haut – la Tour de Blackpool.
> Mark – âgé – Stéphanie.

The next stage

1 *AN IRREGULAR VERB IN* -RE: PRENDRE

▶ **Je, tu, il/elle/on** are regular, but the stem changes in the plural. For other irregular -re and -ir verbs, see Unit 6 **The main points 2.**

prendre *to take*	
je **prends**	nous **prenons**
tu **prends**	vous **prenez**
il/elle/on **prend**	ils/elles **prennent**

▶ re- in verbs like **reprendre** *(to take back, to retake)*

You can add **re-** before many French verbs to mean that you do the action again:

recommencer *to restart,*
refaire *to do again,*
repartir *to go again,*
reprendre *to take again,*
reconnaître *to recognize.*

2 C'EST *OR* IL EST?

Sometimes you have to choose between **c'est** (see **The main points 2**) and **il est**.

Il est/elle est + adjective
▶ **Il est/elle est** is used when you are referring to a specific person:

| **Il/elle** est **riche**. (ton père/ma femme) | *He/she is wealthy. (your father/my wife)* |

or to a specific thing:

| **Elle** est très **importante**. (cette tâche) | *It is very important. (this task)* |

▶ **Il est/elle est** + noun (without an article) is used when you are saying what someone's job or profession is. (See Unit 1 **The main points 2**):

| **Il est** commerçant. | *He is a shopkeeper.* |
| **Elle est** professeur. | *She is a teacher.* |

Il est meaning 'it is'

▶ **Il est** + adjective

There are many impersonal expressions in French based on **il est** meaning *it is*:

Il est important, il est probable, il est possible ... See Unit 10 **The next stage 2, Impersonal expressions** and Unit 17 **The main points 3, Probability and possibility.**

▶ **Il est** + adjective + **de** + infinitive (*it is* + adjective + *to*) is used to refer forward to something later in the sentence:

Il est important d'acheter des cadeaux avant de partir.	*It is important to buy presents before leaving.*
Il est difficile de comprendre cette liste.	*It is difficult to understand this list.*

C'est (it is) + adjective
See **The main points 2**. This refers back to an idea or situation but not to a person.

C'est vraiment très intéressant.	*It is really very interesting.*
C'est vrai, tu sais.	*It is true, you know.*

The structure **c'est** + noun + adjective can be used to refer to a person:

C'est un homme intelligent.	*He is an intelligent man.*
C'est une femme intelligente.	*She is an intelligent woman.*

3 PLUS DE (MORE THAN)

The expression *more than* is not always expressed by **plus que** when you are using figures. **Plus de** is used instead of **plus que** when figures are used:

Il fait **plus de** 30 degrés.	*It is more than (over) 30 degrees.*
Il y a **plus de** 100 élèves.	*There are more than (over) 100 pupils.*

4 BON/BIEN (GOOD/WELL), MEILLEUR/ MIEUX (BETTER)

The adverb **bien** (*well*) is sometimes used in French where in English you would use the adjective *good*:

Ce travail est **bien**.   *This is good work.*

Because there is sometimes a problem for English speakers in choosing between **bon** and **bien**, it might also be difficult to know when to use the comparatives **meilleur** and **mieux**. The adjective **meilleur/e/s** (*better*) is the comparative of **bon/bonne/s** (*good*). It agrees with the appropriate noun in gender and number and goes before the noun it relates to:

Cette confiture est **meilleure** que celle-là.	*This jam is better (literally 'more good') than that.*
Mark a **meilleur** caractère qu'Andrew.	*Mark has a better temper than Andrew.*

The adverb **mieux** (*better*) is the comparative of **bien** (*well/fine*) and remains invariable (does not agree):

Ces nouvelles baskets sont **mieux**.   *These new trainers are better.*

Mieux, being an adverb, follows the verb:

Ça va **mieux**.	*I am better./Things are going better.*
Ça va **mieux**?	*Are you better? Are things any better?*

TEN THINGS TO REMEMBER

1 Make sure you know the present tense endings of regular -**ir** and -**re** verbs.

2 The regular endings of the **nous, vous** and **ils/elles** forms of -**ir** verbs are -**issons**, -**issez** and -**issent**: **nous réussissons, vous choisissez, ils/elles finissent.** Don't forget to add the -**iss**-!

3 Learn the irregular verb **prendre**. Like **faire**, it is very useful in everyday situations: **nous prenons un livre, nous prenons le temps, nous prenons un café.**

4 Note that **comprendre, reprendre** and **apprendre** are also irregular, following the same pattern as **prendre**.

5 Ce used with a noun is a <u>demonstrative adjective</u>. Like all adjectives, it agrees with the noun in gender: **ce livre, cette maison.** In front of a masculine noun beginning with a vowel or vowel sound, **ce** becomes **cet: cet ami. Ce, cet** and **cette** all become **ces** in the plural.

6 When ce is the subject of the verb **est** or **sont**, it is a <u>demonstrative pronoun</u>: **c'est, ce sont.** When it is the subject of other verbs, it becomes **ceci, cela** or **ça: ça m'intéresse** (*that interests me*).

7 In French, object pronouns come before the verb, unlike in English: **il <u>le</u> voit** (*he sees him*).

8 In order to say 'the one' or 'that one', **ce** is combined with **lui, elle, eux** and **elles** to give **celui, celle, ceux** and **celles: celui** (i.e. **le livre**) **dans la vitrine; celle** (i.e. **la maison**) **de Stéphanie, celle que nous aimons.**

9 To compare things or people, use: **moins/plus/aussi** + adjective + **que: Il est aussi grand que moi.** (*He is as tall as me.*) To compare quantities, use: **moins de/plus de/autant de** + noun + **que: Il a autant d'argent que moi.** (*He has as much money as me.*)

10 **Mieux** is an <u>adverb</u> and is used with a <u>verb</u>: **Elle chante mieux que Nicolas.** (*She sings better than Nicolas.*) **Meilleur** is an <u>adjective</u>. It is used with a <u>noun</u> and agrees with it: **Stéphanie est ma meilleure amie.** (*Stéphanie is my best friend.*)

6

Saying what you are going to do

In this unit you will learn
- *To talk about where you are going*
- *To talk about what you are going to do*
- *To ask about people, places and things*
- *To locate people, places and things*

Topic
- *Travel*

Grammar
- ▶ The immediate future: **aller** + infinitive (*going to* + infinitive)
- ▶ Irregular **-ir** and **-re** verbs
- ▶ Prepositions *in, at, to, with*
- ▶ Adverbs
- ▶ **En** + the present participle
- ▶ Superlatives *the least/the most*

The next stage
- ▶ **-ir/-re** reflexive verbs
- ▶ Verbs followed by prepositions
- ▶ More about adverbs in set expressions

Getting started

1 To say where you are going and what you are going to do, you can use the present tense in conversational French.

Je **vais** à Paris la semaine prochaine.   *I am going to Paris next week.*
J'**ai** une réunion dans deux   *I have a meeting in two*
  semaines.   *weeks.*

The future action is indicated by the time expression: *next week/ next year...* In writing, or to emphasize the fact that the action will take place in the future, you will need to use the future tense (see Unit 11). However, just as in English, there is a way of saying that an action will take place in the immediate future (*going to +* infinitive): *I'm going to go abroad soon.*

In French you use the verb **aller** + the infinitive of the verb indicating the action:

Je **vais aller** à Paris la semaine   *I am going to go to Paris*
  prochaine.   *next week.*

You have already learned the present tense of **aller**, which is an irregular verb. If you are unsure refer back to Unit 1 **The main points** 3.

2 In this unit you will also meet more irregular verbs ending in **-ir** and **-re** such as **prendre** (*to take*), **partir** (*to leave*):

Les Français **prennent** souvent un mois   *French people often take a*
  de vacances en juillet ou en août.   *month off in July or August.*
Ils **partent** à la mer ou à la   *They go to the seaside or to*
  montagne.   *the mountains.*

3 To say where you are going to, or to locate people, things or places, you need to use a preposition, for example: *to, in, with, ...*

St-Amand-les-Eaux se trouve   *St-Amand-les-Eaux is situated*
  dans le nord **près de** la   *in the north near the Belgian*
  frontière belge.   *border.*

4 To say **when, where, how, how often** you do something, you use adverbs. In this unit you will find out about common adverbs such as **souvent** (*often*). You will also find out how most other adverbs in French are formed, for example **rarement** (*rarely*).

Isabelle va **souvent** à Paris.	*Isabelle often goes to Paris.*
Elle va à Paris **principalement** pour les expositions dans les musées.	*She goes to Paris mainly for exhibitions in museums.*

5 You have used adjectives for comparisons in Unit 5 **The main points 4** and **Say it in French 2**. In this unit you will learn how to use the superlative form, how to say *the most, the least* and so on:

Paris est **la plus** belle capitale du monde.	*Paris is the most beautiful capital in the world.*

Say it in French

Look more closely at **verb structures**, **prepositions** and **adverbs** in the following examples.

1 *WHERE YOU ARE AND WHERE YOU ARE GOING*

Mark **est** en vacances **à** St-Amand-les-Eaux. St Amand offre de nombreuses attractions touristiques.	*Mark is on holiday in St-Amand-les-Eaux. St Amand has many tourist attractions.*
Mark visite la station thermale. Elle **se trouve près de** la source **du** clos de l'Abbaye.	*Mark visits the spa centre. It is situated near the spring at the Clos de l'Abbaye.*
Mark et Stéphanie se promènent **dans** la forêt de St Amand.	*Mark and Stéphanie are walking in the forest of St Amand.*
La forêt de St Amand est **au centre du** Parc naturel régional.	*St Amand forest is in the centre of the regional country park.*
Mark et Stéphanie **vont visiter** l'Abbaye et écouter le carillon de 48 cloches.	*Mark and Stéphanie are going to visit the Abbey and listen to the peal of 48 bells.*
Ils **vont** aussi **faire** des courses et **prendre** un verre **à** la terrasse d'un café.	*They are also going to go shopping and have a drink at a pavement cafe.*

2 WHAT YOU ARE GOING TO DO

Demain je **vais aller** à la pharmacie **pour** acheter des aspirines.

Tomorrow I am going to go to the chemist to buy some aspirins.

Les parents **de** Mark **vont venir** en France **afin de** rencontrer les parents **de** Stéphanie.

Mark's parents are going to come to France to meet Stéphanie's parents.

Les Dickson **vont suivre** des cours **du** soir en français.

The Dicksons are going to take evening classes in French.

Ils **vont venir** en France **en** juillet.

They are going to come to France in July.

Sandy **va** bientôt **passer** ses examens en français.

Sandy is going to take her French exams soon.

Elle **va** beaucoup **réviser** pendant plusieurs semaines.

She is going to revise a lot for several weeks.

3 ASKING ABOUT PEOPLE, PLACES AND THINGS

Qu'est-ce qu'il y a à voir dans la région?

What is there to see in the area?

Pourquoi la ville porte-t-elle ce nom?

Why does the town have this name?

Où est-elle située?

Where is it situated?

Pourquoi est-elle célèbre?

Why is it famous?

Quelles sont les spécialités de St Amand?

What are the specialities of St Amand?

Qui est le maire de St Amand?

Who is the mayor of St Amand?

Comment est-ce que ça s'appelle?

What's that called?

4 LOCATING PEOPLE, PLACES AND THINGS

Stéphanie et Mark **sont** au café **près de** la gare.

Stéphanie and Mark are at the cafe near the station.

La ville **est située dans** le nord de la France, **à** 30 km de Lille.

The town is situated in the north of France, 30 km from Lille.

Le musée **se trouve sur** la place du marché.

The museum is situated in the market place.

The main points

1 *THE IMMEDIATE FUTURE*

Aller *(to go) + infinitive*
The immediate future tells you what is going to happen in the not
too distant future and replaces the future tense in conversational
French, when no specific point about the future is being made. See
Say it in French 2.

Les Dickson **vont mettre** leur français en pratique durant leurs vacances.	*The Dicksons are going to put their French to use during their holidays.*
Ils **vont faire** la connaissance de la famille de Stéphanie.	*They are going to meet Stéphanie's family.*
Où **allez**-vous **passer** vos vacances?	*Where are you going to spend your holidays?*
Nous n'**allons** pas **passer** les vacances en Italie.	*We aren't going to spend the holidays in Italy.*
Allez-vous **visiter** Marseille?	*Are you going to visit Marseilles?*

2 *IRREGULAR* -IR *AND* -RE *VERBS*

Verbs in **-ir**
A small group of irregular verbs ending in **-ir** add the following
endings to the stem:

-e, -es, -e, -ons, -ez, -ent.

The stem of these verbs does not change in the plural:

cueillir *to pick*	cueille, cueilles, cueille,	cueillons, cueillez, cueillent
offrir *to offer*	offre, offres, offre,	offrons, offrez, offrent
ouvrir *to open*	ouvre, ouvres, ouvre,	ouvrons, ouvrez, ouvrent
souffrir *to suffer*	souffre, souffres, souffre,	souffrons, souffrez, souffrent

Mark **cueille** un brin de muguet pour Stéphanie.

Mark picks a sprig of lily of the valley for Stéphanie.

A group of irregular verbs ending in two consonants before **-ir** have the **-ir** and also one preceding consonant removed to form the stem for the first three persons in the singular. The following endings are added:

-s, -s, -t, -ons, -ez, -ent.

The stem does not change in the plural:

dormir *to sleep*	**dors, dors, dort,**	**dormons, dormez, dorment**
mentir *to lie*	**mens, mens, ment,**	**mentons, mentez, mentent**
partir *to leave*	**pars, pars, part,**	**partons, partez, partent**
sortir *to go out*	**sors, sors, sort,**	**sortons, sortez, sortent**
courir *(to run)* has the same endings:		
	cours, cours, court,	**courons, courez, courent**

Le vendredi soir, Mark et Stéphanie **sortent** à Aberdeen.

On Friday nights Mark and Stéphanie go out in Aberdeen.

Two **-ir** verbs are highly irregular:

tenir *to hold*	**tiens, tiens, tient,**	**tenons, tenez, tiennent**
venir *to come*	**viens, viens, vient,**	**venons, venez, viennent**

Verbs with similar spelling such as **devenir** (*to become*), **revenir** (*to come back*), **retenir** (*to hold back*), etc. follow the same pattern:

Isabelle **tient** les cordons de la bourse.

Isabelle holds the purse-strings.

Les parents de Mark **viennent** de Dundee.

Mark's parents come from Dundee.

Verbs in **-re**

The stem of irregular -re verbs changes in the present tense with plural subjects.

For **prendre,** the stem becomes **pren-** so that the plural forms of the present tense are:

nous prenons, vous prenez, ils prennent

The endings of the present tense of the other irregular **-re** verbs are: **-s, -s, -t, -ons, -ez, -ent.**

Here is a more complete list of irregular verbs in **-re.**

Look at the way the stem changes in the plural:

boire to drink	**bois, bois, boit,**	**buvons, buvez, boivent**
croire to believe	**crois, crois, croit,**	**croyons, croyez, croient**
conduire to drive	**conduis, conduis, conduit,**	**conduisons, conduisez, conduisent**
connaître to know	**connais, connais, connaît,**	**connaissons, connaissez, connaissent**
dire to say	**dis, dis, dit,**	**disons, dites, disent**
écrire to write	**écris, écris, écrit**	**écrivons, écrivez, écrivent**
lire to read	**lis, lis, lit,**	**lisons, lisez, lisent**
prendre to take	**prends, prends, prend,**	**prenons, prenez, prennent**
suivre to follow	**suis, suis, suit,**	**suivons, suivez, suivent**
vivre to live	**vis, vis, vit**	**vivons, vivez, vivent**

Cette année Mark et Stéphanie **prennent** une semaine de vacances en mai.	*This year Mark and Stéphanie are taking a week's holiday in May.*
Les Dickson ne **connaissent** pas encore les Lemaire.	*The Dicksons do not know the Lemaires yet.*
Mark **écrit** quelques cartes.	*Mark writes some postcards.*
Stéphanie les **lit** et ajoute un petit mot.	*Stéphanie reads them and adds a few words.*

For more information on irregular verbs, see the **Verb tables.**

3 PREPOSITIONS (IN, AT, TO, WITH)

Prepositions can go with verbs, for example **sortir de** (*to go out of/ to come from*), but they mainly introduce adverbial phrases which explain *where*, *when*, *how*, *why* things happen. See **The main points 4** below.

Here is a list of prepositions (both single words and groups of words) you have already met in examples in this book:

Prepositions and prepositional groups for place (where)

à	*to/in/at*	**dans**	*in*
à côté de	*beside/next to*	**de**	*of/from/by*
à l'intérieur de	*inside*	**derrière**	*behind*
après	*after*	**devant**	*in front of*
au bord de	*on/at the edge of*	**en**	*to/in/of*
au coin de	*on/at the corner of*	**en face de**	*opposite*
au-dessous de	*below/underneath*	**entre**	*between*
au-dessus de	*above*	**loin de**	*far from*
autour de	*around*	**parmi**	*among*
avant	*before*	**près de**	*near*
chez	*at/at the home of (someone)*	**sous**	*under*
		sur	*on*
contre	*against*	**vers**	*towards*

L'Abbaye se trouve **sur** la place **en face de** l'hôtel de ville.	*The Abbey is situated in the marketplace opposite the town hall.*
L'agence de voyages se trouve **au coin de** la rue, **à côté du** marchand de légumes **près de** l'Abbaye.	*The travel agency is situated on the corner of the street, next to the greengrocer's near the Abbey.*
À St Amand, il y a un marché **sur** la place tous les vendredis **de** 9 heures **à** 13 heures.	*In St Amand there is a market in the square every Friday from 9.00 to 13.00.*

Prepositions for time (when)

à	*at*	**jusque**	*until*
avant	*before*	**pendant**	*during*
après	*after*	**pour**	*for*
depuis	*since/for*		

Insight

In French, be careful to use the preposition **à** (*at/in/to*) correctly with verbs of movement such as *fly to, walk to, travel to,* etc.:

▶ When you say **Je voyage à Paris**, you are actually saying *I am travelling IN Paris,* not *I am travelling TO Paris.* So you need to add how you are travelling: **Je vais me rendre/aller à Paris en train/en avion.** *(I am going to go to Paris by train/by plane.)*

▶ Similarly, **Je marche à l'université** means that you are walking around within the university precinct, whereas **Je vais à l'université à pied** means I am going to the university on foot.

Stéphanie habite à Aberdeen **depuis** six mois.
Avant ça, elle était à l'université de Lille **pendant** deux ans.
Elle va travailler à Aberdeen **jusqu'** à la fin de son stage, puis elle espère y trouver un autre emploi.

Stéphanie has been living in Aberdeen for six months.
Before that she was at the University of Lille for two years.
She is going to work in Aberdeen until the end of her work placement and then she is hoping to find another job there.

Other prepositions and prepositional groups showing how or why:

afin de	*in order to*	**par**	*by/through*
à cause de	*because of*	**pour**	*in order to*
au lieu de	*instead of*	**presque**	*almost*
avec	*with*	**sans**	*without*
comme	*like, such as*	**sauf**	*except*
d'après	*according to*	**selon**	*according to*
de façon à	*in order to*	**suite à**	*following*

Stéphanie travaille **comme** stagiaire pour une compagnie pétrolière à Aberdeen.

Stéphanie works as a trainee for an oil company in Aberdeen.

Elle travaille **avec** Mark. **Selon lui,** elle est très douée et elle se débrouille très bien dans son emploi.

She works with Mark. In his opinion she is very gifted and is doing very well in her job.

Mark a tous les cadeaux **sauf** un pour son meilleur ami.

Mark has all his presents except one for his best friend.

As mentioned in Unit 1 **The main points 8**, when prepositions are followed by personal pronouns, stressed pronouns are used: **moi, toi, lui/elle/soi, nous, vous, eux/elles.** See also Unit 7 **The main points 6.**

Tu viens **avec moi?**

Are you coming with me?

Elle va à la librairie **avec lui.**

She is going to the bookshop with him.

Selon toi, Mark, est-ce que Stéphanie va obtenir un emploi à temps complet à la fin de son stage?

Mark, in your opinion, is Stéphanie going to get a full-time job at the end of her work placement?

Tu y vas **sans moi?**

Are you going without me?

4 ADVERBS

Adverbs describe *where*, *when*, *how*, or *why* something happens. They work with words such as verbs, adjectives or other adverbs to change or explain the basic meaning. There are two main groups of adverbs:

Short, frequently used adverbs

assez	*fairly/enough*	**toujours**	*always*
bien	*well*	**très**	*very*
moins	*less*	**trop**	*too*
plus	*more*	**vite**	*fast*
souvent	*often*	**vraiment**	*really/truly*

Adverbs formed from adjectives

For these adverbs you simply add -**ment**, usually to the feminine form of the adjective:

actif *(m)*	**active** *(f)*	active**ment**
heureux *(m)*	**heureuse** *(f)*	heureuse**ment**
mondial *(m)*	**mondiale** *(f)*	mondiale**ment**
passif *(m)*	**passive** *(f)*	passive**ment**
principal *(m)*	**principale** *(f)*	principale**ment**
régulier *(m)*	**régulière** *(f)*	régulière**ment**

For adjectives which already end in -**e**, add -**ment** without any change:

simple *(m, f)*	simple**ment**
véritable *(m, f)*	véritable**ment**

For adjectives ending in -**ent/-ant**, remove the -**ent/-ant** and add -**emment/-amment**:

fréquent	fréqu**emment**
prudent	prud**emment**
courant	cour**amment**

The position of adverbs
Adverbs can accompany/modify **verbs**, **adjectives** or **other adverbs**.

▶ When adverbs modify **verbs**, they usually come after the verb (or after the auxiliary verb **être** or **avoir** in the perfect tense, see Unit 13 **The main points 3**):

Mark travaille **souvent** sur la plate-forme pétrolière.	*Mark often works on the oil rig.*
Il téléphone **régulièrement** à Stéphanie.	*He phones Stéphanie regularly.*
Il a **déjà** acheté un téléphone portable.	*He has already bought a mobile phone.*

▶ When adverbs modify **adjectives,** they come directly before the adjective:

Mark trouve les parents de Stéphanie **vraiment** sympathiques.	*Mark finds Stéphanie's parents really friendly.*
Il est **très** heureux d'être en France.	*He is very happy to be in France.*

▶ Short adverbs such as **trop, plus, très** can also modify other adverbs and are placed before them:

Certains Français roulent **trop** vite.	*Some French people drive too fast.*
Les Britanniques roulent **plus** prudemment.	*The British drive more cautiously.*

5 ADVERBIAL PHRASES

There are some frequently used adverbial phrases which are formed from a preposition + a **noun:**

avec plaisir	*with pleasure*
en ce moment	*at the moment*
en retard	*late*

Georges et Isabelle accueillent Mark **avec plaisir.**	*Georges and Isabelle welcome Mark with pleasure.*

6 TIME PHRASES

To say when something happened, there are some time phrases which do not start with a preposition in French, although they do in English:

le samedi soir	*on Saturday nights*
le dimanche matin	*on Sunday mornings*
le matin	*in the morning*
lundi	*on Monday*
le lundi	*on Mondays*

7 EN + THE PRESENT PARTICIPLE

See Unit 3 **The next stage 3**.

In English, you form the present participle from the infinitive of the verb by adding *-ing*:

to drive → driving; to go → going

In French, you find the stem of the verb and add **-ant**:

rouler → roul- → roul**ant** (*driving*); **aller** → all- → all**ant** (*going*)

Se couch**ant** tard à cause de ses examens, Sandy est très fatiguée.	*Going to bed late because of her exams, Sandy is very tired.*

To show that one thing causes another (*by/in …ing*), in French you add the preposition **en** before the present participle (the **-ant** form of the verb):

En pren**ant** des cours du soir, les parents de Mark espèrent apprendre assez de français pour communiquer avec les Lemaire.	*By taking evening classes, Mark's parents hope to learn enough French to communicate with the Lemaires.*

8 SUPERLATIVES: THE LEAST, THE MOST

The most …
To say that something or someone is *the most* …, or for adjectives that end in *-est* in English (great*est*, old*est*, new*est*), you use: **le/ la/les plus** + adjective. The adjective agrees in number and gender with the noun, and its position does not change.

Most adjectives go *after* the noun:

Nicolas est le cinéphile **le plus** passionné de toute la famille.	*Nicolas is the keenest cinema enthusiast of the whole family.*

St Amand est une des villes **les plus** connues du nord, ayant participé plusieurs fois aux jeux d'Interville.

St Amand is one of the most famous cities in the north, having taken part in the Interville Games several times.

L'eau de St Amand est une des eaux **les plus** riches en minéraux et en magnésium et c'est **la plus** consommée dans le nord.

St Amand water is among the richest in minerals and magnesium and is the one most people drink in the north.

Here are some examples of adjectives which go before the noun. See Unit 3 **The main points 1**.

Nicolas est **le plus grand** garçon de sa classe.

Nicolas is the tallest boy in his class.

À la maison, il a **la plus petite** chambre.

At home, he has the smallest bedroom.

The least …

To say that something or someone is *the least* you use: **le/la/les moins** + adjective. The adjective agrees in number and gender with the noun:

Nicolas est **le moins** sportif de toute la famille.

Nicolas is the least sporty of the whole family.

L'eau de St Amand est aussi une des eaux minérales **les moins** chères.

St Amand water is also one of the least expensive mineral waters.

The story

In the following conversation, look for **expressions of time** and **of place**, and for verbs **expressing an immediate future**:

Isabelle parle de Paris à Mark.

Isabelle is talking to Mark about Paris.

Isabelle	Mark, connaissez-vous Paris?	*Mark, do you know Paris?*
Mark	Non, mais j'aimerais beaucoup y aller un jour avec Stéphanie. Est-ce que vous allez souvent à Paris?	*No, but I would very much like to go there one day with Stéphanie. Do you go to Paris often?*
Isabelle	Environ une fois par an. J'ai des cousins qui vivent là-bas. Exceptionnellement, je vais y aller la semaine prochaine, afin de rendre visite à ma cousine Jacqueline. Elle est à l'hôpital suite à un accident de la route. Je pars mercredi matin.	*About once a year. I have some cousins who live there. Exceptionally, I'm going to go there next week, to visit my cousin Jacqueline. She is in hospital as the result of a road accident. I'm leaving on Wednesday morning.*
Mark	Est-ce que c'est très grave?	*Is it very serious?*
Isabelle	Assez grave. D'après les docteurs elle a vraiment de la chance d'être en vie. Sa voiture est complètement inutilisable. Elle a les deux jambes cassées et quelques blessures aux bras et au visage. Elle dort très mal et elle se sent plutôt déprimée. Je vais donc aller la voir.	*Fairly serious. According to the doctors she is very lucky to be alive. Her car is a complete write-off. Both her legs are broken and she has a few cuts to her arms and face. She is sleeping very badly and feels rather depressed. So I'm going to go and see her.*
Mark	Combien de temps allez-vous rester à Paris?	*How long are you going to stay in Paris?*
Isabelle	Trois ou quatre jours seulement. Je vais en profiter pour faire quelques courses pendant mon séjour là. Je voudrais aller aux Galeries Lafayette, près de l'Opéra. C'est le magasin le mieux	*Only three or four days. I'm going to take the opportunity to do some shopping during my stay there. I'd like to go to the Galeries Lafayette near the Opera. It is the most convenient and the most popular shop in Paris.*

situé et le plus populaire
de Paris. Il est extrêmement
populaire avec les touristes.

*It is extremely popular with
tourists.*

A quick check

1 Put the words in the following sentences in the correct order,
adding capitals and punctuation as necessary:
- **a** vais St Amand je visiter de l'Abbaye
- **b** est-ce des vas cartes que postales tu acheter
- **c** le j' aller les sangliers aimerais bois dans voir les de
  St Amand

2 Make the verbs in brackets agree with their subject and add the
correct prepositions in the following sentences:
- **a** Mark (écrire) des cartes postales ___ St Amand et les
  (envoyer) ___ sa famille ___ Dundee et ___ ses amis.
- **b** Les parents ___ Mark (vivre) ___ un quartier résidentiel ___
  Dundee.
- **c** Mr Dickson (prendre) le bus ___ se rendre au travail le
  matin.
- **d** Il est directeur ___ un supermarché ___ quelques kilomètres
  ___ centre ville ___ de la rivière Tay.
- **e** Il (partir) ___ 8 heures le matin et (revenir) ___ 18 heures,
  ___ le jeudi soir car il travaille ___ 21 heures.

3 Select adverbs from the lists in **The main points 4** above, and
add them to the following sentences:

Dundee occupe une position _____ privilégiée sur la côte est
de l'Écosse. Les deux collines, Balgay et Law, offrent une vue
_____ superbe de la Tay et de la campagne. Dundee est une
ville _____ connue pour le bateau *Discovery*, et l'observatoire
de Balgay avec ses vues féeriques. Dundee est une ville _____
accueillante pas très loin de St Andrews _____ célèbre pour le
golf.

The next stage

1 -IR/-RE *REFLEXIVE VERBS*

Most reflexive verbs are -**er** verbs. See Unit 3 **The main points**
2 and 3. Some -**ir/-re** verbs can also be used as reflexives. The
extra pronoun **se** which comes in front of the verb changes form
according to the subject of the verb.

Here are a few examples of -**ir** and -**re** reflexive verbs:

s'asseoir *to sit down*	**Tu t'assieds.**
se comprendre *to understand one another*	**Nous nous comprenons.**
se conduire *to behave (oneself)*	**Ils se conduisent bien.**
se connaître *to know oneself/know each other*	**Vous vous connaissez?**
se dire *to tell oneself*	**Je me dis ...**
s'écrire *to write to each other*	**Nous nous écrivons.**
se tenir *to stand/behave/hold*	**Ils se tiennent bien.**

Mark et Stéphanie **se tiennent** la main.	*Mark and Stéphanie hold hands.*
Les Dickson et les Lemaire ne **se connaissent** pas encore.	*The Dicksons and the Lemaires don't know each other yet.*

2 *VERBS FOLLOWED BY PREPOSITIONS*

Prepositions are often used differently in English and French.
This is most noticeable in **verb groups** (**s'habituer à, penser à, se
contenter de**). For example, the preposition **à** can be translated by
at/in and it also means *to*:

Mark s'habitue **à** la vie française. *Mark is getting used to French life.*

à can also mean *of/about* in expressions such as:
penser **à** (*to think of/about*)

de can also mean *with* in expressions such as:
se contenter **de** (*to be satisfied with*)

par can mean *with* in expressions such as:

> commencer **par** (*to begin with*),
> remplacer **par** (*to replace with*)

Mark pense à écrire à ses amis.	*Mark is thinking of writing to his friends.*
Mark et Stéphanie se contentent **de** sortir le week-end.	*Mark and Stéphanie are satisfied with going out at weekends.*

Many French verbs are almost always followed by a preposition, forming a **verb group**.

It is important to remember the verb *with its preposition* and to look up the verb in a good dictionary whenever you are unsure.

Here is a list of French verbs followed by the preposition **à**:

aboutir à	*to lead to*
***aider quelqu'un à**	*to help someone to*
s'amuser à (+ inf.)	*to amuse oneself* (+ verb + *ing*)
appartenir à	*to belong to*
***chercher à**	*to try to*
***commencer à**	*to begin to*
consentir à	*to consent to*
***continuer à**	*to continue to*
s'habituer à	*to become used to*
***inviter quelqu'un à**	*to invite someone to*
***penser à**	*to think of*
***réussir à**	*to succeed in*

Stéphanie s'habitue à vivre à Aberdeen.	*Stéphanie is getting used to living in Aberdeen.*
Elle cherche à rester en Écosse.	*She is trying to stay in Scotland.*

The verbs marked with * above and below are not always followed by a preposition, either in English or in French. Some can also be followed by a direct object:

Il commence **son travail** à 8 h 30. *He starts work at 8.30.*

Here is a list of French verbs followed by the preposition **de**. As you can see, this preposition can be translated in many ways: *to*, *from*, *of*, *for*, *with*. Note that the equivalent English verb may not be followed by a preposition.

s'arrêter de (+ inf.)	*to stop (doing something)*
avoir l'air de	*to look like*
avoir besoin de	*to need*
avoir envie de	*to be afraid of*
se contenter de	*to be satisfied with*
se dépêcher de	*to hurry to*
douter de	*to doubt*
*éviter de	*to avoid (doing something)*
s'excuser de	*to apologize for*
*finir de	*to finish*
*offrir de	*to offer to*
*ordonner à quelqu'un de	*to order someone to*
parler de	*to talk about*
se passer de	*to do without*
penser de	*to have an opinion about*
se souvenir de	*to remember*

The reflexive verbs (**s'arrêter, se contenter, se dépêcher** …) have a preposition when they are followed by an infinitive. You would say:

Je me dépêche.   *I hurry up*

but

Je me dépêche **de faire** quelque chose.	*I hurry to do something.*
Mark se dépêche **de téléphoner** à Stéphanie.	*Mark rushes to phone Stéphanie.*

There are some verbs which are followed by a preposition in English, but not in French:

chercher	*to look for*
écouter	*to listen to*

| **entrer** | *to come in* |
| **regarder** | *to look at* |

| Nous cherchons St-Amand-les-Eaux. | *We're looking for St-Amand-les-Eaux.* |
| Nicolas écoute la radio. | *Nicolas is listening to the radio.* |

Only a few prepositions can be followed by a verb – usually the infinitive:

▶ à, de
▶ compound prepositions containing de, such as loin de, avant de, au lieu de
▶ pour, sans, par
▶ après can be followed by avoir or être (See Unit 15 **The next stage 3**):

| **Après avoir** acheté ses cadeaux, il ne lui reste plus beaucoup d'argent. | *After buying his presents he doesn't have a lot more money left.* |

3 MORE ABOUT ADVERBS

Cher
The adjective **cher** can become an adverb. It is invariable when it is used in the set expression **coûter cher**:

| Cette robe coûte **cher**. | *This dress costs a lot.* |
| Ces logiciels coûtent **cher**. | *These software packages are expensive.* |

Vite
Vite is an adverb and not an adjective.

You say:

| Ces trains sont **rapides**. | *These trains are fast.* |

(adjective qualifying the noun *trains*-masc. plural)

But if you use **vite,** it is invariable:

Stéphanie roule **vite.**   *Stéphanie drives fast.*

(adverb modifying the verb **roule**)

Mal
Mal is also an adverb, not an adjective, so it does not show agreement:

Cela fait **mal.**   *It hurts.*
La cousine d'Isabelle se   *Isabelle's cousin feels rather*
  sent plutôt **mal.**   *unwell.*

Beaucoup trop
You can say **beaucoup trop** (*far too much*).

Mark aime **beaucoup**   *Mark likes sweet things (far) too*
  trop les sucreries.   *much.*

Adjectives used as adverbs
Some adjectives can be used as adverbs in certain phrases (see **cher** above), in which case they do not show agreement:

Parler **fort/haut**   *To speak loudly*

TEN THINGS TO REMEMBER

1 The preposition **à** can be a bit confusing. It can mean *in*, *at*, *to* or *with*: **Je suis à Dundee** (*in Dundee*), **Il fait des études à l'université** (*at the university*), **Je vais à St Amand** (*to St Amand*), **Alison porte une robe à fleurs** (*with flowers on it*).

2 They are many irregular **-ir**, **-re** and **-oir** verbs. Learn them as you progress through the book and keep details in the irregular verb section of your notebook.

3 If you want to say *the most* or *the least*, use **le/la/les** (depending on the gender and number of the noun) + **plus/moins** in front of the adjective: **le plus beau** (**jardin**) (*the most beautiful (garden)*), **les moins chers** (**vins**) (*the least expensive (wines)*, **la plus intéressante** (**histoire**) (*the most interesting (story)*.

4 Long adverbs are formed by adding **-ment** to the feminine form of the adjective: **intellectuellement**.

5 To make an adverb from adjectives ending in **-ant** or **-ent**, add the endings **-amment** or **-emment**: **courant** → **couramment** (*fluently*), **prudent** → **prudemment** (*prudently*).

6 Just as it is important to remember the gender of each noun as you learn it, for verbs it is important to remember whether they are followed by **de** or **à**.

7 If the verb structure includes a noun, the preposition used is more likely to be **de**: **j'ai l'intention de**, **j'ai besoin de**.

8 Note that **vite** and **mal** are adverbs and are therefore used to modify verbs, not nouns: **je roule vite/mal** (*I drive fast/badly*). With nouns, you must use an adjective: **j'ai une voiture rapide** (*I have a fast car*), **j'ai une mauvaise** note (*I've got a bad mark*).

9 Je viens de literally means 'I come from', but it can mean 'I have just done (something)': **Je viens d'acheter une nouvelle voiture.** (*I've just bought a new car.*)

10 To say that you are about to do something soon, in the immediate future, you can use the structure **aller** + infinitive: **Je vais acheter une nouvelle voiture.** (*I'm going to buy a new car.*)

7

Saying who owns what

In this unit you will learn
- *To speak about personal ownership*
- *To say and ask who owns something*

Topic
- *Homes and possessions*

Grammar
▶ More about possessive adjectives *my*, *your*, *her/his/its*
▶ Possessive pronouns *mine*, *his*, *hers*
▶ The preposition **de** to show possession
▶ The preposition **à** to show belonging
▶ Useful verbs for possession and ownership: **être** (*to be*), **avoir** (*to have*), **appartenir** (*to belong to*) in the present tense
▶ Stressed pronouns after **à** and **de**

The next stage
▶ More about possessive adjectives and pronouns
▶ More about possession

Getting started

You have already met possessive adjectives which show ownership. See Unit 2 **The main points 6**.

| Voilà l'appartement de **mes** amis. | *That is my friends' flat.* |
| **Leur** appartement est situé près des magasins. | *Their flat is situated near the shops.* |

As you can see from the above examples, possessive adjectives always come before the noun and agree in gender and number with the noun they precede and **not with the owner.**

| Stéphanie cherche **son** livre. | *Stéphanie is looking for her book.* |
| « Où est **mon** livre? » demande-t-elle à Nicolas. | *'Where is my book?' she asks Nicolas.* |

1 You use possessive pronouns to avoid repeating a noun:

Leur appartement is replaced by **le leur**.
Mon livre is replaced by **le mien**.

| Cet appartement est **le leur**. | *This flat is theirs.* |
| Ce livre est **le mien**. | *This book is mine.* |

2 In English, possession can also be expressed by the use of *'s* or *s'*. In French, the preposition **de** is used to show ownership:

| Les amis **de** mes parents ont une propriété sur la Côte d'Azur. | *My parents' friends have a property on the Côte d'Azur.* |

3 In this unit, you will also meet the preposition **à** to show ownership, useful verbs to show ownership and possession – **être** (*to be*), **avoir** (*to have*), **appartenir** (*to belong to*) – and will learn to ask questions about ownership and possession: *Whose is it/this?*, *Who do they/these belong to?*

| C'est à Nicolas? Non, c'est à Stéphanie. | *Is it Nicolas'? No, it is Stéphanie's.* |

4 As mentioned in Unit 6 **The main points** 3, if a preposition is followed by a personal pronoun, the stressed pronoun is used: **moi, toi, lui/elle/soi, nous, vous, eux/elles.**

The other grammatical structures you will find useful to express possession are:

▶ Demonstrative adjectives (Unit 2 **The main points** 5)
▶ Demonstrative pronouns (Unit 5 **The main points** 2)

Ce livre est à moi. Es-ce que **celui-ci** est à toi? *This book is mine. Is this one yours?*

Say it in French

The following examples show the different structures used in French to express possession. Look at them and check with the English translation if necessary before going on to the **The main points**.

1 *SHOWING PERSONAL OWNERSHIP*

Voici la maison **de** la famille Lemaire.	*This is the Lemaires' house.*
Leur maison est individuelle.	*Their house is detached.*
La chambre **de** Stéphanie est la plus grande.	*Stéphanie's room is the biggest.*
Voici la chambre **de son** frère.	*This is her brother's bedroom.*
Sa chambre est toujours en désordre.	*His bedroom is always untidy.*
Isabelle et George ont la chambre la plus spacieuse. **La leur** a un balcon et une salle de bains complète.	*Isabelle and George have the most spacious room. Theirs has a balcony and an en suite bathroom.*
Nicolas trouve **la sienne** trop petite.	*Nicolas thinks his is too small.*
Comment est **la tienne**?	*What is yours like?*

2 ASKING WHO OWNS SOMETHING

À qui est cette chambre?	*Whose is this bedroom?*
À qui appartient la plus grande chambre?	*Who does the biggest bedroom belong to?*
Tu **as** la plus grande chambre?	*Do you have the biggest bedroom?*
C'est l'ordinateur **de qui**?	*Whose computer is it?*
À qui sont ces logiciels?	*Who does this software belong to?*
Est-ce que ces logiciels **appartiennent** à Nicolas?	*Does this software belong to Nicolas?*

The main points

1 MORE ABOUT POSSESSIVE ADJECTIVES

Possessive adjectives must agree in both gender and number with the noun they accompany, so there are more variations in French than in English:

mon, ma, mes	*my*
ton, ta, tes	*your*
son, sa, ses	*his/her/its*
notre, nos	*our*
votre, vos	*your* (plural and formal)
leur, leurs	*their*

Nicolas, est-ce que c'est **ta** chambre ou celle de **ta** sœur?	*Nicolas, is this your bedroom or your sister's?*
Stéphanie ne trouve pas **son** album de photos.	*Stéphanie can't find her photo album.*
Nos livres sont dans le bureau en bas.	*Our books are in the office downstairs.*
Leurs voisins se plaignent souvent du bruit.	*Their neighbours often complain about the noise.*

Insight

In English, we say 'They are carrying their umbrellas', whereas French says **Ils portent leur parapluie** (i.e. they are carrying one umbrella each). **Ils portent leurs parapluies** would mean that they are carrying several umbrellas each.

In English, 'They like their cars' could mean that several people each like their own car or, for example, that a family own several cars and like all of them. In French, you would say either **Ils aiment leur voiture** (they each like their own car) or **Ils aiment leurs voitures** (they own several cars and like them all).

2 POSSESSIVE PRONOUNS (MINE, HIS, HERS, OURS, ...)

As you can see from the words in bold in the following examples (**la mienne, la sienne,** etc.), possessive pronouns agree in number and gender with the noun they replace. They *agree* in both number and gender *with whatever is owned* – not with the owner as in English. They are like nouns because they are accompanied by the definite articles **le/la/les,** which also vary according to the gender and number of the thing owned.

Forms of the possessive pronoun				
masc. sing.	*fem. sing.*	*masc. plural*	*fem. plural*	
le mien	la mienne	les miens	les miennes	*mine*
le tien	la tienne	les tiens	les tiennes	*yours (informal)*
le sien	la sienne	les siens	les siennes	*his/her/its*
le nôtre	la nôtre	les nôtres	les nôtres	*ours*
le vôtre	la vôtre	les vôtres	les vôtres	*yours (plural, formal)*
le leur	la leur	les leurs	les leurs	*theirs*

À qui est ce MP3?	*Whose MP3 is this?*
C'est **le mien**.	*It's mine.*
Nicolas emmène **le sien** au lycée.	*Nicolas takes his to the secondary school.*
Ce CD n'est pas **le tien**.	*This CD is not yours.*
Nos voisins se plaignent souvent. Comment sont **les vôtres** (plural)?	*Our neighbours often complain. What are yours like?*

3 THE PREPOSITION DE TO SHOW POSSESSION OR OWNERSHIP

Very often in French **de** is used, particularly with a person's name, to show that someone owns something. There is no equivalent structure to the English *'s, s'*.

La chambre **de** Stéphanie est toujours très bien rangée.	*Stéphanie's room is always very tidy.*
Celle **de** Nicolas est toujours en désordre.	*Nicolas' is always untidy. (i.e. the one of Nicolas ...)*
La chambre **de** leurs parents offre une jolie vue sur la campagne.	*Their parents' room has a lovely view over the countryside.*

4 THE PREPOSITION À TO SHOW BELONGING

In French, the preposition à is used in questions to ask *Whose is ...?* or *Whose are ...?* **À qui est ...?**, **À qui sont ...?** as shown in these examples. It is also used to say to whom something belongs.

À qui sont ces magazines?	*Whose are these magazines?*
À qui est cette vidéo-ci?	*Whose is this video?*
Ces logiciels ne sont pas **à toi.**	*This software isn't yours.*
Ils sont à ton ami.	*It belongs to your friend.*
À qui est la nouvelle voiture garée devant la maison de nos voisins?	*Whose is the new car parked in front of our neighbours' house?*

5 USEFUL VERBS FOR POSSESSION AND OWNERSHIP

▶ **Avoir**: as with the English verb *to have*, **avoir** can be used to show ownership or possession:

Nicolas **a** deux CD de Westlife.	*Nicolas has two Westlife CDs.*
Mark **a** aussi leur dernier album.	*Mark also has their latest album.*

Être + à: can be used to show possession. See **The main points 4**.

C'est à qui?	*Whose is it?*
C'est à Nicolas.	*It's Nicolas'.*

▶ **Appartenir + à + noun**: this can be used in similar situations to **être à**:

La voiture garée juste en face de la maison **appartient aux*** parents de Stéphanie.	*The car parked right in front of the house belongs to Stéphanie's parents.*

*As usual, **à + les** contract to make **aux**.

6 STRESSED PRONOUNS AFTER À

If you want to indicate possession using à + a pronoun, you use
the stressed form of the pronoun: **toi, moi, lui/elle**, etc. See Unit 1
The main points 8; Unit 6 **The main points 3**.

Cette voiture est à eux.	*This car belongs to them.*
Est-ce que ce CD est à toi?	*Does this CD belong to you?*
Non, c'est à lui.	*No, it belongs to him.*
Stéphanie a sa voiture bien à elle, mais elle n'est pas assurée en ce moment.	*Stéphanie has her very own car but it is not insured at present.*

The story

Look for **possessive adjectives** and **possessive pronouns** in the
following conversation between Stéphanie and Nicolas.

Stéphanie cherche son album de photos pour le montrer à Mark.
Stéphanie is looking for her photo album to show it to Mark.

Stéphanie	Où est mon album de photos? Il n'est pas à sa place habituelle. Je me demande si Nicolas l'a. Nicolas, as-tu mon album de photos?	*Where is my photo album? It isn't in its usual place. I wonder if Nicolas has it. Nicolas, have you got my photo album?*
Nicolas	J'ai un album mais c'est le mien.	*I've got an album but it is mine.*
Stéphanie	Mais non, ce n'est pas le tien, c'est le mien. Le tien est sûrement enfoui sous un tas de vêtements. Tu es si désordonné! Et ça? Ce n'est pas à toi non plus. C'est mon logiciel.	*No, it isn't yours, it's mine. Yours is probably buried under a pile of clothes. You are so untidy! And this? This doesn't belong to you either. It's my software.*

| Nicolas | Non, tu te trompes. Ce n'est pas le tien. C'est celui de mon copain, Claude. Le tien est sûrement bien rangé sur ton étagère. | *No, you're wrong. It is not yours. It is my friend Claude's. Yours is probably put away neatly on your shelf.* |
| Stéphanie | Mark, est-ce que tu veux voir des photos amusantes de Nicolas? | *Mark, do you want to see some funny pictures of Nicolas?* |

A quick check

1 Replace the expressions in bold (**possessive adjectives + nouns**) with the corresponding possessive pronouns in the following sentences.

Exemple: C'est **leur maison**. C'est **la leur**.

Où se trouve **votre maison**?	Où se trouve _____?
Andrew ne trouve pas ses **disques compacts**.	Andrew ne trouve pas _____.
Il prend **mes CD**.	Il prend _____.
J'oublie souvent de rendre **tes DVD**.	J'oublie souvent de rendre _____.

2 Complete the following sentences with the words in the box.

> de, les nôtres, appartient, toi, eux, la leur, à, le mien, leurs, toi, leurs

C'est le dictionnaire ___ Sandy.

Ce magazine appartient ___ Sandy.

Ce livre n'est pas à ___. C'est _____.

_____ voisins sont plus aimables que _____.

Ce catalogue *La Redoute* _____ à Sandy.

« Est-ce qu'il y a des photos de ___ dans ce catalogue? », demande Andrew.

La voiture garée en face de la maison des Dickson est à ___.
La nouvelle Peugeot 406 n'est pas _____. C'est celle de _____
voisins.

The next stage

1 *MORE ABOUT POSSESSIVE ADJECTIVES AND PRONOUNS*

Agreement

Possessive adjectives and pronouns agree with *what is owned* and
not the owner. This means that some sentences can be ambiguous
in French, as it is not clear who the owner is. This is usually made
clear by the context or situation, since the listener/reader would
automatically know who the possessor was.

Son logiciel est le même que **le sien.**	*His/her software is the same as his/hers. (i.e. Nicolas' friend's software is the same as Stéphanie's – see* **The story** *above)*

Votre can either refer to several owners or to one owner addressed
in a formal way:

Où est **votre** voiture?	*Where is your car?*

Here again the context will show who the owner(s) is/are.

The possessive adjectives (**son, sa, ses**) and possessive pronouns
(**le sien, la sienne, les siens, les siennes**) can also be used in a
general sense to mean *one's, your* or *everyone's*:

On a besoin de **son** lecteur laser pour écouter ses disques compacts.	*You need your CD player to listen to your CDs.*

Clarifying ownership

To make clear who the owner is, especially in spoken French, you can add the preposition à with a stressed pronoun:

Ce sont **ses** baskets à **elle**.	*These are her trainers.*
Mark a **son** appartement à **lui**.	*Mark has his own flat.*
Son dessin à **elle** a gagné le premier prix.	*Her drawing won first prize.*

A similar situation can arise with the possessive adjective *their* in English, and with **leur** and **leurs** in French. French can make matters clearer by using à **eux** or à **elles**.

Voici leur appartement à **eux**.	*Here is their flat.* (at least two people, one or both of whom are masculine)
Voici leurs photos à **elles**.	*Here are their photos.* (the girls' photos)

Their/theirs

Number agreements with the possessive adjective **leur/leurs** and the possessive pronouns **le (la) nôtre/les nôtres, le (la) vôtre/les vôtres, le (la) leur/les leurs** can sometimes cause a problem for English speakers. This is because English adds an **-s** to change the adjective into the pronoun (*your book* → *yours, our magazine* → *ours, their television* → *theirs*).

The possessive agrees with the owner in English, so you tend to think of *their* as always plural. In French, you add an **-s** only when the thing owned is plural.

Possessive adjective + noun	**Possessive pronoun**
Voici leur platine laser et leurs disques compacts. *This is their CD player (*one*) and their CDs (*several*).*	**Voici la leur. (platine laser)** *This one is theirs.* but **Ce sont les leurs? (DVD)** *Are they theirs? (*several*)*

Les copains de Nicolas écoutent souvent **leurs** disques compacts.	*Nicolas' friends often listen to their CDs.*
S'ils n'apportent pas **leur** platine laser, ils peuvent se servir de **la nôtre**.	*If they do not bring their CD player they can use ours.*
Ils peuvent aussi écouter **les nôtres**.	*They can also listen to ours. (our CDs)*

2 MORE ABOUT POSSESSION

Possession with parts of the body

Possessive adjectives are used in English with parts of the body (*my* hand, *your* head, etc.). In French the definite article is more likely, especially in written and more formal French:

Elle a une bague **au** doigt.	*She's got a ring on her finger.*
Il a mal **au** pied droit.	*His right foot hurts.*
Il met la main à **la** poche.	*He puts his hand in his pocket. (i.e. to pay)*

Saying 'of mine', 'of yours', 'of his', 'of theirs', etc.

The preposition **à** followed by a stressed pronoun (**moi, toi**) or a name (Nicolas) is also used to express possession in this way in French. See **The main points 6.**

Ce sont des copains **à moi**.	*They are friends of mine.*
Non. Ce sont des copains **à Nicolas**.	*No. They're friends of Nicolas'.*
J'ai trouvé des livres **à toi**.	*I found some books of yours.*

Appartenir à *(to belong to)*
Ce livre **appartient** à Stéphanie.	*This book belongs to Stéphanie.*

If the object of the verb **appartenir** is a pronoun, the pronoun comes before the verb:

Il **lui** appartient.	*It is hers/belongs to her.*

See Unit 9 **The main points 3.**

TEN THINGS TO REMEMBER

1 The preposition **à** is used to show belonging: **ce livre est à moi** (*this book belongs to me*). The preposition **de** is used to show possession: **c'est le livre de mon frère** (*it's my brother's book*), **c'est à moi** (*it belongs to me*).

2 In French, there is no equivalent of the apostrophe that we use in English to express possession: *my friend's book, my friends' house*. You need to say 'the (noun) of (person)': **le livre de mon copain, la maison de mes amis**.

3 **Appartenir, tenir, retenir** and **détenir** are all irregular verbs and follow the same pattern as **tenir** (see **Verb tables**).

4 To say 'it is mine', you can either use **à** + stressed pronoun (**c'est <u>à moi</u>, c'est <u>à eux</u>**) or replace the noun with a possessive pronoun (**c'est <u>le mien</u>, ce sont <u>les leurs</u>**).

5 Possessive adjectives come before nouns and agree in gender and number with them: **mon livre, ta radio, leur DVD, leurs voitures**.

6 **Leur voiture** means one car each, or a car that is shared by several people; **leurs voitures** means they have several cars (see **The main points 1**). In English, we say 'The people in this street leave their cars outside'. In French, you say either **Ils laissent leur voiture dehors** (each person leaves one car out) or **Ils laissent leurs voitures dehors** (each person owns more than one car and leaves them out).

7 Possessive pronouns agree in gender and number with the nouns they replace: **c'est la mienne (la radio), ce sont les miens (les DVD), ce sont les miennes (les erreurs)**.

8 In spoken French, you can stress ownership by saying: **ce sont ses DVD <u>à elle</u>** (*they are her DVDs*). Because **ses** (meaning either 'his' or 'her') agrees with the noun and not with the owner like in English, only the context tells us if the owner is masculine or feminine. You can use **à elle** or **à lui** to clarify the gender of the owner.

9 – In **Il le voit** (*He sees him/it*), **le** is a direct object pronoun: He sees whom?/what?
– In **Il lui appartient** (*It belongs <u>to him</u>*), **lui** is an indirect object pronoun: It belongs <u>to</u> whom? – It belongs <u>to</u> him.

(More about different types of pronoun in Unit 9 **The next stage 2.**)

10 Stressed pronouns **moi, toi, elle, lui, soi, nous, vous, eux, elles** are used not only with **à** but with all prepositions: **après toi, sans eux, pour elles.**

8

....

Permission and obligation

In this unit you will learn
- *To say what you can do*
- *To give and refuse permission*
- *To say what needs to be done*
- *To give orders and instructions*

Topic
- *Leisure activities and plans*

Grammar

▶ Verbs followed by an infinitive: **pouvoir** (*to be able to*), **savoir** (*to know, to know how to*), **vouloir** (*to want to*), **devoir** (*to have to*)

▶ Impersonal expressions: **il faut** (**falloir** *to need something/ to be necessary*), **il pleut** (**pleuvoir** *to rain*)

▶ Other verbs ending in **-oir**: **valoir** (*to be worth*), **voir** (*to see*), **recevoir** (*to receive*), **s'asseoir** (*to sit down*)

▶ Expressions with **avoir**

The next stage

▶ The difference between **savoir** and **connaître**

▶ **Devoir** (*to have to* or *to owe*)

....

Getting started

1 You have already met the structure **aimer** + infinitive (*to like doing something*) in Unit 2 **The main points** 3:

Nous **aimons jouer** aux échecs.   *We like to play chess.*
J'**aime faire** du sport.   *I like to do/I am keen on sport.*

and the immediate future **aller** + infinitive (*to be going to do something*) in Unit 6 **The main points** 1:

Je **vais acheter** des cadeaux.   *I am going to buy presents.*

In this unit, you will meet similar structures, i.e. verbs followed by infinitives which are used to say what:

> ▸ *you can do/are able to do:* **pouvoir** + infinitive
> ▸ *you are allowed to do:* **pouvoir** + infinitive
> ▸ *you are able/have the knowledge to do:* **savoir** + infinitive
> ▸ *you want to do:* **vouloir** + infinitive
> ▸ *you must do/have to do:* **devoir** + infinitive

Georges **doit** se lever tôt pour aller travailler, car il commence à 8 h 00.

Il **peut** rentrer plus tôt le soir, s'il n'y a pas de travail urgent et il peut faire soit du ball-trap soit du jardinage pour se distraire. Il **doit** souvent travailler le samedi et Isabelle ne **sait** jamais à quelle heure il va rentrer.

Isabelle **sait** très bien cuisiner et fait souvent de la pâtisserie pour l'église de la Croix du Petit Dieu. Elle travaille

Georges has to get up early to go to work, because he starts at 8 o'clock.

He can come home earlier in the evening if there is no urgent work and he can enjoy either clay-pigeon shooting or gardening. He often has to work on Saturdays and Isabelle never knows at what time he is going to come home.

Isabelle is a very good cook and often bakes cakes for the Croix du Petit Dieu church. She works on a voluntary basis

bénévolement pour une
entreprise caritative car elle
veut aider les défavorisés.

for a charity, because she wants
to help the underprivileged.

2 In this unit, you will also meet the impersonal way of saying what
you need, what is necessary, what must be done or has to be done:

Il faut beaucoup d'adresse et de
précision pour faire du ball-trap.
Il faut beaucoup s'exercer pour
gagner les premiers prix.

You need a lot of skill and accuracy
to do clay-pigeon shooting.
You must train a lot to win the
first prizes.

3 You will meet other **-oir** verbs which are also irregular:

Georges aime faire les concours
de ball-trap mais quand **il pleut**
on ne **voit** pas très bien les
assiettes et les concours sont
annulés.

Georges likes clay-pigeon
shooting competitions but
when it rains you cannot see
the plates very well and the
competitions are cancelled.

4 In this unit, you will also learn a few set expressions with **avoir**:

Quand Georges va à la chasse
il prend de la boisson et de
la nourriture pour faire un
pique-nique. Quand il a **soif** ou
quand il **a faim** il peut s'arrêter
et casser la croûte.

When Georges goes shooting
he takes food and drink for a
picnic. When he is thirsty or
hungry he can stop and have a
snack.

Say it in French

1 SAYING WHAT YOU CAN DO

Les Lemaire ne **peuvent** pas partir
en vacances cette année car ils
ont beaucoup de dépenses.

The Lemaires cannot go on
holiday this year because they
have many expenses.

Ils **peuvent** se distraire dans la région car il y a beaucoup de choses à faire, des randonnées en forêt, à la campagne ...

They can enjoy themselves in the area because there are many things to do, walks in the forest, in the country ...

Ils **peuvent** se rendre à la mer, à Malo-les-bains ou à St Omer en un peu plus d'une heure.

They can go to the seaside to Malo-les-bains or St Omer in just over an hour.

Est-ce que Georges **peut** faire du ball-trap toute l'année?

Can Georges go clay-pigeon shooting all the year around?

Oui, mais il ne **peut** chasser que durant une période limitée.

Yes, but he can only shoot during a limited period.

2 GIVING AND REFUSING PERMISSION

Nicolas a envie d'aller faire du camping avec quelques amis.

Nicolas feels like going camping with some friends.

« Est-ce que je **peux** aller camper avec des copains? » demande-t-il à Isabelle.

'Can I go camping with some friends?' he asks Isabelle.

« Oui, tu **peux** si ton père veut bien. »

'Yes, you can if your dad agrees.'

« Vous **pouvez** emprunter notre tente. »

'You can borrow our tent.'

3 WHAT NEEDS TO BE DONE

Avant de partir, Nicolas **doit** ranger sa chambre.

Before leaving Nicolas must tidy his bedroom.

Isabelle veut aller à la mer avec Stéphanie et Mark. Georges **doit** travailler.

Isabelle wants to go to the seaside with Stéphanie and Mark. Georges has to work.

Elle **doit** préparer toutes les affaires de plage. Elle ne **doit** pas oublier le paravent.

She must prepare all the beach things. She must not forget the wind break.

Avant de partir, ils **doivent** vérifier la pression des pneus et le niveau d'huile.

Before leaving they have to check the tyre pressure and the oil level.

4 GIVING ORDERS AND INSTRUCTIONS

Nicolas, tu **dois** ranger tes affaires.

Nicolas, you must tidy your things.

Il **faut** aussi ranger tes vêtements.

You must also tidy your clothes.

Tu **dois** prendre soin de la tente.

You must take care of the tent.

Il **faut** la déplier et l'aérer avant de l'emporter.

You have to unfold it and air it before taking it.

The main points

1 VERBS FOLLOWED BY AN INFINITIVE

These are known as *modal verbs*. They are irregular and the spelling of the stem changes in the **nous** and **vous** forms.

Pouvoir

Just as in English, **pouvoir** (*to be able to*) can mean both *to have the ability to* and *to have permission to* do something. The exact meaning is indicated by the context.

pouvoir *to be able to*	
je peux	**nous pouvons**
tu peux	**vous pouvez**
il/elle/on peut	**ils/elles peuvent**

Stéphanie **peut** conduire la voiture de ses parents.

Stéphanie can drive her parents' car.

Pouvoir either means *to be able to* or *to be allowed to* in the above example. Only the context will determine the exact meaning.

Stéphanie **peut** conduire la voiture de ses parents car la voiture est assurée.

Stéphanie is able to drive her parents' car because it is insured.

For other examples refer to **Getting started 1**.

Stéphanie **peut** conduire leur voiture car ils savent que c'est une bonne conductrice.	*Stéphanie is allowed to drive their car because they know she is a good driver.*

See other examples in **Say it in French 2**.

Savoir or pouvoir
In French, you use **savoir** and not **pouvoir** if you want to stress the fact that you *have the knowledge/the ability to do* something, and that *you know how to* do something:

savoir to know (how to)	
je sais	**nous savons**
tu sais	**vous savez**
il/elle/on sait	**ils/elles savent**

Alison **sait** cuisiner.	*Alison knows how to cook.*
Stéphanie **sait** bien conduire.	*Stéphanie can (knows how to) drive well.*
Est-ce qu'elle **sait** aussi bien conduire en Écosse? Ses parents ne le **savent** pas.	*Can she drive as well in Scotland? Her parents do not know.*

Vouloir
This verb forms the present tense like **pouvoir**.

vouloir to wish, want	
je veux	**nous voulons**
tu veux	**vous voulez**
il/elle/on veut	**ils/elles veulent**

Vouloir is used

▶ in the **present tense** to say that someone *would like* something/ *would like to do* something or to ask if they *would like* something/*would like to do* something:

Nicolas, **veux**-tu venir avec nous demain? Nous allons à St Omer.	*Nicolas, would you like to come with us tomorrow? We are going to St Omer.*
Non, je ne **veux** pas y aller.	*No, I don't want to go there.*
À quelle heure **voulez**-vous partir?	*What time do you want to leave?*
Mark **veut** visiter la région.	*Mark wants to visit the area.*

▶ in the **conditional tense** (see Unit 18 **The main points** 3) to say that you *would like* something in a less direct and more polite way.

You have already met **vouloir** in expressions such as: **je voudrais** (*I would like*). Refer back to Unit 4 **The main points** 3.

Mark, où **voudrais**-tu aller?	*Mark, where would you like to go?*
Je **voudrais** bien aller sur la côte.	*I'd like to go to the coast.*

Devoir
In English, there is a choice between *have to* and *must to* express the necessity or the moral obligation to do something. In French there is only one verb, **devoir**.

devoir *to have to*	
je dois	**nous devons**
tu dois	**vous devez**
il/elle/on doit	**ils/elles doivent**

Nicolas **doit** montrer le respect à ses parents et **doit** être poli.	*Nicolas must show respect to his parents and be polite.*
Georges est très strict.	*Georges is very strict.*
Lorsque Stéphanie conduit en France elle **doit** se souvenir des priorités à droite.	*When Stéphanie drives in France she has to remember to give way on the right.*

2 IMPERSONAL EXPRESSIONS

Falloir/Il faut *(one must/one has to/needs something)*
Falloir is called an impersonal verb. It is only used with the subject pronoun **il**.

It can be used in different tenses. See **Verb tables**. It is used as follows:

▶ To say that something is needed: **Il faut** is followed by a noun with a definite, indefinite or partitive article **le, la, les, un, une, des, du, de la, de l', d'**. See Unit 4 **The main points 2**.

Il faut de la nourriture pour la route, le plan de St Omer et un guide touristique.	*We need food for the road, the street map of St Omer and a tourist guide.*

▶ To say that you need something or that someone needs something:

Il me faut un plan de la ville.	*I need a street map of the city.*
Est-ce qu'**il vous faut** des directions précises?	*Do you need precise directions?*

In this case, **il faut** is used with the indirect object pronoun, which is placed between **il** and **faut**. See Unit 9 **The main points 3**.

▶ To say that *something has to/must be done*. **Il faut** can also be followed by an infinitive:

Mark, **il faut** se lever de bonne heure demain matin.	*Mark, we must get up early tomorrow morning.*
Il faut partir avant l'heure de pointe.	*We must leave before the rush hour.*

Pleuvoir *(to rain)*
This is another impersonal verb used only with **il**.

Et s'**il pleut** beaucoup, qu'est-ce qu'on fait?	*If it rains a lot, what do we do?*

Stéphanie, comment dit-on « *It's raining cats and dogs* » en français?	*Stéphanie, how do you say 'It's raining cats and dogs' in French?*
On dit: « Il pleut des cordes/des hallebardes. »	*You say: 'Il pleut des cordes/des hallebardes.'*

3 OTHER VERBS ENDING IN -OIR

Valoir *(to be worth)*
Valoir is usually used with the third person singular or plural subject pronouns (**il/elle/ils/elles**) or with **ça/cela** (*this, that*) or with a noun:

Combien est-ce que **ça vaut**?	*How much is that worth?*
Combien **valent** ces plans de St Omer?	*How much do these street plans of St Omer cost?*
Ils **valent** €2,30 chacun.	*They cost €2.30 each.*
S'il pleut **cela** ne **vaut** pas la peine de partir.	*If it rains it's not worth going.*

Voir *(to see)*
This verb is conjugated like **croire**. See Unit 6 **The main points 2**.

voir *to see*	
je vois	**nous voyons**
tu vois	**vous voyez**
il/elle/on voit	**ils/elles voient**

Quand il pleut beaucoup on ne **voit** pas bien la route et il y a plus de risques d'accident.	*When it is raining hard you don't see the road well and there is more risk of an accident.*

Other verbs, which are formed by adding a prefix to the verb **voir**, have the same endings as **voir**, but alter the stem. Check them in a good dictionary:

apercevoir	*to notice*
concevoir	*to conceive*

décevoir	to disappoint
percevoir	to cash in, to perceive
recevoir	to receive

Stéphanie se lève et **aperçoit** des nuages menaçants. Deux minutes plus tard, il pleut à verse. Un tel temps **déçoit** vraiment!	*Stéphanie gets up and notices threatening clouds. Two minutes later it is pouring down. Such weather is really disappointing!*
Stéphanie **reçoit** souvent des nouvelles de France.	*Stéphanie often receives news from France.*

S'asseoir *(to sit down)*

The verb **s'asseoir** is a highly irregular reflexive verb which you can see in full in the **Verb tables**.

Mark **s'assied** à côté de Stéphanie et regarde la carte de France pour voir où se trouve St Omer.	*Mark sits down next to Stéphanie and looks at the map of France to see where St Omer is.*

4 EXPRESSIONS WITH AVOIR

Expressions where **avoir** corresponds to 'to have' in English

▶ **avoir rendez-vous**

Isabelle a **rendez-vous** chez le coiffeur.	*Isabelle has an appointment at the hairdresser's.*

▶ **avoir mal à la tête**

Elle **a mal à la tête** et elle prend deux aspirines.	*She has a headache and takes two aspirins.*

▶ **avoir le courage de**

Georges a **le courage de** ses opinions.	*Georges has the courage of his convictions.*

Expressions where **avoir** + noun corresponds to 'to be' +
adjective in English
You have already come across some phrases using **avoir** which do
not mean *have* in English:

J'ai faim.	*I am hungry.*
J'ai soif.	*I am thirsty.*
J'ai 21 ans.	*I am 21.*

Other expressions:

avoir de la chance	*to be lucky*
ne pas avoir de chance	*to be unlucky/unfortunate*
avoir la chance de	*to be lucky/fortunate (enough) to*
avoir du courage	*to be courageous*
avoir peur/avoir peur de	*to be afraid/afraid of*
avoir l'habitude de	*to be used to*
avoir honte/avoir honte de	*to be ashamed/ashamed of*
en avoir marre de	*to be fed up with*
avoir sommeil	*to be tired*

Stéphanie, Mark et Isabelle **n'ont pas de chance** car le temps est affreux.	*Stéphanie, Mark and Isabelle are unlucky because the weather is awful.*
Isabelle **en a marre de** ce temps variable. Elle voudrait habiter dans un pays chaud.	*Isabelle is fed up with this changeable weather. She would like to live in a hot country.*

The story

From this stage, you should feel confident enough to read and
understand the French in the dialogues in **The story**. If you
have any problems, look up unknown words or expressions
in your dictionary. If you are completely at a loss, refer to the
Transcriptions near the back of this book.

In this conversation between Mark and Stéphanie, look for **verbs followed directly by an infinitive**, the modal verbs **pouvoir** and **devoir**.

Mark et Stéphanie prévoient de faire de l'équitation.

Stéphanie	Qu'est-ce que tu veux faire demain, s'il ne pleut pas? Tu veux faire de l'équitation ou des randonnées?
Mark	Je ne sais pas monter à cheval.
Stéphanie	Tu peux apprendre; ce n'est pas difficile.
Mark	Est-ce qu'il y a des centres équestres à St Amand?
Stéphanie	Il y en a plusieurs, mais je peux monter chez mon amie Monique, qui a plusieurs chevaux. Tu vois les pâtures, là-bas? Ce sont les siennes. On aperçoit les chevaux d'ici.
Mark	Il faut porter des vêtements spéciaux?
Stéphanie	Oui et non. Tu peux porter un jean et des baskets, mais tu dois porter une bombe. Mon père peut te prêter la sienne. Je vais téléphoner à Monique pour voir si nous pouvons monter demain. Au fait, quand tes parents veulent-ils venir?
Mark	Ils peuvent venir en juillet. Ils veulent visiter le nord et peut-être aller passer quelques jours à Paris.

A quick check

1 Add the missing verbs and/or expressions in the following sentences: You will need savoir, **devoir, pouvoir, avoir envie de, vouloir.**

S Je vais demander à mes parents s'ils _____ rester chez nous à ce moment-là. Je crois que Papa ne _____ pas travailler le 14 juillet car c'est férié. Est-ce que tu _____ combien de temps ils _____ rester?

M Je ne _____ pas exactement. Une quinzaine de jours. Ils _____ inviter tes parents à venir en Écosse l'année prochaine. Est-ce que tu crois que tes parents _____ venir à Dundee?

S Oui, j'en suis sûre. Cette année ils ne _____ pas partir en vacances.

2 Ask questions about the following phrases using the pronouns and verbs in brackets.

Exemple: chanter (tu, savoir) – Est-ce que tu sais chanter?

parler français (vous, savoir)
aller au cinéma (tu, vouloir)
rentrer tard (il, pouvoir)
ranger nos affaires (nous, devoir)

The next stage

1 *THE DIFFERENCE BETWEEN* SAVOIR *AND* CONNAÎTRE

These two verbs often create problems as they both mean *to know*.
Savoir means *to have knowledge of, to know how to* and **connaître**
means *to be acquainted with, to be familiar with*.

Je **connais** le chemin.	*I know (am familiar with) the way.*
Je **sais** quel chemin prendre.	*I know which way to go.*

The idea of *having the knowledge of* is introduced in this second
sentence.

You use **connaître** when talking about people:

Est-ce que Mark **connaît** les amis de Stéphanie?	*Does Mark know (is he acquainted with) Stéphanie's friends?*

2 DEVOIR *(TO HAVE TO, TO OWE)*

Devoir does not always mean *to have to/must*, it can also mean
to owe.

The meaning will only be made clear by the context. When **devoir**
means *to owe*, it is not followed by an infinitive. Look at the
difference between these two examples:

Isabelle **doit** acheter une bouteille de shampooing chez le coiffeur.	*Isabelle must buy a bottle of shampoo at the hairdresser's.*
Je vous **dois** combien, s'il vous plaît?	*How much do I owe you, please?*

TEN THINGS TO REMEMBER

1 All verbs ending in **-oir** are irregular (see **Verb Tables**).

2 Verbs like **recevoir, concevoir** and **décevoir** can be difficult to remember: **je reçois, nous recevons; je conçois, nous concevons; je déçois, nous décevons.** Don't forget the cedilla on the letter **c** to make the 's' sound: **-çois** is pronounced [sswa].

3 **Je peux** can mean *I am able to* or *I am allowed to*.

4 **Je dois** can mean *I must* or *I have to*. It can also mean *I owe*: **je dois 20 euros** (*I owe 20 euros*).

5 **Je veux** can sound quite direct and assertive. When you want to ask for something politely in a shop, restaurant, etc., use **je voudrais** (*I would like*) instead.

6 The verb **valoir** means *to be worth*: **cela vaut 20 euros** (*it costs 20 euros*), **cela ne vaut rien** (*it's worth nothing*), **cela n'en vaut pas la peine** (*it isn't worth the worry*).

7 All modal verbs such as **pouvoir** (*to be able to, to be allowed to*) and **devoir** (*to have to*) are followed by an infinitive in French: **nous pouvons <u>venir</u>, je dois <u>faire</u>** …

8 **Il faut** is an impersonal expression used only with the subject **il**. It can be followed by a noun (**il faut du vin**), an infinitive (**il faut aller vite**) or **que** + the subjunctive mood (Unit 16).

9 Similar impersonal expressions are **il est important que** (*it is important that*) and **il s'agit de** (*it is about …*).

10 To talk about knowing people or concrete words/facts, use the verb **connaître: je connais cette personne, je connais le problème.** To say you know how to do something, or to express a more abstract idea, use **savoir: je sais comment faire, nous savons nager.**

9

Directions, instructions
and advice

In this unit you will learn
- **To ask for and give directions**
- **To advise and tell someone to do/not to do something**

Topics
- **Travel plans**
- **Directions**

Grammar
▶ Verbs to give directions: **continuer** (*to continue*), **tourner** (*to turn*), **prendre** (*to take*) and useful expressions such as **il faut**, **vous devez/tu dois** (*you need to/you have to*)
▶ Using imperatives to give directions: **prenez** (*take*)
▶ Indirect object pronouns **me**, **te**, **lui** (*to me, to you, to her/him*)
▶ The pronoun **y** (*there, about this*)

The next stage
▶ **Aller** and **donner** in the imperative
▶ Functions of object pronouns
▶ The difference between **y** and **en**

Getting started

1 Useful verbs to give directions

The **present tense**, which you met in Units 1, 3, 5 and 6, is used to give directions. Look back at these units if you are not sure of verb endings, especially those of irregular verbs such as **prendre** (*to take*) (see Unit 6 **The main points** 2). You will also need to look back at ordinal numbers: **le premier/la première** (*the first*), etc. (Unit 3 **The main points** 4) and at prepositions of place (Unit 6 **The main points** 3) **à côté de** (*next to*), **près de** (*near*), **en face de** (*opposite*).

Vous **prenez** la première à droite.	*You take the first on the right.*
Vous **continuez** tout droit et vous **tournez** à gauche. C'est près d'ici.	*You go straight ahead and you turn left. It is near here.*
L'Abbaye **est** sur la place en face de l'hôtel de ville.	*The Abbey is in the market place opposite the town hall.*

The impersonal expression **il faut** (*one must/one has to/one needs to*) (Unit 8 **The main points** 2) is also useful when giving directions and telling people what to do:

Il faut tourner à droite.	*You'll need to turn right.*
Il faut prendre la quatrième rue à gauche.	*You'll need to take the fourth street on the left.*

Another useful verb for giving directions is the verb **devoir** (Unit 8 **The main points** 1):

Vous **devez** continuer tout droit, traverser la rue et continuer jusqu'à la rue de Lille.	*You have to go straight ahead, cross the road and continue as far as the Rue de Lille.*

2 To give directions, you can use a form of the verb called the **imperative**. The imperative will be covered in Unit 12

The main points 1. In this unit, you will only learn how to use some imperatives to give directions.

Prenez à droite.	*Take a right-hand turn.*
Prends la première à droite.	*Take the first on the right.*
Continuez/continue tout droit.	*Go straight ahead.*

3 Finally, to give directions to someone, you need to learn different personal pronouns. You have already met **subject pronouns** and **stressed pronouns** in Unit 1 **The main points 1** and **8**.

Je ne sais jamais donner les directions.	*I never know how to give directions.*
Et **toi,** tu sais donner les directions?	*Do you know how to give directions?*

You met **direct object pronouns** in Unit 5 **The main points 3**, answering the question *what?*:

Je **le** prends.	*I take it. (I take what?)*
Je **l'**aime.	*I like him/her/it.*
Je sais **les** donner.	*I know how to give them.* (directions)

The pronouns you need to answer the question *to whom?* are called **indirect object pronouns**. You will meet these pronouns in this unit:

Je **lui** donne des directions précises.	*I give him/her precise directions.*
Un homme demande les directions pour aller à la gare.	*A man asks the way to the station.*
Stéphanie **lui** indique le chemin.	*Stéphanie shows him the way.*
Un couple **lui** demande le chemin pour aller à la mairie. Elle **leur** dit de continuer tout droit et de prendre la première rue à droite.	*A couple asks her the way to the town hall. She tells them to go straight on and to take the first on the right.*

Say it in French

1 ASKING FOR AND GIVING DIRECTIONS

Excusez-moi, monsieur, où se **trouve** le chemin de l'Empire, s'il vous plaît?

Excuse me, where is the Chemin de l'Empire, please?

Ce n'**est** pas loin d'ici.

It's not far from here.

Vous **continuez** tout droit et juste après le pont vous **prenez** la première à gauche.

You go straight on and just after the bridge you take the first on your left.

Vous **allez** jusqu'au bout de la rue Salengro, puis vous **tournez** à gauche. Et vous êtes au chemin de l'Empire.

You go right down to the end of the Rue Salengro, then you turn left. And you're at the Chemin de l'Empire.

Et pour **aller** au gîte Le Luron?

And to go the gîte Le Luron?

C'est dans la forêt de St Amand.

It is in the St Amand forest.

Du chemin de l'Empire, **prenez la** première à droite. **Continuez** tout droit, **traversez** la rocade du Nord.

From the Chemin de l'Empire, you take the first right. Go straight ahead, cross the northern bypass.

Ensuite **il faut continuer** tout droit jusqu'au bout de la rue Basse.

Then you'll have to go straight ahead, right to the end of the Rue Basse.

Vous **arrivez** place du Mont des Bruyères.

You arrive at Mont des Bruyères square.

Là vous **continuez** tout droit.

There you go straight on.

Prenez la rue Transvaal et vous êtes à la forêt de St Amand.

Take the Rue Transvaal and you are at the forest of St Amand.

Le gîte Le Luron **est** à votre droite.

The gîte Le Luron is on your right.

2 ADVISING SOMEONE TO DO/NOT TO DO SOMETHING

Andrew, si tu veux rester à Dundee chez un copain, tu **dois** être raisonnable.

Andrew, if you want to stay at a friend's in Dundee, you must be sensible.

Tu **dois** t'occuper de la maison.

You must look after the house.

Il faut sortir la poubelle le mardi matin.

You must take the dustbin out on Tuesday mornings.

Il faut te lever de bonne heure pour aller en classe.

You must get up early to go to your classes.

Il ne faut pas trop te servir du téléphone.

You must not use the telephone too often.

Si tu as des problèmes tu **dois** contacter ton oncle. Tu **lui** téléphones et tu **lui** dis de venir te chercher.

If you have any problems you must contact your uncle. Ring him and tell him to come and fetch you.

Il peut **nous** passer un coup de fil si nécessaire. Toi aussi, tu peux **nous** donner de tes nouvelles.

He can give us a ring if necessary. You can also keep in touch with us.

The main points

1 VERBS FOR GIVING DIRECTIONS

Irregular verbs
aller (*to go*), **être** (*to be*) (Unit 1), **prendre** (*to take*) (Unit 6)

Regular verbs
continuer (*to continue*), **descendre** (*to go down*), **remonter** (*to go up*), **tourner** (*to turn*), **traverser** (*to cross*)

To give information and/or advice to someone formally, these verbs are used with **vous**:

Vous continuez tout droit, **vous** tournez à gauche, puis **vous** prenez la deuxième à gauche. **Vous** y êtes.

You go straight on, turn left, then you take the second on the left. You are there.

To give information to someone you know well or to direct someone in an informal way, you would use the pronoun **tu** (Unit 1 **The main points 5**):

Tu traverses la rue de Tournai et **tu** remontes le chemin du Corbeau.

You cross the Rue de Tournai and go up the Chemin du Corbeau.

Falloir and **devoir**

You met both these verbs in Unit 8 **The main points 1, 2.**

▶ **Falloir:** The impersonal structure **Il faut** is often followed by the infinitive of a verb of direction but could also be followed by **que** + verb in the subjunctive. You will meet expressions like these in Unit 16 **The main points 2.**

Il faut tourner à droite et prendre la quatrième à gauche.
You'll need to turn right and to take the fourth on the left.
Il ne faut pas tourner à gauche car c'est un sens interdit.
You must not turn left, as it is a one-way street.

▶ **Devoir:** This modal verb is used to tell people what they *have to do* to get to the place they are inquiring about. Unlike **il faut**, which cannot be used with other subject pronouns, **devoir** can be used with any of the subject pronouns. (See Unit 8 **The main points 1.**)

Vous devez vous arrêter aux feux, puis vous tournez à gauche.
You must stop at the traffic lights, then you turn left.
Tu dois remonter la rue de Condé jusqu'au rond-point.
You have to go back up the Rue de Condé as far as the roundabout.
Nous devons prendre un bus sur la place?
Do we have to catch a bus in the market place?

2 USING IMPERATIVES TO GIVE DIRECTIONS

This is the easiest and the most frequent way of giving directions.
You just use the verbs *without* a subject pronoun, i.e. instead
of saying *you continue* **vous continuez**, you just say *continue*
continuez. Instead of saying **tu continues**, you just say *continue*.

For -er verbs, including the verb **aller**, you drop the -s when **tu** is
the subject:

Continuez tout droit, **prenez** à gauche, **passez** devant la mairie et c'est à votre gauche.	*Go straight ahead, turn left, pass the town hall and it is on your left.*
Continue, prends à droite, **va** un peu plus loin et c'est à droite.	*Go straight on, go right, go a bit further and it is on the right.*

Here are the imperative forms of the verbs to give directions:

Tu form	**Vous** form	
va	**allez**	*aller*
continue	**continuez**	*continuer*
descends	**descendez**	*descendre*
passe	**passez**	*passer*
prends	**prenez**	*prendre*
remonte	**remontez**	*remonter*
tourne	**tournez**	*tourner*
traverse	**traversez**	*traverser*

Prenez la première à gauche. **Allez** jusqu'au carrefour. Au carrefour **continuez** tout droit jusqu'aux feux et **prenez** la première à droite.	*Take the first on the left. Go to the crossroads. At the crossroads go straight ahead to the traffic lights and take the first right.*

If you are speaking in an informal or friendly way, you say:

Prends la première à gauche. **Va** jusqu'au carrefour. Au carrefour
continue tout droit jusqu'aux feux et **prends** la première à droite.

3 INDIRECT OBJECT PRONOUNS

Here is a list of the **personal pronouns** you have already met:

▶ subject pronouns Unit 1 **The main points 1**
▶ reflexive pronouns Unit 3 **The main points 2**
▶ direct object pronouns Unit 5 **The main points 3**

In the fourth column in the following grid, you will find **indirect pronouns** – the pronouns used to answer the question *to whom?* Where the direct and indirect objects are different, they are in italic:

subject	reflexive	direct object	indirect object
je	me	me	me
tu	te	te	te
il/elle/on	se	*le/la*	*lui*
nous	nous	nous	nous
vous	vous	vous	vous
ils/elles	se	*les*	*leur*

As you can see, object pronouns only differ in the third person singular (**il/elle/on**) and plural (**ils/elles**). With indirect pronouns, you use **lui** and **leur** whether you are speaking about a male or a female person:

Les Dickson demande les directions pour aller chez les Lemaire.

The Dicksons ask for directions to go to the Lemaires'.

Mark va **leur** donner un plan de St Amand à son retour.

Mark is going to give them a street map of St Amand on his return.

Il va aussi **leur** écrire pour confirmer qu'ils sont les bienvenus chez les Lemaire.

He is also going to write to them to confirm that they are welcome at the Lemaires'.

Les Dickson vont venir en juillet. Isabelle demande à Georges si cela **lui** convient.

The Dicksons are going to come in July. Isabelle asks Georges if this is all right with him.

| Stéphanie **lui** explique que les Dickson souhaitent venir le 7 juillet. | *Stéphanie explains to him that the Dicksons wish to come on 7 July.* |

In Unit 12 **The main points 6,** you will find out about word order when using more than one object pronoun.

Verbs which take indirect object pronouns

appartenir à quelqu'un	*to belong to someone*
Cela **m**'appartient.	*This belongs to me.*
apporter quelque chose à quelqu'un	*to bring someone something, to bring something to someone*
Le facteur **nous** apporte le courier à 7 h.	*The postman brings us the mail/the mail to us at 7 a.m.*
donner quelque chose à quelqu'un	*to give someone something, to give something to someone*
Il **te** donne beaucoup de cadeaux.	*He gives you a lot of presents.*
écrire à quelqu'un	*to write to someone*
Il **lui** écrit souvent.	*He often writes to her/him.*
envoyer quelque chose à quelqu'un	*to send someone something, to send something to someone*
Il **vous** a envoyé un mél?	*Did he send you an e-mail?*
expliquer quelque chose à quelqu'un	*to explain something to someone*
Il **leur** explique la situation clairement.	*He explains the situation clearly to them.*

montrer quelque chose à quelqu'un	*to show someone something, to show something to someone*
Il **lui** montre le chemin.	*He shows him the way.*
offrir quelque chose à quelqu'un	*to present someone with something*
Mark **lui** offre des fleurs.	*Mark presents her with some flowers.*
poser des questions à quelqu'un	*to ask someone questions*
Elle **me** pose souvent la même question.	*She often asks me the same question.*

4 THE PRONOUN Y

This pronoun means *there* in examples such as: **Vous y êtes.**
(See **The main points 1.**)

| Vous **y** allez quand? | *When are you going there?* |

Y also means *about this/it.*

| J'**y** pense souvent. | *I often think about it.* |

Y comes before the verb except when the verb is in the imperative.

| Restez-**y**. | *Stay there.* |

For **y** with other object pronouns, see Unit 12 **The main points 6.**

The story

From this discussion about Mark's parents and their visit to France, make a list of the **instructions** and identify the **indirect object pronouns**.

Mark demande à Stéphanie si ses parents peuvent venir en juillet.

Mark	Stéphanie, ma mère vient de me demander si elle et Papa peuvent venir chez vous le 7 juillet. Est-ce que cela convient à tes parents?
Stéphanie	Je vais leur poser la question tout de suite et tu peux lui retéléphoner plus tard pour lui donner la réponse.

Stéphanie appelle sa mère et elle lui donne la nouvelle.

Stéphanie	Maman, est-ce que les parents de Mark peuvent venir chez nous le 7 juillet? Ils aimeraient passer trois ou quatre jours chez nous, puis visiter la région et aussi Paris.
Isabelle	Bien sûr, avec plaisir. Ton père peut peut-être prendre quelques jours de congé. Comment vont-ils voyager?
Stéphanie	Ils vont prendre l'avion de Glasgow à Paris et louer une voiture à l'aéroport. Mark va leur donner une carte routière et un plan de St Amand pour les aider.

Voici les instructions que Mark va donner à ses parents:

Vous arrivez à l'aéroport Roissy-Charles de Gaulle et vous prenez l'autoroute du nord, la A1, jusqu'à Péronne.

Ensuite, prenez la A2 jusqu'à la sortie Cambrai/Valenciennes. Quittez la A2 à Valenciennes et continuez jusqu'à la Sentinelle. Là, vous devez prendre la A23 jusqu'à la sortie St Amand/Lille.

Quittez la A23 à l'entrée de St Amand et prenez la voie rapide jusqu'à la forêt de Raismes. Au deuxième rond-point, tournez à gauche et vous êtes au chemin de l'Empire.

A quick check

1 Mark's instructions at the end of **The story** are given in the **vous** form as he is talking to his parents. Give them in the **tu** form.

2 Make up four instructions using the **vous** forms of the imperative and the vocabulary given below. The verbs are in bold.

Exemple: **Passez devant la mairie.**

tourner	à	la première	**continuer**	Lille
droite	**prendre**	à	gauche	
tout	devant	droit	**passer**	
descendre	la	jusqu'	mairie	
au	coin	de	rue	

3 Replace the expressions in bold below with the appropriate pronouns.

    a Tu dis **à tes parents** que c'est d'accord.
    b Tu téléphones **à Andrew** pour dire quand tu vas revenir.
    c Tu donnes les directions **à Alison et Patrick**.
    d Patrick demande les directions exactes **à Mark**.

The next stage

1 ALLER *AND* DONNER *IN THE IMPERATIVE*

For -**er** verbs, including **aller**, in the imperative you drop the -**s** from the **tu** form. **Va vite!** (*Go quickly!*) However, you retain the -**s** before vowels or vowel sounds to make it easier to pronounce:

Vas-y!   *Go! (there).*
Donnes-en un peu!   *Give a bit/some of it!*

2 *FUNCTIONS OF OBJECT PRONOUNS*

Reflexive and object pronouns
If you look back to indirect pronouns in **The main points 3**, you can see that **me, te, nous** and **vous** can serve different functions. They can be used as **reflexives**, **direct objects** or **indirect objects**:

Je **me** pose des questions.   *I am asking **myself** questions.* (to myself)
Il **me** regarde.   *He is looking at/watching **me**.* (me)
Il **me** pose des questions.   *He is asking **me** questions.* (to me)

To identify what type of pronoun it is, you ask the following questions:

- ▶ Are the subject and the object the same person? (= reflexive)
- ▶ Does the pronoun answer the question *who?* (*whom?*)/*what?* (= direct object)
- ▶ Does the pronoun answer the question *to whom?* (= indirect object)

Use of indirect object pronouns

Learners often have difficulty in using **indirect object pronouns** in French because English and French verbs are sometimes different. See Unit 12 **Getting started 3**. Be particularly careful with the following verb structures:

demander à   *to ask*
téléphoner à   *to phone*

Nous **leur** demandons les directions.   *We ask them for directions.*

Il **leur** téléphone.   *He rings them up. (telephones to them)*

You can choose the correct pronoun by identifying the verb and asking *who?* (*whom?*)/*what?* or *to whom?* after it. In the sentence **je le donne**, **le** answers the question *what?*:

verb = **donne**; **donne** *what?* → **le**; so **le** is a **direct object**.

In **je lui donne**, **lui** answers the question *to whom?*:

verb = **donne**; **donne** *to whom?* → **lui**; therefore **lui** is an **indirect object**.

3 *THE DIFFERENCE BETWEEN* Y *AND* EN

They can both mean *of this* but y replaces à + noun.

J'y pense souvent. = Je pense à cela.   *I often think of/about this.*

whereas **en** (Unit 5 **The main points** 3) replaces **de** + noun.

J'en mange = Je mange **de cela**.   *I eat some (of it).*

TEN THINGS TO REMEMBER

1 Check the present tense of irregular verbs **aller, devoir** and **prendre,** as they are often used in giving directions.

2 The expression **il faut** + infinitive (**il faut tourner à droite**) is very useful and easy to use for directions.

3 Ordinal numbers (Unit 3) will be useful in explaining which street to take.

4 You will need to be able to use expressions that tell you where something is: **à droite, à gauche, à côté de, devant, derrière, en face de,** etc. (See Unit 6 **The main points 3.**)

5 You need to know the present tense of regular verbs (Units 1, 3, 5, 6) to be able to give orders (use the imperative).

6 The imperative has two main forms depending on the person you are speaking to: the **tu** form (**prends, continue**) and the **vous** form (**prenez, continuez**). There is also a **nous** form (more about this in Unit 12) when you want to say *'Let's …'*: **Allons au cinéma.** (*Let's go to the cinema.*)

7 Can you recognize the difference between direct and indirect objects?: **il le voit** (*he sees him*), **il lui donne** (*he gives to him*). English and French verbs do not always take the same kind of object: for example English says 'I phone him', whereas French says **Je lui téléphone** (*I phone (a message) to him*). **Je le téléphone** would mean 'I phone it' (i.e. 'it' is the message that I'm phoning through).

8 The indirect object pronouns **y** and **en** are very handy to avoid repetition: **Tu vas à Londres. Oui, j'y vais.** (*Are you going to London? Yes, I'm going there.*) **Tu parles de la visite des Dickson? Oui, j'en parle.** (*Are you talking about the Dicksons' visit? Yes, I'm talking about it.*)

9 Object pronouns usually come before the verb (Unit 5), but if the verb is in the imperative they come after it: **Donne-le-moi.** (*Give it to me.*)

10 The object pronouns **me, te, nous** and **vous** are the same whether they are direct, indirect or reflexive: **ils <u>nous</u> appellent, tu <u>nous</u> dis, nous <u>nous</u> appelons.** In the third person, the direct object pronouns are **le, la, l'** and **les**, and the indirect object pronouns are **lui** and **leur**. The third person reflexive pronoun **se** is used for both singular and plural (**il se lève, ils se lèvent**).

10

Describing a sequence of events

In this unit you will learn
- *To describe and ask about a process that involves several stages*
- *To describe and ask about a series of actions and events*
- *To ask and say why something happened*

Topic
- *Planning a visit*

Grammar

▶ Expressions of time: **hier** (*yesterday*), **aujourd'hui** (*today*), **demain** (*tomorrow*)

▶ Structuring adverbs: **d'abord** (*first*), **ensuite** (*then*), **finalement** (*finally*)

▶ Time prepositions: **pendant** (*during*), **avant** (*before*), **après** (*after*), **depuis** (*since*)

▶ Cause and effect: **parce que** (*because*), **donc** (*so*), **car** (*for*)

The next stage

▶ More about time expressions

▶ Speaking impersonally:

▶ Impersonal expressions: **Il faut** (*It is necessary*), **Il est important** (*It is important*), **Il est difficile** (*It is difficult*)

▶ The present passive: **ils sont invités par ...** (*they are invited by ...*), **l'invitation est envoyée par ...** (*the invitation is sent by ...*)

Getting started

1 To talk or write about a series of events or actions, you use words such as **d'abord** (*first*), **ensuite** (*then*), **finalement** (*finally*). These words are adverbs of time (you have already met some of them in Unit 6) and they are used to make the sequence of events clear:

D'abord, tu organises le voyage, *First you plan the trip, next*
ensuite tu achètes les billets. **Puis** tu *you buy the tickets. Then you*
prépares les valises et **enfin** tu prends *pack and finally you get a*
un taxi pour aller à l'aéroport. *taxi to go to the airport.*

2 You can also express the idea of a sequence of events using a preposition + a noun: **avant l'aube/six heures** (*before dawn/six o'clock*), **après le coucher du soleil/19 heures** (*after sunset/7 p.m.*), **pendant l'après-midi** (*during the afternoon*). See prepositions of time in Unit 6 **The main points 3.**

Insight

These expressions let you write and speak about things which usually take place in an established order.

3 Events are sometimes related by a process of cause and effect, rather than by time. To show this kind of relationship between events or stages in a process you need to use conjunctions, words such as **parce que** (*because*), **donc** (*so*), **car** (*for*).

La famille Dickson va en France *The Dickson family is going to*
parce qu'ils veulent rencontrer *France because they want to*
la famille de la copine de leur *meet the family of their son*
fils Mark. Ils pensent que *Mark's girlfriend. They think*
Mark et Stéphanie vont bientôt *that Mark and Stéphanie are*
se fiancer, **donc** ils veulent *going to get engaged soon so*
rencontrer ses parents et voir *they want to meet her parents*
son pays. Les parents de Mark *and see her country. Mark's*
sont un peu inquiets, **car** ils ne *parents are a bit worried, since*
connaissent pas bien Stéphanie. *they don't know Stéphanie well.*

4 If you want to know how events are related to one another, you will need to be able to ask questions.

▸ For time relationships, you can use **quand?** (when) or questions such **as Qu'est-ce qui se passe d'abord/ensuite?** (*What happens first/then?*) with the adverbs you have already learned (Unit 6 **The main points 4**).

Quand souhaitent-ils y aller?   *When do they wish to go there?*
Qu'est-ce qui se passe d'abord?   *What happens first?*

▸ For cause and effect, you can use questions beginning with **Pourquoi?** (*Why?*).

Pourquoi veulent-ils aller en France?   *Why do they want to go to France?*

Say it in French

1 *ASKING ABOUT SEVERAL STAGES*

Qu'est-ce qui se passe d'**abord** à l'agence de voyage?

What happens first at the travel agency?

Premièrement je dis que nous voulons aller en France.

First of all I say that we want to go to France.

Et **ensuite/après/puis**?

And then?

Il faut **ensuite** leur dire combien de personnes, l'âge de chacun et à quelle période nous voulons y aller.

Then I'll have to explain how many of us there are, how old we are and when we want to go.

Puis tu te renseignes sur les prix et les horaires et **finalement** tu fais la réservation.

Then you get information on prices and times and finally you make the booking.

2 ASKING ABOUT A SERIES OF ACTIONS OR EVENTS

Comment pouvez-vous vous payer des vacances en France?

How can you afford a holiday in France?

En décembre dernier nous avons gagné un peu d'argent à la loterie. Ta mère a aussi donné plusieurs cours particuliers en février et en mars.

Last December we won a bit of money on the lottery. Your mother also gave several private lessons in February and March.

Ce mois-ci nous n'allons pas au restaurant et nous limitons les sorties coûteuses, **donc** nous faisons des économies. **De plus, le mois prochain** mon patron va me donner une augmentation. Pas de problème donc pour payer le billet!

This month we aren't eating out and we're cutting down on expensive outings, so we're saving money. In addition, next month my boss is going to give me a pay rise. So, no trouble paying the fare!

3 ASKING WHY SOMETHING HAPPENED

Pourquoi est-ce que les Lemaire veulent rencontrer les Dickson à l'aéroport?

Why do the Lemaires want to meet the Dicksons at the airport?

Parce qu'il est très difficile de conduire à Paris en raison de la circulation intense.

Because it is very difficult to drive in Paris due to the heavy traffic.

Pour quelle raison les Dickson veulent-ils aller en France?

Why (For what reason) do the Dicksons want to go to France?

Ils veulent y aller pour faire la connaissance des Lemaire.

They want to go there to make the acquaintance of the Lemaires.

Pourquoi est-ce qu'ils veulent les rencontrer cet été?

Why do they want to meet them this summer?

Mark et Stéphanie vont peut-être se fiancer cette année. **Par conséquent** ils pensent qu'il est important de les rencontrer le plus vite possible.

Mark and Stéphanie are maybe going to get engaged this year. So they think it is important to meet them as soon as possible.

Comme il y a de la place chez les parents de Stéphanie, les Dickson vont y rester quelques jours.		*As there is room at Stéphanie's parents', the Dicksons are going to stay there for a few days.*	
Puisqu'ils ont envie de connaître la région, ils vont aussi visiter différents endroits.		*Since they are keen to know the area, they are also going to visit different places.*	

The main points

1 *EXPRESSIONS OF TIME*

To say when one thing happened in relation to another, you need to be able to use time expressions such as **hier** (*yesterday*), **aujourd'hui** (*today*), **demain** (*tomorrow*), the adjectives **dernier** (*last*) and **prochain** (*next*) and the demonstrative adjectives – **ce, cet, cette, ces** (see Unit 2 **The main points** 5).

> ### Insight
> You will learn the tenses you need to use with these time expressions in Units 11, 13 and 14.

		past	present	future
matin	*morning*	**hier matin**	**ce matin**	**demain matin**
après-midi	*afternoon*	**hier après-midi**	**cet après-midi**	**demain après-midi**
soir	*evening*	**hier soir**	**ce soir**	**demain soir**
nuit	*night*	**la nuit dernière**	**cette nuit**	**la nuit prochaine**
semaine	*week*	**la semaine dernière**	**cette semaine**	**la semaine prochaine**
mois	*month*	**le mois dernier**	**ce mois-ci**	**le mois prochain**
été	*summer*	**en été dernier**	**cet été**	**l'été prochain**
année	*year*	**l'année dernière**	**cette année**	**l'année prochaine**

| L'année dernière Stéphanie a débuté son stage en Écosse. | *Last year, Stéphanie started her work placement in Scotland.* |
| Cette année la famille Dickson va en France et l'année prochaine les parents de Stéphanie passeront les vacances d'été chez les Dickson. | *This year the Dickson family is going to France and next year Stéphanie's parents will spend the summer holidays at the Dicksons'.* |

See also **Say it in French 2.**

2 STRUCTURING ADVERBS

Verbs show whether they refer to the present, past or future by their form:

Mark **rencontre** Stéphanie.	*Mark **meets** Stéphanie.*
Mark **a rencontré** Stéphanie.	*Mark **met/has met** Stéphanie.*
Mark **va rencontrer** Stéphanie.	*Mark **is going to meet** Stéphanie.*
Mark **rencontrera** Stéphanie.	*Mark **will meet** Stéphanie.*

To show more precisely where the verb comes in a series of events, you can use an **adverb of time.** Adverbs usually tell us more about verbs so they are often found near verbs: **Je la rencontre souvent** (*I often meet her*). You can change the word order depending on what you want to emphasize:

Je vais **d'abord** l'inviter à prendre un café.	*I'll invite her first of all to have coffee.*
D'abord, je vais l'inviter à prendre un café.	*First I'll invite her to have coffee.*
Je vais l'inviter à prendre un café, **d'abord.**	*I'll ask her to have a coffee first.*

3 *TIME PREPOSITIONS*

To explain where in a sequence an event occurs, occurred or will
occur, you can use a **time preposition** plus a noun:

Après les examens je vais aller plus souvent au cinéma.	*After the exams, I will go to the cinema more often.*
Avant les vacances, nous sommes toujours fatigués.	*Before the holidays we are always tired.*
Pendant les vacances nous nous reposons et **après** notre retour à la maison nous sommes en pleine forme.	*During the holidays we rest and after coming home we are in top form.*
Je dois étudier sérieusement **avant** les vacances.	*I have to study seriously before the holidays.*

Prepositions showing the order of a series of events (**avant, après,
jusqu'à**) can be followed by the time instead of a noun:

Je téléphone souvent à mes parents **après neuf heures** et nous parlons **jusqu'à dix heures**.	*I often phone my parents after nine o'clock and we talk until ten o'clock.*
L'avion de Londres arrive **avant 18 heures**, puis il part pour Berlin.	*The London plane arrives before 6 p.m., then it leaves for Berlin.*
Sandy travaille **jusqu'à dix heures**. Ensuite elle se couche.	*Sandy works until ten o'clock. Then she goes to bed.*

176

4 CAUSE AND EFFECT

Events can also be related through the effects they produce. The simplest way to show this is by using the expression **parce que** (*because*). You can ask a question to find out about cause and effect using **pourquoi?** (*why?*).

Pourquoi choisissez-vous de prendre l'avion?
Why do you choose to go by plane?

Parce que c'est plus rapide.
Because it's quicker.

Other **linking expressions** can be used to show the effect or the result of something:

L'avion va plus vite que le train, **donc** nous le prenons pour aller en France.
The plane goes quicker than the train, so we will take it to go to France.

Comme l'avion est plus rapide que le train, nous avons décidé de le prendre pour aller en France.
Since the plane is faster than the train, we decided to fly to France.

C'est parce que l'avion est plus rapide que le train **que** nous avons décidé de le prendre pour aller en France.
It's because the plane is faster than the train that we decided to fly to France.

Puisque l'avion va plus vite que le train, nous avons décidé d'aller en France en avion.
As the plane is faster than the train, we decided to go to France by plane.

See also **Say it in French 3**.

The story

Look particularly for **structuring adverbs** and expressions of cause and effect.

Les Lemaire se préparent à recevoir les Dickson.

Isabelle	Comment les choses vont-elles se passer? D'abord ils vont louer une voiture à l'aéroport. Ensuite il y a deux heures de route avant d'arriver chez nous. Puis il faut dîner, …
Georges	Qu'est-ce qu'on fait d'habitude quand on a des invités? On leur montre la ville et puis on visite un peu la région. Les Dickson vont sûrement s'intéresser aux environs de St Amand. On peut donc les conduire en forêt et à Valenciennes. Et on peut aussi leur présenter nos amis.
Isabelle	Oui, bien sûr, mais on prend des vacances pour se reposer! Il faut leur laisser le temps de se détendre et ne pas essayer de faire trop de choses. D'ailleurs, comme c'est la première fois qu'ils viennent en France, il faut leur montrer ce qui est typiquement français.
Georges	Il est difficile de décider ce qui est intéressant pour des Écossais parce que nous ne connaissons pas l'Écosse.
Isabelle	Il est préférable donc de leur demander ce qu'ils veulent voir – la campagne, la mer, les villes, …
Georges	Et puis, il est important de leur présenter des amis de Stéphanie car ils veulent sûrement mieux la connaître.

A quick check

1 Check **The main points 1, 2, 3, 4** and identify the expressions of time, and of cause and effect in the extracts below. Then put the ten elements in the correct order to make a brief story entitled **Les vacances**.

– nous essayons de nous lever le plus tard possible.
– Il est donc midi et nous n'avons pas pris une décision.
– car nos parents commencent à se fâcher.
– Pendant les vacances, nous voulons nous reposer, mais nos parents préfèrent être très actifs.
– Après avoir mangé, il faut accepter de sortir …
– Finalement, tout le monde est prêt, et nous pouvons enfin partir.
– Puis nous prenons une douche et nous nous habillons très lentement.
– C'est pour cette raison que …
– Alors nous discutons interminablement le programme du jour.
– D'abord nous mangeons un petit déjeuner copieux.

The next stage

1 *MORE ABOUT TIME EXPRESSIONS*

Expressions such as **avant** (*before*), **après** (*after*), **pendant** (*during*) (see **The main points 3**), are not only found in sentences where the present tense is used. They are also used when talking about past, recently past and future events.

Avant mon stage en Grande-Bretagne je ne m'intéressais pas à l'histoire écossaise.

Before my work experience in Great Britain, I wasn't interested in Scottish history.

J'ai téléphoné à Stéphanie ce matin **après** neuf heures et nous nous sommes rencontrés **avant** dix heures.

I phoned Stéphanie after nine o'clock and we met before ten o'clock.

Pendant notre séjour nous ferons beaucoup de randonnées en forêt.

During our stay we'll take a lot of walks in the forest.

Exception: **depuis**

To indicate how long something has been going on, or when it started, you can use: **depuis** *(for/since)*.

Les Lemaire **attendent** les Dickson depuis plus de deux heures.	*The Lemaires have been waiting for the Dicksons for more than two hours.*
Depuis 1996, nous **allons** tous les ans à Annecy en juillet.	*We've been going to Annecy in July every year since 1996.*

Insight

The verb tenses in English and French are different here: in French, the present tense is used with **depuis**. (More about this in Unit 15 **The next stage 2**.)

2 SPEAKING IMPERSONALLY

It is useful to be able to speak about events without necessarily using the personal forms of the verb. There are two main ways of doing this:

▶ using **impersonal expressions** and
▶ using a form of the verb called the passive. The passive is based on the verb **être** (see Unit 1 **The main points 2**).

Impersonal expressions
Some of these were used in earlier sections of this unit in **The story**:

Il faut dîner ...
Il faut leur laisser le temps de se détendre.
Il faut leur montrer ce qui est typiquement français.
Il est difficile de décider ...
Il est préférable donc de leur demander ...
Il est important de leur présenter ...

Il faut (*It is necessary*) is followed directly by an infinitive:

Il **faut apprendre** le français   *We'll have to (it is necessary to)*
  avant les vacances.   *learn French before the holidays.*

See Unit 8 **Say it in French 4, The main points 2.**

Other impersonal expressions are followed by **de** and an infinitive:

Il **est difficile de comprendre**   *It's hard to understand Nicolas*
  Nicolas, car il parle très vite.   *because he speaks very fast.*
Il **est préférable de prendre** vos   *It's better to take your holidays*
  vacances en été.   *in the summer.*
Il **est facile de voir** pourquoi   *It's easy to see why Mark likes*
  Mark aime Stéphanie.   *Stéphanie.*
Il **est important de connaître** les   *It's important to know*
  parents de Stéphanie.   *Stéphanie's parents.*
Il **est ridicule de refuser** de parler   *It is stupid to refuse to speak*
  français.   *French.*

The present passive

Another way of speaking impersonally or indirectly is to say that
something *is done by someone*. This is called the passive voice. You
need to be able to use **être** + the past participle of another verb,
followed by the preposition **par** (*by*):

Les Dickson **sont accueillis par**   *The Dicksons are welcomed by*
  les Lemaire.   *the Lemaires.*
Les valises **sont faites par** Alison   *The packing is done by Alison*
  parce que les autres n'aiment   *because the others don't like*
  pas les faire.   *doing it.*

Notice that the past participle acts like an adjective and agrees with
the person(s) or thing(s) it is telling you about:

Les Dickson (masc. plural) sont accueillis.

Les valises (fem. plural) sont faites.

The past participles of regular verbs are formed in the following way:

-er verbs		-ir verbs		-re verbs	
infinit.	past part.	infinit.	past part.	infinit.	past part.
donner	donné	accueillir	accueilli	vendre	vendu
inviter	invité	atterrir	atterri	rendre	rendu

Insight

For more information on past participles, see Unit 13 **The main points 1** and **The next stage 1**.

Here are some examples of the use of the **present passive** (for the past tenses of the passive, see Unit 15 **The main points 4**).

Je **suis** toujours **accueilli** à la gare par mes parents.	*I'm always collected at the station by my parents.*
Tu es **invité**(e) par mes parents à venir dîner à la maison demain.	*You are invited by my parents to come and have dinner at home tomorrow.*
Il est très **attiré** par Stéphanie.	*He is very attracted to Stephanie.*
Cette voiture **est louée** par nos amis écossais.	*This car is hired by our Scottish friends.*
Nous **sommes invités** par les Lemaire.	*We are invited by the Lemaires.*
Vous êtes souvent **photographié** par votre copine.	*You are often photographed by your girlfriend.*
Les Dickson **sont invités** par les Lemaire à passer leurs vacances en France.	*The Dicksons are invited by the Lemaires to spend their holidays in France.*
Les valises **sont faites** par Alison.	*The packing is done by Alison.*

TEN THINGS TO REMEMBER

1 When things happen in a fixed order, you can describe the sequence using prepositions (**avant, après**) + nouns: **avant les vacances, pendant les vacances, après les vacances.**

2 You can also use adverbs to describe a sequence of events or the different stages of an event you have recently been involved in (**d'abord/premièrement, ensuite/puis, enfin/finalement**).

3 To talk about cause and effect, use conjunctions (**parce que, donc, car**).

4 Remember the useful question words **Quand?** (for time) **and Pourquoi?** (for purpose/reason).

5 Check that you are familiar with the different times of the day (**le matin, l'après-midi, le soir**) and with other time words (**le jour, la journée, la semaine, le mois, l'an, l'année**).

6 Word order for adverbs in French is flexible. You can change the emphasis by changing the place of the adverb: **Je vais l'inviter à prendre un café <u>d'abord</u>. → <u>D'abord</u> je vais l'inviter à prendre un café.**

7 The question word **Pourquoi?** and its answering **Parce que …** are the basis of many conversations.

8 **Depuis** is a word to watch out for. Unlike in English, it is followed by the present tense to show that something has been going on for some time: **Nous <u>apprenons</u> le français depuis le commencement de l'année.** (*We <u>have been learning</u> French since the beginning of the year.*)

9 French has a number of useful impersonal expressions (**il faut, il est difficile/préférable/important**). When you use them, you don't have to worry about using different subject pronouns and forms of the verb.

10 The passive is another form of the verb that is easy to use. All you need is the present tense of **être** and the past participle: **Nous sommes invités par nos amis.**

11

Future plans and events

In this unit you will learn
* *To speak and write about the future*
* *To ask about future events*
* *To talk about your hopes and plans*

Topic
* *Hopes for the future*

Grammar
▶ Regular verbs in the future tense (**le futur**)
▶ Common irregular verbs in the future
▶ Irregular verbs in **-er** in the future: **manger** (*to eat*), **appeler** (*to call*), **acheter** (*to buy*)
▶ Time expressions and the future
▶ Relative pronouns **qui** and **que**

The next stage
▶ The future: differences between French and English
▶ Other time expressions and the future
▶ Relative pronouns after **de**: **dont** (*of which/whom*)
▶ Relative pronouns referring to people, after other prepositions: **avec qui**, **pour qui**
▶ Relative pronouns referring to things, after other prepositions: **lequel**, etc.

Getting started

1 When you are speaking, you can often choose to use the present tense to refer to something you are going to do. If you do this, you will usually need to use a time expression as well, to show that you are referring to the future:

Je vais en France **cet été**.   *I'm going to France this summer.*
Tu vas au cinéma **ce soir**?   *Are you going to the cinema this evening?*
Il arrive demain matin **à**   *He's arriving tomorrow morning at*
  huit heures.   *eight o'clock.*

2 You have already learned (Unit 6 **The main points** 1) how to use **aller** (*to go*) with an infinitive to speak about the immediate future.

Je **vais acheter** un dictionnaire   *I'm going to buy a French-English*
  français-anglais.   *dictionary.*
Mes parents **vont téléphoner** à   *My parents are going to phone*
  Madame Lemaire ce soir.   *Madame Lemaire this evening.*
La semaine prochaine Mark   *Next week, Mark is going to start*
  va commencer à travailler sur   *working on a Shell platform.*
  une plate-forme Shell.

Go back to Unit 6 and make sure you can use this form without any difficulty.

3 As well as learning to use the future tense in this unit, you will also learn some of the time expressions you need so that you can talk about and ask questions about the future. Some of them you have already learned in Unit 10 **The main points** 1, 2. In the examples in 1 (above), these expressions are in bold. Locate the two time expressions in **Getting started** 2.

4 The irregular verbs you have already covered use the same future endings as the regular verbs, but have an irregular stem:

avoir *to have*   **vouloir** *to wish/want*
être *to be*   **pouvoir** *to be able*

aller *to go*
venir *to come*
faire *to make/do*

savoir *to know*
devoir *to be obliged/have to*
falloir *to be necessary*

Say it in French

1 *SPEAKING AND WRITING ABOUT THE FUTURE*

Les parents de Mark **arriveront** à l'aéroport Roissy-Charles-de-Gaulle. Là, ils **loueront** une voiture.

Mark's parents will arrive at Roissy-Charles-de-Gaulle airport. There they will hire a car.

Les Lemaire les **rencontreront** à l'aéroport et les Dickson les suivront en voiture.

The Lemaires will meet them at the airport and the Dicksons will follow them in the car.

Ils **arriveront** à St Amand deux heures plus tard.

They will arrive in St Amand two hours later.

Je leur **préparerai** un bon repas français.

I will prepare them a good French meal.

Je leur **ferai** une bonne mousse au chocolat.

I will make them a nice chocolate mousse.

Ils n'**auront** peut-être pas faim à cette heure-là.

Perhaps they won't be hungry at that time.

2 *ASKING ABOUT FUTURE EVENTS*

À ton avis, qu'est-ce qu'ils **feront** durant leur séjour?

What do you think they will do during their stay?

Qu'est-ce qu'on leur **montrera**?

What shall we show them?

Seront-ils intéressés? **Voudront**-ils visiter St Amand et ses environs?

Will they be interested? Will they want to visit St Amand and its surroundings?

Souhaiteront-ils rencontrer des amis de Stéphanie?

Will they want to meet some of Stéphanie's friends?

Peut-être **auront**-ils déjà des plans précis.

Perhaps they'll already have specific plans.

Nous leur **demanderons** ce qu'ils veulent faire.	*We'll ask them what they want to do.*
Ce **sera** la meilleure solution.	*That'll be the best way.*

3 TALKING ABOUT YOUR HOPES/YOUR PLANS

J'espère qu'ils se **plairont** chez nous.	*I hope (that) they'll enjoy being here.*
Nous **ferons** tout notre possible pour les mettre à l'aise.	*We'll do our best to put them at their ease.*
Je ne sais pas comment nous **communiquerons,** mais nous **ferons** de notre mieux.	*I don't know how we will communicate, but we'll do our best.*
J'**achèterai** un bon dictionnaire demain ou bien j'**emprunterai** celui de Nicolas.	*I'll buy a good dictionary tomorrow or I'll borrow Nicolas'.*
J'espère que Nicolas nous **aidera.**	*I hope that Nicolas will help us.*
Nous **pourrons** toujours nous faire comprendre par des gestes et nous **demanderons** à Nicolas d'être interprète.	*We'll always be able to make ourselves understood with gestures and we'll ask Nicolas to be our interpreter.*
Stéphanie **reviendra** peut-être en France à ce moment-là.	*Stéphanie will perhaps come back to France at that time.*

The main points

1 REGULAR VERBS IN THE FUTURE TENSE

For regular verbs, and many irregular verbs, the stem for this tense is the infinitive – **aimer** (to love), **finir** (to finish). Regular verbs ending in -re – **entendre** (*to hear*), **apprendre** (*to learn*), **vendre** (*to sell*) – drop the e (**entendr-, apprendr-, vendr-**) before adding the endings.

> **Insight**
> The endings for the future tense are the same for all French verbs.

Subject pronoun	Stem (= infinitive)	Endings
je/j'	aimer-	**AI**
tu	finir-	**AS**
il	apprendr-	**A**
elle	visiter-	**A**
on	rencontrer-	**A**
nous	vendr-	**ONS**
vous	partir-	**EZ**
ils	grossir-	**ONT**
elles	entendr-	**ONT**

J'aimerai Stéphanie toute ma vie. *I'll love Stéphanie all my life.*
Tu finiras avant moi. *You'll finish before me.*
Il apprendra à faire de la planche *He'll learn to windsurf.*
à voile.
Isabelle **visitera** le musée avec les *Isabelle will visit the museum*
Dickson. *with the Dicksons.*
On les **rencontrera** à l'aéroport. *We'll meet them at the airport.*
Nous vendrons la BMW à notre *We'll sell the BMW when we get*
retour. *back.*
Vous partirez tôt le matin. *You'll leave early in the morning.*
Ils grossiront s'ils mangent trop. *They'll get fat if they eat too*
much.
Elles entendront de la musique *They'll hear some French music.*
française.

See **Say it in French** 1, 2, 3.

2 COMMON IRREGULAR VERBS IN THE FUTURE

The stem of the future tense of the following verbs is very irregular
and has to be learned in each case:

avoir *to have*, **être** *to be*, **aller** *to go*, **venir** *to come*, **faire** *to make/
do*, **vouloir** *to wish/want*, **pouvoir** *to be able*, **savoir** *to know*,
devoir *to be obliged/have to*, **falloir** *to be necessary*.

Although the stems are not the infinitives, they all end in **-r**.

Infinit.	Stem	
avoir	aur-	aurai, auras, aura, aurons, aurez, auront
être	ser-	serai, seras, sera, serons, serez, seront
aller	ir-	irai, iras, ira, irons, irez, iront
venir	viendr-	viendrai, viendras, viendra, viendrons, viendrez, viendront
faire	fer-	ferai, feras, fera, ferons, ferez, feront
vouloir	voudr-	voudrai, voudras, voudra, voudrons, voudrez, voudront
pouvoir	pourr-	pourrai, pourras, pourra, pourrons, pourrez, pourront
savoir	saur-	saurai, sauras, saura, saurons, saurez, sauront
devoir	devr-	devrai, devras, devra, devrons, devrez, devront
falloir	faudr-	il faudra
voir	verr-	verrai, verras, verra, verrons, verrez, verront

Stéphanie

En l'an 20.., j'**aurai** mon diplôme.	*In 20.., I will have my degree.*
Est-ce que j'**aurai** d'autres examens à passer?	*Will I have other exams to take?*
Non. Je ne **serai** plus étudiante et j'**irai** en Grande-Bretagne chercher du travail.	*No, I will no longer be a student and will go to Great Britain to look for work.*
Mark **viendra** me voir quand il ne **sera** pas sur la plate-forme de forage.	*Mark will come and see me when he is not on the oil rig.*
Ferons-nous des promenades ensemble?	*Will we go for walks together?*
Nous **ferons** peut-être du sport.	*Perhaps we will take up sport.*
Il ne **voudra** pas m'accompagner à mes cours d'équitation mais on **pourra** aller à des matchs de foot ensemble.	*He will not want to go with me to my horse-riding lessons, but we will be able to go to football matches together.*

You can also use the future in the **negative** (il ne **voudra** pas, je ne **devrai** pas) and in the **interrogative** (Est-ce que j'**aurai** ...? Ferons-nous ...?).

> ## Insight
> Look for the irregular verbs in **Say it in French 1, 2, 3.**

3 *IRREGULAR VERBS IN -ER IN THE FUTURE*

Verbs spelled like **manger, appeler, acheter** follow the spelling rules you learned for the present tense (Unit 1 **The next stage 2; Verb tables**).

Quand nous serons en France, *When we are in France, maybe* nous **mangerons** peut-être des *we'll eat some snails.* escargots.

(The **g** in **manger** remains soft because it is followed by **e**.)

Je t'**appellerai** chez toi ce soir. *I'll ring you at your place tonight.*

(To avoid two neutral **e**'s following one another, the consonant **l** is doubled.)

Mon père m'**achètera** le billet et *My father will buy me the ticket* je **viendrai** te voir en Écosse. *and I'll come to see you in* *Scotland.*

(To avoid two neutral **e**'s following one another, a grave accent is added to the **e** in the second last syllable of the verb.)

4 *TIME EXPRESSIONS AND THE FUTURE*

When you use a verb in the future tense, you are referring, either explicitly or implicitly, to a period of time after the moment when you are speaking or writing.

Prepositions with time

Note the **prepositions** used in the time expressions in bold below:

En 3000 le monde fêtera le commencement du quatrième millénaire.	*In 3000 the world will celebrate the start of the fourth millennium.*
En été nous irons à la plage, mais **au printemps** nous serons dans le Massif central.	*In summer we shall go to the beach, but in spring we'll be in the Massif Central.*
Elle viendra nous voir **en janvier**.	*She will come to see us in January.*
Nos amis les Dickson arriveront **lundi**.	*Our friends the Dicksons will arrive on Monday.*
Leur avion atterrira **à 13 h 15**.	*Their plane will land at 1.15 p.m.*

Prochain

You can also use the adjective **prochain** (next) (see Unit 10 **The main points 1**) with the names of months or days:

Vendredi **prochain** je terminerai mon stage et je rentrerai chez moi.	*Next Friday I'll finish my work placement and I'll go home.*

The future with **dans** and **en**

The prepositions **dans** and **en** are both used for future time. **Dans** is used in speaking about a point of time in the future:

Dans quinze jours mon patron sera en vacances et nous pourrons travailler plus calmement.	*In a fortnight's time my boss will be on holiday and we'll be able to work more calmly.*
Nous nous verrons **dans** huit jours et je te raconterai tout.	*We'll see one another in a week and I'll tell you everything.*

| Je serai chez toi **dans** dix minutes. | *I'll be at your place in ten minutes time.* |

En is used to say how long it will take to do something:

| Il viendra **en** moins de dix minutes. | *He'll come in less than ten minutes.* (i.e. it will take him less than ten minutes) |
| Elle finira son doctorat **en** quatre ans. | *She'll finish her doctorate in four years.* (i.e. it will take her four years) |

5 *RELATIVE PRONOUNS* QUI *AND* QUE

Insight

Relative pronouns are useful to make your French more polished.

Like other pronouns (e.g. personal pronouns, Unit 1 **The main points** 1 and Unit 5 **The main points** 3), they also make it possible for you to avoid repetition and to construct longer sentences. They are particularly useful in writing.

Qui

Qui is a **subject** pronoun. It can replace people (*who*):

| Mon chef, **qui** travaille souvent en France, sera très content de vous rencontrer. | *My boss, who often works in France, will be very pleased to meet you.* |
| Est-ce que tu connais le directeur **qui** m'a interviewée? | *Do you know the director who interviewed me?* |

or things (*which/that*):

| Je veux vous parler de votre CV **qui** m'intéresse beaucoup. | *I should like to talk to you about your CV which interests me very much.* |
| Vous travaillerez dans le bureau **qui** se trouve à côté du mien. | *You'll be working in the office (that is) beside mine.* |

Que
Que is an **object pronoun** which can replace people (*whom*):

J'ai attendu dans le bureau de la secrétaire **que** j'ai rencontrée la semaine dernière.	*I waited in the office belonging to the secretary (whom) I met last week.*

or things (*which/that*):

Je suis très content(e) de l'ordinateur **que** j'utilise pour mon travail.	*I'm very happy with the computer (that) I use for my work.*

Insight
In English, the relative pronoun is often not expressed

- ▶ *the office (that is) beside mine*
- ▶ *the secretary (whom) I met last week*
- ▶ *the computer (that) I use for my work.*

Some verbs are always followed by a preposition
téléphoner à quelqu'un (*to phone someone*)
demander à quelqu'un (*to ask someone*).

Where verbs like this are followed by a relative pronoun, **qui** (*whom*) is used for people:

M. Monnoury est la personne **à qui** j'ai téléphoné ce matin.	*Mr Monnoury is the person (whom) I phoned this morning.*

The story

In this passage, look for the **verbs in the future tense**, the **time expressions** and the **relative pronouns**.

Qu'est-ce que tu fais? Stéphanie, Mark, Alison et Georges parlent de leur travail et de leurs projets d'avenir.

Stéphanie	Le travail que je fais actuellement ne m'intéresse pas beaucoup, mais après mon stage je pourrai trouver un emploi quand je rentrerai en France. C'est mon chef, Mr Williams, qui m'encourage à apprendre l'anglais et à me perfectionner en informatique. « Vous utiliserez toujours l'anglais et l'informatique » me dit-il.
Mark	À présent le poste que j'occupe m'oblige à passer beaucoup de temps sur plate-forme. Mais j'aurai besoin de cette expérience du forage en mer. C'est l'expérience pratique qui sera nécessaire si je veux avoir plus tard un poste de cadre.
Alison	Le travail d'un professeur devient de plus en plus dur. Pendant les vacances, qui passent toujours beaucoup trop vite pour moi, on ne se repose pas. Il faut préparer les cours car il est difficile de trouver le temps qu'il faut pendant le trimestre. Ce soir, comme d'habitude, je corrigerai des copies et je préparerai des polycopies que j'utiliserai demain.
Georges	Un plombier ne dort jamais tranquille car à tout moment le téléphone peut sonner. Il faut toujours dépanner des gens qui ont des problèmes – des problèmes qui n'arrivent que la nuit ou pendant le week-end. J'espère que mon fils aura un emploi qui lui permettra de bien dormir et de ne pas travailler à des heures impossibles.

A quick check

Change the verbs and the **time expressions** in the following passages to the future:

Stéphanie	Aujourd'hui je travaille au bureau. Je tape des lettres pour mon chef et j'assiste à une réunion des membres du département de ressources humaines. Est-ce que tu viens me chercher à 17 heures 30? On achète de quoi manger à Marks et Spencer.
Mark	Ce soir je mange avec Stéphanie. Mardi je ne suis pas ici car je prends l'hélicoptère et je recommence à travailler sur une plate-forme BP. Je règle l'appareil de forage et je le contrôle par ordinateur. Nous sommes sur plate-forme pour trois semaines. Je ne vois pas Stéphanie et elle me manque beaucoup.
Alison	Aujourd'hui à 4 heures nous avons une réunion de tous les enseignants. Elle dure au moins deux heures et demie et je ne rentre pas avant 19 heures 30. Vous préparez vous-mêmes le dîner – et il ne faut pas oublier de faire la vaisselle!
Georges	Est-ce que nous pouvons manger à 21 heures ce soir? La réparation de la tuyauterie chez Madame Vincent n'est pas terminée et je dois aussi remplacer les robinets dans sa salle de bains.

The next stage

1 THE FUTURE: DIFFERENCES BETWEEN FRENCH AND ENGLISH USAGE

Using the future in place of the present

Insight

After **quand** (*when*), **lorsque** (*when*), **aussitôt que** (*as soon as*) and **dès que** (*as soon as*), French uses a verb in the future

(**Quand vous arriverez ...**) whereas in English we use a verb in the present (*When you arrive ...*).

Nous les **accueillrons** quand ils **arriveront**.	*We'll welcome them when they arrive.*
Lorsque Mark **partira**, Stéphanie se **sentira** très triste.	*When Mark leaves, Stéphanie will feel very sad.*

Accueillir follows the same pattern as the verb **cueillir**. See **Verb tables**.

The future perfect

In French, a tense called the **future perfect** (Quand **j'aurai terminé** mon travail) is used where in English you would use a past tense. This emphasizes that one action will come after the other:

Je te téléphonerai quand j'**aurai terminé** mon travail.	*I'll ring you when I've finished work.*
Dès que j'**aurai réparé** le tuyautage de Madame Vincent, je rentrerai à la maison.	*As soon as I've repaired Madame Vincent's pipes, I'll come home.*

2 OTHER TIME EXPRESSIONS AND THE FUTURE

Some useful expressions are found in the table in Unit 10 **The main points 1**. In addition, you may need:

après-demain *the day after tomorrow*
le lendemain *the following/next day*
demain en huit *a week tomorrow/tomorrow week*
mercredi en quinze *a fortnight on Wednesday*

3 RELATIVE PRONOUNS AFTER DE: DONT

If you want to use a relative pronoun:

▶ with expressions which always include the preposition **de**: **avoir besoin de** *to need*, **avoir peur de** *to be afraid of*
▶ with verbs which can be followed by **de**: **parler de** *to speak about/of*, **rêver de** *to dream about*

the relative pronoun **dont** replaces **de + qui** (*of whom, of which*):

Les employés **dont** nous avons besoin sont difficiles à trouver dans cette région de l'Écosse.	*The employees we need are hard to find in this part of Scotland.*
Les résultats **dont** il a peur seront publiés la semaine prochaine.	*The results he's afraid of will be published next week.*
Je ferai ce soir les exercices **dont** le professeur nous a parlé.	*This evening, I'll do the exercises the teacher spoke about.*
La carrière en marketing **dont** je rêve me permettra de voyager partout en Europe.	*The career in marketing I dream of will allow me to travel all over Europe.*

The word order with **dont** is important.

noun		subject	verb
les employés	**dont**	nous	avons besoin
les résultats	**dont**	il	a peur
les exercices	**dont**	le professeur	a parlé
la carrière	**dont**	je	rêve

4 RELATIVE PRONOUNS REFERRING TO PEOPLE, AFTER PREPOSITIONS

La collègue **avec qui** je viens au bureau habite près de chez moi.	*The colleague I come to work with (with whom I come to work) lives near me.*
Le client **pour qui** je fais des recherches veut améliorer ses logiciels.	*The client I'm doing research for (for whom I'm doing research) wants to improve his software.*

5 RELATIVE PRONOUNS REFERRING TO THINGS, AFTER PREPOSITIONS

Insight

Check back to Unit 4 **The main points 4** for **lequel**, **laquelle** and **lesquelles** as interrogative pronouns.

When they follow a preposition, relative pronouns referring to **things** have the following form.

They agree with the word they replace in number and gender:

	Masculine	Feminine
Singular	lequel	laquelle
Plural	lesquels	lesquelles

As-tu vu l'ordinateur **sur lequel** je travaille? (ordinateur: masc. sing. → **lequel**)

Have you seen the computer I work on (on which I work)?

Les compagnies pétrolières **avec lesquelles** nous traitons sont rarement françaises. (compagnies: fem. plur. → **lesquelles**)

The oil companies we work with (with which we work) are rarely French.

Les salles de bain **dans lesquelles** je travaille sont très révélatrices de la vie des gens. (salles de bain: fem. pl. → **lesquelles**)

The bathrooms I work in (in which I work) reveal a lot about people's lives.

TEN THINGS TO REMEMBER

1 All verbs (except some of the irregular ones) form the future in the same way: infinitive + the following endings: -ai, -as, -a, -ons, -ez, -ont.

2 It is a good idea to revise all parts of the main irregular verbs when you learn their future stem: **avoir, aur-; être, ser-; vouloir, voudr-.**

3 The same stems are used for the conditional tense (Unit 18) so you're getting two for the price of one!

4 A simple way of talking about the immediate future is to use the present tense of **aller** (Unit 6) + infinitive: **Je vais apprendre le français.** (*I'm going to learn French.*)

5 To talk about future time, you will need to use appropriate time expressions: **demain, après-demain, l'année prochaine.**

6 If you want to say someone will do something (future) in a certain amount of time, you need to know when to use **dans** and when to use **en. Dans** is used when referring to a specific point of time in the future: **Dans trois ans, j'aurais terminé mes études.** (*In three years, I'll have finished my studies.*) **En** is used to say how long it will take to do something: **Je serai chez vous en dix minutes.** (*I'll be at your place in ten minutes.*)

7 Use relative pronouns to make longer and more interesting sentences. The most common ones are **qui** and **que**. To use them correctly, you need to know when the pronoun is a subject and when it is an object.

8 English often leaves out relative pronouns, but in French they are never omitted: **le livre que je lis** (*the book (that) I'm reading*).

9 Another difference between English and French is in their use of the future tense. French is probably more logical: **Lorsque Mark <u>partira</u>** (future tense), **Stéphanie se sentira très triste.** (*When Mark <u>goes away</u>* (present tense), *Stéphanie will feel very sad.*)

10 Remember that the word order with the relative pronoun **dont** is: noun + **dont** + subject + verb: **le voyage dont elle m'a parlé.**

12

....

Orders and instructions

In this unit you will learn
- *To ask someone to do or not to do something*
- *To give orders and instructions*

Topics
- *Money*
- *The bank*

Grammar
- ▶ The imperative of regular verbs
- ▶ The imperative of irregular verbs
- ▶ The present tense for giving instructions
- ▶ The infinitive and giving instructions
- ▶ Giving negative instructions
- ▶ Two object pronouns
- ▶ The imperative with two object pronouns

The next stage
- ▶ Other ways of giving orders
- ▶ Polite requests

Getting started

1 The imperative form of the verb is used for giving instructions (see Unit 9 **The main points** 2). To form the imperative, you use parts of the present (indicative) tense.

2 In this unit, you will learn how to use verbs which have more than one object pronoun. You learned about direct object pronouns in Unit 5 **The main points** 3, and indirect object pronouns in Unit 9 **The main points** 3. You should revise them before beginning this unit.

Alors, est-ce que tu **les** prends ou est-ce que tu ne **les** prends pas?	*Well, are you taking them or are you not taking them?*
Stéphanie laisse tomber son carnet de chèques et Mark **le** ramasse.	*Stéphanie drops her cheque book and Mark picks it up.*
Mark **leur** téléphonera et **leur** dira que les Lemaire **les** rencontreront à l'aéroport.	*Mark will phone them and tell them that the Lemaires will meet them at the airport.*

3 The distinction between direct and indirect objects is sometimes difficult for English speakers. See Unit 9 **The next stage** 2. You can identify the **direct object** by asking *what?* or *whom?* after the verb:

I gave the teller the cheque. → verb = *gave* → *gave **what**?* → *the cheque*

So '*cheque*' is the **direct object**.

The **indirect object** is not related directly to the verb, but to a preposition, usually *to*. Because the preposition is often not expressed in English, it can take a moment to work out what is the indirect object.

You can decide whether an object is indirect by asking the question *to/for whom?* after the verb:

I gave the cheque → to/for whom? → *(to) the teller*

So '*teller*' is the **indirect object**.

Study the following examples and ensure that you can recognize the difference between the two types of object in English.

Give him the money! → *'money'* = direct object: *'him'* = indirect object.

Give it to George!
Let's buy them this book!
I'll give him the money.
Sandy brought her a cup of tea.

Say it in French

1 *ASKING SOMEONE TO DO SOMETHING*

Est-ce que nous pouvons nous arrêter à la banque? J'ai besoin de retirer de l'argent.	*Can we stop at the bank? I need to draw some money out.*
Arrête, s'il te plaît, car je voudrais acheter un petit cadeau pour Madame Lemaire.	*Please stop, because I would like to buy a small gift for Madame Lemaire.*
N'oublie pas les conseils de notre prof de français pour demander à quelqu'un de répéter quelque chose.	*Don't forget our French teacher's advice for asking someone to repeat something.*
Pourriez-vous répéter, s'il vous plaît?	*Could you repeat, please?*
Pouvez-vous parler plus lentement, s'il vous plaît?	*Can you speak more slowly, please?*

2 GIVING ORDERS

Andrew, **occupe-toi** bien de la maison.	*Andrew, look after the house well.*
Sors la poubelle le mardi matin.	*Put the bin out on Tuesday mornings.*
Ne te lève pas trop tard.	*Don't get up too late.*
Toi et tes amis, **n'utilisez pas** trop le téléphone.	*You and your friends must not use the phone too much.*
Contacte ton oncle si tu as des problèmes.	*Contact your uncle if you have any problems.*
Suivons les conseils de Mark.	*Let's follow Mark's advice.*
Il ne **faudra** pas rouler trop vite car il est important de lire les panneaux routiers.	*We mustn't drive too fast, as it is important to read the road signs.*
Insérer la carte bancaire, **taper** le numéro personnel. **Choisir** le montant.	*Insert your bank card, key in your personal number. Select the amount.*
Retirer la carte avant d'obtenir l'argent.	*Take your card out before the money is issued.*

The main points

1 THE IMPERATIVE OF REGULAR VERBS

The verbs you have studied so far have been in the **indicative** (or standard) **mood**. It is used for making statements. See Unit 9 **The main points** 2. The **imperative mood** is used for giving instructions or orders. In French, there are three forms of the imperative, depending on the situation the speaker is in:

▶ speaking to a friend
▶ speaking to someone you don't know well or to a group of people
▶ speaking to a group of people in which you are included.

Look back at **Say it in French** and see if you can find examples of the first two.

In each of the three situations described, you can use part of the present tense of the verb (without a subject) to give an instruction:

▶ speaking to a friend, use the **tu** form of the verb:

Donne cet argent à ton frère!	*Give that money to your brother!*
Finis tes devoirs!	*Finish your homework!*
Viens ici!	*Come here!*

For -**er** verbs only, the **s** of the **tu** form is dropped in the imperative: **Donne!** (*Give!*), **Achète!** (*Buy!*), **Chante!** (*Sing!*).

▶ speaking to someone you don't know well or to a group of other people, use the **vous** form of the verb:

Insérez votre argent dans la fente à droite!	*Insert your money in the slot on the right!*
Protégez votre carte des regards indiscrets!	*Hide your card from prying eyes!*
N'**oubliez** pas votre carte de crédit!	*Don't forget your credit card!*

▶ speaking to a group of people in which you are included (*Let's do something in English*), use the **nous** form of the verb:

Allons à la banque ce matin!	*Let's go to the bank this morning!*
Essayons ma carte bancaire!	*Let's try my bank card!*
Apprenons à mieux parler français!	*Let's learn to speak French better!*

Insight

The **tu** and **vous** forms are more common than the **nous** form. Although it expresses a suggestion rather than an order, the **nous** form is thought of as an imperative in French.

In the boxes below, the imperative forms are in bold:

| **jouer** *to play* |
| je joue |
| tu **joue**(s) |
| il/elle/on joue |
| nous **jouons** |
| vous **jouez** |
| ils/elles jouent |

| **finir** *to finish* |
| je finis |
| tu **finis** |
| il/elle/on finit |
| nous **finissons** |
| vous **finissez** |
| ils/elles finissent |

| **rendre** *to give back* |
| je rends |
| tu **rends** |
| il/elle/on rend |
| nous **rendons** |
| vous **rendez** |
| ils/elles rendent |

Ne joue pas avec Pierre!	*Don't play with Pierre!*
Jouons le concerto numéro 3 ce soir!	*Let's play Concerto No 3 tonight!*
Jouez dans le jardin!	*Play in the garden!*
Finis tes devoirs!	*Finish your homework!*
Finissons le gâteau!	*Let's finish the cake!*
Ne **finissez** pas tout aujourd'hui!	*Don't finish the lot today!*
Rends ton amie heureuse!	*Make your friend* (f.) *happy!*
Rendons grâce à Dieu!	*(Let's) give thanks to God!*
Rendez ce livre à Andrew, s'il vous plaît.	*Give this book back to Andrew, please.*

2 THE IMPERATIVE OF IRREGULAR VERBS

Avoir *and* être
Some irregular verbs such as **avoir** and **être** have special forms in the imperative:

| **avoir** | Aie! | Ayons! | Ayez! |
| **être** | Sois! | Soyons! | Soyez! |

Irregular -er **verbs**
Irregular -er verbs (Unit 1 **The next stage 2**) have an irregular **tu** form (see **Verb tables**):

Achète trois kilos de cerises!	*Buy three kilos of cherries!*
Appelle ce numéro à huit heures!	*Phone this number at eight o'clock!*

Jette ce papier dans la poubelle!	*Throw that paper in the bin!*
Lève-toi et marche!	*Arise and walk!*
Répète ce que je dis!	*Repeat what I say!*

Some of the irregular verbs in **-er**, e.g. **manger** (*to eat*), **placer** (*to place/put*), are also irregular in the **nous** form, if the pronunciation of the consonant becomes hard before the vowel o. This is avoided by inserting an **e** before the ending for verbs ending in **-ger** (e.g. **manger**) or by adding a cedilla to the **c** for verbs ending in **-cer** (e.g. **placer**):

Mangeons cette tarte!	*Let's eat this tart!*
Plaçons notre argent en lieu sûr!	*Let's invest our money in a safe place!*

Other irregular verbs

aller	Va!	Allons!	Allez!
faire	Fais!	Faisons!	Faites!
savoir	Sache!	Sachons!	Sachez!

3 THE PRESENT TENSE FOR GIVING INSTRUCTIONS

When you are speaking, you can use the present tense (including the subject – **tu** or **vous**) to give a direct order:

Tu ouvres un compte et **tu y verses** l'argent.	*You open an account and you put the money in.*
Tu prépares le terrain et **tu plantes** les fraises.	*You prepare the soil and you plant the strawberries.*
Tu tonds le gazon avant de sortir.	*(You) mow the lawn before you go out.*
Vous chantez tous ensemble.	*You all sing together.*
Vous rangez les bicyclettes et vous nettoyez vos baskets.	*(You) put the bikes away and (you) clean your trainers.*

4 THE INFINITIVE FOR GIVING INSTRUCTIONS

In formal situations, where written instructions are given, the infinitive is sometimes used to issue a direct instruction:

Composer votre numéro personnel.	*Type in your PIN.*
Demander une liste de nos services bancaires.	*Ask for a list of our banking services.*
Retirer votre carte et votre argent.	*Take your card and your money.*
Se munir d'une pièce d'identité.	*Provide yourself with some ID.*

See **Say it in French 2.**

5 *GIVING NEGATIVE INSTRUCTIONS*

The negative of the imperative is formed, as for the indicative, by using **ne** and **pas** (see Unit 1). As in other tenses, **ne** precedes the verb and **pas** follows it:

Ne mettez **pas** vos cartes de crédit dans votre porte- monnaie!	*Don't put your credit cards in your purse!*
Ne gaspillez **pas** votre argent!	*Don't waste your money!*
Ne dépensons **pas** sans réfléchir!	*Let's not spend without thinking about it!*

Insight

For negative commands using the infinitive (see **4** above), both **ne** and **pas** come before the verb:

Ne pas utiliser la carte après la date d'expiration!	*Do not use the card after the expiry date!*

6 *TWO OBJECT PRONOUNS*

You learned how to use direct object pronouns in Unit 5 **The main points 3,** and indirect object pronouns in Unit 9 **The main points 3.** A verb can sometimes have both a direct and an indirect object. See above, **Getting started 3.**

Je donnerai **un chèque** (direct object) **à Mark** (indirect object).	*I'll give a cheque to Mark. (I'll give Mark a cheque.)*

If both the objects are pronouns, they both go before the verb:

Je **le** (the cheque) **lui** (to Mark)   *I'll give it to him.*
  donnerai.

There is a fixed order when two object pronouns are used. It is not related to whether the pronouns are direct or indirect objects – you have to learn the order in which the pronouns are used in French.

The following grid, which looks a bit like the placings for a football team, shows you the order to follow, from left to right, when you are using two object pronouns. The most usual combinations are from columns 1 and 2:

Je **vous les** enverrai.   *I'll send them to you.*

and from columns 2 and 3:

Mark **le lui** achète.   *Mark buys it for him/her.*
Les Dickson **les** (les cadeaux)   *The Dicksons take them (the*
  leur (aux Lemaire) apportent.   *gifts) to them (the Lemaires).*

subject	object pronouns					Verb
	1	2	3	4	5	
	me					
	te					
Je	se	le	lui			envoie
Mark	nous	la	leur	y	en	achète
Les Dickson	vous	les				apportent
	se					

7 THE IMPERATIVE WITH TWO OBJECT PRONOUNS

Using two object pronouns with the direct imperative is simple. The objects follow the verb (as they do in English) and the direct object comes before the indirect object. The indirect object pronouns are: **moi, toi, lui, nous, vous, leur,** the same forms (except for **leur**) as the stressed pronouns (see Unit 1 **The main points** 8). The verb and the pronouns are joined by hyphens:

Envoie-**le-lui**!	*Send it to him/her!*
Apportons-**les-leur**!	*Let's take them to them!*
Achetez-**la-moi**!	*Buy it for me!*

Insight

If the imperative verb is in the negative, follow the word order rules given in 6 above:

Ne le lui envoyez pas!	*Don't send it to him/her!*
Ne les leur apportons pas!	*Let's not take them to them!*
Ne me l'achetez pas!	*Don't buy it for me!*

The story

In the conversation below, pick out the **verbs in the imperative** and the **object pronouns**.

Nicolas, son père et sa mère essaient de calculer comment il peut se permettre d'aller en Grande-Bretagne l'année prochaine.

Georges	Tu devrais changer complètement tes habitudes. Tu mets de l'argent de côté, tu ouvres un nouveau compte en banque, tu y verses au moins 150 euros par mois et tu ne dépenses rien!
Nicolas	C'est facile pour toi! Fais ceci! Fais cela! Ne fais pas ceci! Tu commandes et moi j'obéis. Mais pour moi, ce n'est pas facile. Imagine un peu! Je me prive de sorties, de vêtements, de livres, de cinéma. Pense à l'effet que tout cela aura sur moi!
Isabelle	Oui, écoute Georges! Aide-le! Ne lui donne pas d'ordres! Donne-lui plutôt des conseils!
	(Contd)

Georges	C'est ce que j'essaie de faire. Je veux l'aider. Ne me le reprochez pas! D'ailleurs j'allais suggérer qu'on lui donne l'argent que nous avons mis de côté pour la nouvelle voiture. Donnons-le-lui! Il en a vraiment besoin.
Isabelle	Alors là, non! Ne nous affolons pas! Il a une année pour trouver cet argent. Il faut imaginer d'autres solutions parce que moi, je veux une nouvelle voiture!
Nicolas	Ne vous fâchez pas! Restons calmes. Je vous en prie, n'imaginez pas que je suis complètement stupide. Je me trouverai un petit boulot, je ferai du baby-sitting et bientôt j'aurai l'argent qu'il me faut.

A quick check

1 Choose one word from each of the three lists below. Put the verb (Column 1) into the imperative (**tu** form) and make a list of five instructions for a friend going to France.

verbs	*nouns*	*places*
utiliser	**une carte bancaire**	**la banque**
acheter	**une carte Visa**	**les restaurants**
changer	**tes euros**	**les magasins**
	des devises	**un grand magasin**
	une ceinture porte-monnaie	

Exemple: **Achète une ceinture porte-monnaie dans un grand magasin!**

2 In the same way, make a second list of five negative instructions using the imperative (vous) form:

verbs	nouns	places
ouvrir	votre porte-monnaie	le métro
changer	votre carte de crédit	l'hôtel
laisser	votre argent	votre chambre
	votre passeport	

Exemple: **Ne laissez pas votre argent dans votre chambre!**

3 Look at the pronouns in bold in the following sentences, and imagine the nouns they might be replacing:

Exemple: Mark **les lui** achète → **Mark achète des roses à Stéphanie.**

Tu **nous** le donnes.
Il **la lui** apporte.
Nous **te les** offrons.

4 Answer the following questions, using two object pronouns in your answer:

Exemple: **Mark, offre-t-il les fleurs à Stéphanie?** → Oui, il **les lui** offre.

Est-ce que tu donnes cet argent à notre fils?
Ces cadeaux, vous les apportez aux Lemaire?
Nous recommandons cet hôtel à nos amis?

The next stage

1 OTHER WAYS OF GIVING ORDERS

As well as using the imperative, you can also give instructions using
some impersonal expressions such as **il faut** and **il est nécessaire/
essentiel de** followed by an infinitive. (See Unit 9 **The main points** 1
and Unit 10 **The next stage** 2.)

Il faut épargner quand on est jeune.	*You have to save when you are young. (It is necessary to save …)*
Il est nécessaire d'encaisser le chèque cette semaine.	*You have to pay the cheque in this week. (It is necessary to pay …)*

See **Say it in French** 2.

2 POLITE REQUESTS

If you want to make a polite request, rather than give an order, you
can use set expressions based on the conditional tense of the verb
vouloir.

> **Insight**
>
> You will find more information on the conditional in Unit 18
> **The main points** 1, 3.

Voudriez-vous fermer la fenêtre?	*Would you close the window, please?*
Voudrais-tu me prêter quelques euros?	*Would you lend me a few euros, please?*

To make an order or an instruction even more polite, you can add
an expression which makes it less direct:

n'est-ce pas?	Tu partages cet argent avec ton frère, n'est-ce pas?	*You're sharing that money with your brother, aren't you?*

s'il vous plaît **s'il te plaît**	Rends ce livre à Andrew, s'il te plaît.	*Give that book back to Andrew, please.*
je vous en prie **je t'en prie**	Je vous en prie, ne parlez pas de la crise économique!	*Please (I beg you), don't talk about the economic crisis!*

See **Say it in French** 1.

TEN THINGS TO REMEMBER

1 The present tense of regular and irregular verbs, which you already know well, is used for giving orders (the imperative). The imperative uses the second person singular and plural forms (**tu, vous**) and the first person plural (**nous**).

2 Être and avoir have special forms for the imperative: **sois, soyez, soyons; aie, ayez, ayons.**

3 In speech, instead of using the imperative you can sometimes use the present tense: **Tu lui donnes l'argent.** (*Give him/You give him the money.*)

4 When you give an instruction in the negative, **ne** comes before the verb and **pas** immediately after it: **Ne laisse pas ton argent dans ta chambre. Ne donnez pas votre numéro personnel à un ami.**

5 Vouloir is a very useful verb for making requests more polite: **Voulez-vous m'aider?**

6 To make a request more polite, you can also use **pouvoir** (**Pouvez-vous ...?**) or s'il vous/te plaît: **Pouvez-vous me prêter votre livre? Prête-moi ton livre, s'il te plaît.**

7 If you are trying really hard not to upset someone, you can be even more polite by using the conditional + **s'il vous/te plaît**: **Voudrais-tu m'accompagner à la banque, s'il te plaît? Voudriez-vous m'attendre quelques minutes, s'il vous plaît?**

8 Verbs can have more than one object pronoun. Revise direct object pronouns (Unit 5) and indirect object pronouns (Unit 9) and make sure you know the difference.

9 When there are two object pronouns, word order (before the verb) is very important. In normal sentences (statements in the indicative), the word order is fixed, irrespective of whether the pronoun is a direct or an indirect object: **Tu le lui donnes.** (*You give it to him.*) **Elle me le donne.** (*She gives it to me.*)

10 In the imperative, the word order for object pronouns is different. It is the same as in English – but note the hyphens: **Donne-le-lui!** (*Give it to him.*)

13

....

Talking about past events

In this unit you will learn
- *To talk and write about past events*
- *To talk and write about a series of events that happened in the past*
- *To say that things took place over a period of time*
- *To present events that happened in the recent past*

Topics
- *Travel preparations*
- *Arrivals*

Grammar
▶ The past participle
▶ The perfect tense with **avoir**
▶ The perfect tense with **être**
▶ The immediate past: **venir de**
▶ Other time expressions for sequencing events in the past

The next stage
▶ Agreement of the past participle
▶ Uses of **il y a** (*ago*)

Getting started

1 To form the perfect tense of most verbs, you use the present tense of **avoir** (Unit 1 **The main points 2**) plus a past participle (**2** below). Notice the use of the present tense of **avoir** in the following examples:

Mark **a** rencontré Stéphanie à Aberdeen.	*Mark met Stéphanie in Aberdeen.*
Stéphanie **a** présenté Mark à ses parents.	*Stéphanie introduced Mark to her parents.*
Nous **avons** rendu visite aux Lemaire en France.	*We visited the Lemaires in France.*

2 To speak about the past, you will need to know the past participle of each verb. In earlier units, you learned a number of infinitives – the basic form of the verb – such as **donner, finir, vendre**. The past participle is formed from the infinitive:

donner	Il a **donné** un cadeau à sa mère.	*He gave his mother a gift.*
finir	Nous avons **fini** de dîner.	*We've finished eating.*
vendre	Vous avez **vendu** votre maison.	*You've sold your house.*

Insight

Check the irregular verbs you learned in Units 1, 5, 6, 8, 11, and those you have in your notebook. Sometimes the past participle of these verbs is irregular too:

pouvoir → **pu**
vouloir → **voulu**
savoir → **su**
dire → **dit**

3 A small number of verbs do not use the present tense of **avoir**, but of **être**, to form the perfect tense. You have learned the present tense of **être** (Unit 1 **The main points** 2), so you will easily recognize it when you find it as part of the perfect tense:

Nicolas **est** sorti à 20 heures. *Nicolas went out at 8 p.m.*
Il **est** allé voir son copain Pierre. *He went to see his friend Peter.*
Ils **sont** montés dans la chambre *They went up to Peter's room.*
  de Pierre.

4 In many ways, past participles function as adjectives and follow the same rules for agreement.

▶ If they are used with a noun, they agree with it in number and gender:

un rendez-vous manqué (m. sing.) *a missed meeting*
une lettre tapée (fem. sing.) *a typed letter*
des bureaux partagés (m. plural) *shared offices*
des réunions chargées (fem. plural) *packed meetings*

▶ If past participles are used with **avoir** or être to form the perfect tense, there are rules about agreement as these examples show:

J'ai rencontré votre secrétaire. Je *I met your secretary.*
  l'ai rencontrée la semaine dernière. *I met her last week. She*
Elle s'est excusée et nous avons *apologized and we talked*
  parlé du problème. *about the problem.*

Insight
You will gradually learn more about agreement of past participles. **The next stage** 1 will help you on your way.

5 In Unit 6 **The main points** 1, you saw how the present tense of **aller** + infinitive can be used to show that something is going to happen in the immediate future. In a similar way, the present tense of **venir + de +** an infinitive can be used to describe something in the immediate past – something which *has just* happened. (You learned the present tense of **venir** in Unit 6 **The main points 2**.)

Nicolas **vient de** rentrer. Il est 23 heures.	*Nicolas has just come in. It is 11 o'clock.*
Georges **vient de** se réveiller. Il n'est pas content. Isabelle vient de se coucher.	*Georges has just woken up. He isn't happy. Isabelle has just gone to bed.*
Ils **viennent de** se rendre compte que Nicolas grandit.	*They have just realized that Nicolas is growing up.*

6 In Unit 11 **The main points 4**, you met a set of time prepositions which are used to talk about the future. Similarly, there are prepositions – some of them the same – which are frequently used in speaking about the past:

Après le déjeuner, j'ai pris le bus pour aller en ville.	*After lunch, I got the bus to go to town.*
Avant le commencement du film, j'ai acheté des bonbons.	*Before the film started, I bought some sweets.*
Pendant le film, je me suis endormi.	*During the film, I went to sleep.*

7 Just as there are time expressions which are associated with the future (Unit 10 **The main points 1**, Unit 11 **The main points 4**), there are time expressions which you will find useful for speaking about the past:

Nicolas? Je l'ai vu **hier**. Il m'a téléphoné **avant-hier** et **hier soir** je l'ai vu au cinéma.	*Nicolas? I saw him yesterday. He phoned me the day before yesterday and last night I saw him at the cinema.*
La semaine dernière je l'ai rencontré en ville et nous sommes allés au parc.	*Last week I met him in town and we went to the park.*

Say it in French

1 PAST EVENTS

Les Lemaire **ont décidé** d'aller
accueillir les Dickson à
l'aéroport.

*The Lemaires decided to go
and meet the Dicksons at the
airport.*

L'avion **a atterri!**... Les voilà! Dis
donc! Ils **ont apporté** beaucoup
de bagages! ...

*The plane has landed! ... There
they are! Goodness! They've
brought a lot of luggage! ...*

Comment allez-vous?

How are you?

Avez-vous **fait** bon voyage?

Did you have a good trip?

Très bien, merci. Nous **n'avons
pas eu** trop de problèmes.

*Fine, thank you. We didn't have
too many problems.*

Vous **êtes arrivés** à l'heure. Nous
avons laissé la voiture dans le
parking, car souvent l'avion est
en retard.

*You arrived on time. We've left
the car in the car park, because
the plane is often late.*

2 A SERIES OF EVENTS IN THE PAST

Avant le départ de l'avion, nous
avons pris un café. Ensuite,
nous **avons suivi** les indications
pour la salle de départ. Là nous
avons attendu quelques minutes,
et finalement ils **ont annoncé** le
départ de l'avion.

*Before the plane left, we had a
coffee. Then we followed the
signs to the departure lounge.
We waited there a few minutes,
and finally they announced the
departure of the flight.*

3 EVENTS THAT TOOK PLACE OVER A PERIOD OF TIME

Le voyage **a demandé** beaucoup
de préparation. Entre décembre
et mars je **suis allée** plusieurs
fois à l'agence de voyage. J'ai
téléphoné souvent aussi. Mon
mari **s'est occupé** de l'argent.

*The trip needed a lot of
preparation. Between December
and March I went to the travel
agency several times. I phoned
often as well. My husband
looked after the money.*

Quand on lui **a expliqué** *When they explained how the*
comment fonctionne la carte *Maestro card works, he decided*
Maestro, il **a décidé** de ne pas *not to buy a lot of euros.*
acheter beaucoup d'euros.

4 EVENTS IN THE RECENT PAST

Le vol a été assez intéressant … *The flight was quite interesting …*
L'avion **vient de** décoller, quand *The plane has just taken off,*
un passager **se lève, sort** un *when a passenger gets up, gets*
pistolet, et **commence à** menacer *out a gun, and starts threatening*
l'hôtesse. *the stewardess.*

The main points

1 THE PAST PARTICIPLE

The past participle is used as part of the **perfect tense** in both
French and English. Examples in English are: I have **given**, they
have **brought**, it has **landed**, we have **waited**.

Regular verbs
For all regular French verbs, and for some irregular verbs such as **aller**
(*to go*), **sortir** (*to go out*), **partir** (*to leave*), the past participle is formed
from the infinitive, the part of the verb that ends in -er, -ir, -re:

apporter *to bring*	→	**apporté** *brought*
atterrir *to land*	→	**atterri** *landed*
attendre *to wait*	→	**attendu** *waited*

See also Unit 10 **The next stage 2** (The present passive).

Irregular verbs and the past participle
For irregular verbs, you will have to learn the past participles, just
as you learned them for irregular verbs in English: **gone**, **hung**, **ate**,
for example.

Infinitive		Past participle	Infinitive		Past participle
avoir	to have	eu	**prendre**	to take	pris
écrire	to write	écrit	**suivre**	to follow	suivi
faire	to make/do	fait	**venir**	to come	venu
mettre	to put	mis	**voir**	to see	vu

As you have seen (4 above), there are rules about the agreement of past participles with subjects or objects. Some of the rules for agreement are given in **The next stage 1**.

See also Unit 10 **The next stage 2** (The present passive).

2 THE PERFECT TENSE WITH AVOIR

Look back at **Say it in French 1, 2 and 3**. The verbs in the perfect tense are in bold.

The perfect tense is used to speak about events that happened in the past. It is a **compound tense**. That means it is composed of more than one verb: the present tense of **avoir** (the **auxiliary verb**) and the past participle of a second verb (the main verb).

Most verbs in French form the perfect tense using the appropriate part of the present tense of **avoir** (Unit 1 **The main points 2**) and the past participle.

Since you can already use the present tense of **avoir**, the formation of the perfect tense is not difficult:

J'**ai** acheté les billets.	*I (have) bought the tickets.*
Tu **as** préparé les valises.	*You did the packing.*
Elle **a** envoyé une lettre.	*She (has) sent a letter.*
Nous **avons** fini les préparatifs.	*We've finished the preparations.*
Vous **avez** choisi quelle agence de voyage?	*Which travel agency did you choose?*
Ils **ont** attendu l'arrivée de l'avion.	*They waited for the arrival of the plane.*

Now look again at the examples in **Getting started** 1 and 2 and **Say it in French** 1 and 2.

The negative
If you are using this tense in the **negative,** you put **ne** after the subject and **pas** after the auxiliary verb (the present tense of **avoir**):

Mon mari **n'a pas** acheté les billets.	*My husband hasn't bought the tickets.*
Nous **n'avons pas** téléphoné à Stéphanie.	*We didn't ring Stéphanie.*

Inversion
To ask more formal questions with inversion, reverse the order of the subject and the auxiliary verb (**avoir**):

As-tu envoyé la lettre?	*Did you send the letter?*
Pourquoi **ont-ils** attendu l'arrivée de l'avion?	*Why did they wait for the plane to arrive?*

3 THE PERFECT TENSE WITH ÊTRE

There are two groups of verbs which *do not* use **avoir** to form the perfect tense.

Verbs which express a change of state or movement

aller	*to go*	**je suis allé(e)**
entrer	*to enter*	**tu es entré(e)**
arriver	*to arrive*	**elle est arrivée**
monter	*to go up*	**on est monté(e)s**
tomber	*to fall*	**nous sommes tombé(e)s**
naître	*to be born*	**ils sont nés**
venir	*to come*	**elle est venue**
sortir	*to go out*	**tu es sorti(e)**
partir	*to leave*	**il est parti**
descendre	*to descend*	**elle est descendue**
rester	*to remain*	**vous êtes resté(e)(s)**
mourir	*to die*	**ils sont morts**

Insight

You may find it easier to remember these verbs if you learn them as six pairs:

aller	venir
arriver	partir
entrer	sortir
monter	descendre
naître	mourir
rester	tomber

The negative and question forms are the same as those shown above for **avoir**:

Nicolas, **tu n'es pas arrivé** à l'heure.	*Nicolas, you didn't arrive on time.*
Est-elle arrivée avec ses parents?	*Did she arrive with her parents?*

Reflexive verbs
(See Unit 3 **The main points 2.**)

All reflexive verbs form the perfect tense with **être**:

s'habiller	ils se sont habillés	*they got dressed*
se lever	nous nous sommes levé(e)s	*we got up*
se promener	je me suis promené(e)	*I went for a walk*

The negative and question forms of these verbs are the same as for the other verbs, but because of the reflexive pronoun, they look different:

Nous **ne nous sommes pas** levé(e)s pour le déjeuner. — *We didn't get up for breakfast.*

Se sont-ils habillés chaudement avant de sortir? — *Did they dress warmly before going out?*

Agreements

As you can see from these examples, and from those in **Getting started**, when the perfect tense is formed with **être** as the auxiliary verb, the past participle agrees in *number* and in *gender* with the *subject*.

Insight

Check the examples above, and in **The story**, for this new type of agreement.

Avoir *and* **être** *form the perfect tense with* **avoir**

Isabelle n'**a** pas **eu** le temps de nettoyer la cuisine. — *Isabelle did not have time to clean the kitchen.*

Patrick **a été** surpris quand Alison a commencé à parler français. — *Patrick was surprised when Alison started to speak French.*

The position of adverbs with the perfect tense

Short adverbs can go between the auxiliary verb and the past participle:

Ils l'ont **vite** fait.	*They did it quickly.*
Il a **rarement** voyagé.	*He has seldom travelled.*
Il a **vraiment** été surpris.	*He was really surprised.*

Longer adverbs (Unit 6 **The main points 4**) normally go after the past participle:

Ils ont préparé leur voyage **méticuleusement**.	*They prepared their trip carefully.*
Ils ont appris les bases de la grammaire française **remarquablement** vite.	*They have learned the basics of French grammar remarkably quickly.*

4 *THE IMMEDIATE PAST:* VENIR DE

The present tense of **venir** (Unit 6 **The main points 2**) followed by **de** and an infinitive is used to say that something has just happened or has just been done:

Je **viens de descendre** de l'avion.	*I've just got off the plane.*
Nous **venons de rencontrer** les Lemaire.	*We have just met the Lemaires.*
Georges et Isabelle **viennent de** nous **accueillir**.	*Georges and Isabelle have just greeted us.*

Look back at **Say it in French 4** for another example.

5 *OTHER TIME EXPRESSIONS*

To say when you did something in the past, you need to be able to use expressions to show when you did it. See Unit 10 **The main points 1**:

avant-hier *the day before yesterday*	**hier** *yesterday* **hier matin** *yesterday morning* **hier soir** *yesterday evening*	**aujourd'hui** *today*

Hier matin nous sommes allés
à Lille.

*Yesterday morning we went
to Lille.*

The story

In this conversation, identify the **verbs in the perfect tense** (with both **avoir** and **être**).

> ### Insight
> Make a list in your notebook of **past participles** and add any that are new to your list. Note the agreements.

Isabelle raconte à une amie, Chloé, l'arrivée des Dickson à l'aéroport.

Isabelle	Nous avons essayé d'apprendre un peu d'anglais. Heureusement que les Dickson ont appris le français avant d'arriver.
Chloé	Est-ce qu'ils ont parlé français tout de suite?
Isabelle	Non. Ils ont commencé par quelques mots en anglais, mais après, ils se sont souvenus de leurs cours de français.
Chloé	Mais qu'est-ce que tu as fait? Vous ne vous êtes pas sentis un peu gênés?
Isabelle	Si, si. J'ai trouvé la situation très difficile. Des gens qu'on n'a jamais rencontrés, et des étrangers en plus. Et il ne faut pas oublier que Stéphanie a beaucoup insisté sur l'importance de cette visite! Quand ils sont descendus de l'avion, j'ai eu peur.
Chloé	Je t'admire vraiment! Je n'ai jamais pu parler avec des gens que je ne connais pas, et comme je n'ai jamais appris l'anglais …
	(Contd)

Isabelle	Le commencement n'a pas été facile. Mais avec de la bonne volonté on a réussi à communiquer. Ce sont peut-être les futurs beaux-parents de notre fille, après tout. Et ils ont été charmants avec elle. Ils l'ont accueillie chez eux et Alison, surtout, l'a beaucoup aidée. Nous nous sommes bien entendus finalement.

A quick check

1 Imagine that you are Georges Lemaire. Write five sentences about what happened when you went to meet the Dicksons at the airport. (You will find some suggestions in **The story**.)

2 Fill in the appropriate auxiliary verb (**avoir** or **être**) in the following sentences:

Quel voyage! D'abord le taxi n'_____ pas arrivé à l'heure. Nous _____ téléphoné à la compagnie et ils _____ envoyé un autre taxi, mais nous _____ arrivés à la gare deux minutes avant le départ du train. Nous _____ couru et nous _____ attrapé le train de justesse. Avec des valises très lourdes et tous les paquets des enfants, nous _____ eu du mal à trouver des places. Finalement, nous nous _____ assis dans un wagon fumeurs. Naturellement ça m'_____ donné la migraine!

3 Write answers to the following questions:

Q Vous êtes parti(e)s en vacances cette année?
A Oui, nous …

Q Où êtes-vous allé(e)?
A Nous …

Q Qu'est-ce que vous avez vu?
A Nous …

Q Tu as acheté des souvenirs?
A Non, je …

Q Et ta sœur, elle en a acheté?
A Bien sûr que oui! Elle …

The next stage

1 AGREEMENT OF THE PAST PARTICIPLE

When the perfect tense is formed with **avoir**, the past participle agrees with the **direct object** if the object comes before the verb:

J'ai acheté les billets.	(Direct object = **les billets**. No agreement – it follows the verb.)
Je **les** ai achetés.	(Direct object = **les**, replacing **les billets**. It comes before the verb, so the past participle agrees.)
Où sont les valises? (fem. plural)	*Where are the cases?*
Mark **les** a mises dans la voiture.	*Mark put them in the car.*
Et les passeports? (masc. plural)	*And what about the passports?*
Tu ne **les** as pas perdus, j'espère!	*You haven't lost them, I hope!*
Mais non! Quelle idée! Je **les** ai fourrés dans mon sac avec toutes **les** choses que nous avons préparées pour le voyage.	*Of course not! What an idea! I shoved them in my handbag with all the other things we got ready for the trip.*

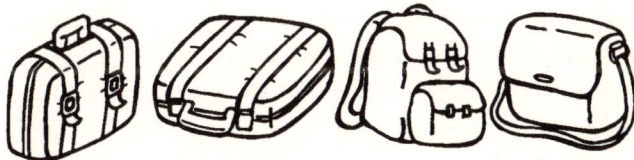

2 USE OF IL Y A (AGO)

To say how long ago something happened, you can use **il y a** (*ago*).

Ils sont arrivés **il y a** huit jours.	*They arrived a week ago.*
Nous sommes allés à Lille **il y a** cinq jours.	*We went to Lille five days ago.*
Stéphanie a téléphoné **il y a** trois heures.	*Stephanie phoned three hours ago.*

TEN THINGS TO REMEMBER

1 The most important thing for talking about past time is the past participle of the verb.

2 The past participle is formed from the infinitive (the basic form of the verb) which usually ends in **-er**, **-ir** or **-re**.

3 But remember that the past participles of irregular verbs have to be learned individually. Take this opportunity to revise the irregular verbs you have met so far.

4 Are you absolutely sure of the present tense of **être** and **avoir**? Together with the past participle, they are essential for speaking about the past.

5 Make sure you know the 12 or so verbs that form the perfect tense with **être**. It is easier to remember them if you think of them as six pairs.

6 By now, you should be using reflexive verbs with confidence. Remember that they all form the perfect tense with **être**.

7 Learn to be aware of the need to make the past participle agree – either with a preceding direct object (verbs that form the perfect tense with **avoir**) or with the subject (verbs that form the perfect tense with **être**).

8 To get the agreement of the past participle right, you will need – yet again! – to be sure of recognizing the difference between a direct and an indirect object.

9 There is a set of adverbs and prepositions you will frequently need for talking about the past. Note especially **hier, avant-hier** and **la semaine/l'année dernière**.

10 The expression **venir de** + infinitive is useful for expressing something that has happened very recently: **Vous venez d'apprendre comment utiliser le passé composé.** (*You have just learned how to use the perfect tense.*)

14

Repeated actions in the past

In this unit you will learn
* *To talk and write about past habits/things you used to do regularly*
* *To discuss situations in the past which lasted for some time*
* *To discuss single events set in the past*
* *To say how often you did things, or how frequently things were done*

Topic
* *Memories*

Grammar
  ▶ The imperfect tense
  ▶ Time expressions used with the imperfect
  ▶ Using the perfect and the imperfect together

The next stage
  ▶ Other time expressions used with the imperfect
  ▶ More about the perfect and the imperfect used together
  ▶ The use of the imperfect in direct and indirect (reported) speech

Getting started

1 In Unit 13, you learned how to use the perfect tense. French has another past tense – the imperfect – which is used to express other aspects of the past:

Quand il **était** jeune, Patrick *When he was young, Patrick*
travaillait à Londres. Tous les *worked in London. Every day he*
jours il **prenait** le métro. *took the tube.*

> ### Insight
> The imperfect is used with some of the same time expressions as the perfect tense (Unit 13 **The main points** 5).

2 There are other time expressions which show that something was done frequently (**tous les week-ends**) or that a situation in the past lasted some time (**pendant cette période**). The imperfect is the correct tense to use after these expressions:

Avant son mariage, Patrick ne *Before he got married, Patrick*
s'intéressait pas au bricolage. *wasn't interested in DIY.*
Pendant cette période, il habitait *During that time, he lived in*
un petit appartement désagréable. *a horrible little flat. Every*
Tous les week-ends il faisait du *weekend he played sport.*
sport. **À cette époque-là,** il sortait *At that time he went out a lot*
beaucoup et **le samedi** il allait *and on Saturdays, he always*
toujours au match de foot. *went to the football match.*

3 Sometimes when you are speaking about the past, you have to choose whether to use the perfect or the imperfect, depending on what kind of past event you want to speak about. For single events (**s'est marié, est né, a cessé**) use the perfect (Unit 13 **The main points** 1, 2, 3). For something that happened frequently (**il voyageait**) use the imperfect:

Patrick s'**est marié** avec Alison *Patrick got married to Alison in*
en 1983. Au début, il **voyageait** *1983. At first, he used to travel*

beaucoup, mais, quand Mark
est né, il a cessé de voyager.

a lot, but, when Mark was born,
he stopped travelling.

4 When you are talking about the past, you use the imperfect
for things which happened often. There are a number of time
expressions you can use to show how frequently something
happened:

Tous les jours Patrick allait à son
travail. **Le samedi,** il allait au
match de foot. **Deux fois par
mois,** il emmenait Mark et Alison
au zoo. **Une fois par an,** ils
prenaient des vacances.

Every day Patrick went to
work. On Saturdays, he went
to the football match. Twice
a month, he took Alison and
Mark to the zoo. Once a year
they went on holiday.

Say it in French

In the following passages, you will find examples of when to
use the structures in **Getting started**. Note particularly the time
expressions that are followed by the imperfect.

1 *PAST HABITS/THINGS YOU USED TO DO REGULARLY*

Isabelle:

Après la naissance de Nicolas,
nous n'**allions** plus au cinéma.
Le samedi, nous **prenions** le
bus pour aller chez mes parents
et **le dimanche** nous nous
promenions dans le parc près
de chez nous. **Le vendredi soir,**
mes parents **gardaient** Nicolas,
et Georges et moi, nous **faisions**
les courses.

After Nicolas was born, we
didn't go to the cinema any
more. On Saturdays we used to
get the bus to go to my parents'
place and on Sundays we went
for a walk in the park near our
house. On Friday evenings, my
parents looked after Nicolas,
and Georges and I did the
shopping.

2 SITUATIONS IN THE PAST WHICH LASTED FOR SOME TIME

Isabelle:

Je me souviens des années 80. Nous n'**avions** pas beaucoup d'argent mais nous **étions** fous de musique rock. Il n'**était** pas facile d'acheter les disques que nous **voulions** à St Amand, et nous ne **pouvions** pas aller tous les week-ends à Lille.

I remember the 80s. We didn't have much money but we were mad on rock music. It wasn't easy to buy the records we wanted in St Amand and we couldn't go to Lille every weekend.

3 SINGLE EVENTS IN THE PAST SET AGAINST A BACKGROUND

Georges:

Oui, la vie n'**était** pas facile à cette époque-là, et comme nous **voulions** acheter une voiture, il **fallait** faire des économies. Quand nous nous **sommes mariés,** mes parents nous **ont donné** de l'argent et c'est cet argent qui nous **a permis** d'acheter notre première maison.

Yes, life wasn't easy then, and as we wanted to buy a car, we had to save money. When we got married, my parents gave us some money and it was that money that made it possible for us to buy our first house.

4 TALKING ABOUT HOW OFTEN YOU DID THINGS

Isabelle:

Vous vous souvenez? Nous allions **tous les ans** à St Omer. Oui, c'était **chaque année,** en août, pendant les vacances scolaires. Il faisait beau **tous les jours** et **le matin,** nous allions nous promener

Do you remember? We used to go to St Omer every year. Yes, every year, in August, during the school holidays. The weather was good every day and in the morning we used

sur la plage de bonne heure. Après, nous allions toujours nous baigner **plusieurs fois par jour**. **Une fois par semaine** il y avait un vieux film au cinéma. C'était **toujours** débile, mais on y allait quand même.

to go for a walk on the beach early. Afterwards, we always went for a swim several times a day. Once a week there would be an old film at the cinema. It was always pathetic, but we used to go just the same.

The main points

1 *THE IMPERFECT TENSE*

The imperfect tense of the verb is a single word, formed from a **stem**. You form the stem by taking the **nous** form (the first person plural) of the present tense (Unit 1). You take off the -**ons** ending:

avoir	nous **avons**	→	av-
parler	nous **parlons**	→	parl-
finir	nous **finissons**	→	finiss-
prendre	nous **prenons**	→	pren-
Exception:	**être**	→	ét-

To the stem, you add the following endings:

-**ais**, -**ais**, -**ait**, -**ions**, -**iez**, -**aient**

Stéphanie:

Quand nous **étions** petits je te **détestais**.
When we were little I hated you.

Tu ne **cessais** pas de pleurer.
You wouldn't stop crying.

Notre père (il) t'**aimait** mieux que moi.
Our father liked you better than me.

Maman (elle) te **donnait** tout ce que tu voulais.
Mum gave you everything you wanted.

Toi et Papa (vous) **étiez** toujours ensemble.
You and dad (you) were always together.

Maman et moi (nous) **faisions** souvent la cuisine.	*Mum and I (we) were often doing the cooking.*
Nos parents (ils) ne **savaient** pas que tu me **frappais**.	*Our parents didn't know that you used to hit me.*

The imperfect is used for:

▶ repeated actions or habits in the past

Tu me battais **tous les jours**.	*You used to hit me every day.*
Je me plaignais **souvent** à nos parents.	*I often used to complain to our parents.*

▶ situations which lasted a long time, or an indefinite time, in the past:

Nous partagions une chambre.	*We used to share a room.*
Nos parents n'avaient pas beaucoup d'argent.	*Our parents didn't have much money.*

Insight

Look back at **Say it in French** and decide why the imperfect was used in each case.

2 TIME EXPRESSIONS WITH THE IMPERFECT

Since this tense is used for things which were done frequently in the past, it is found with time expressions showing how often things were done:

souvent *often*
fréquemment *frequently*
tous les jours *every day*
tous les mois *every month*
tous les ans *every year*
le samedi *every Saturday/on Saturdays*
deux fois par jour *twice a day*
cinq fois par trimestre *five times a term*

Le **samedi** nous allions au cinéma.	*On Saturdays, we used to go to the cinema.*
J'allais **souvent** voir mes parents.	*I often went to see my parents.*
Tous les jours Patrick allait à son travail.	*Every day Patrick went to work.*
Il fallait passer un contrôle continu **deux fois par trimestre**.	*There was continuous assessment twice a term.*

The imperfect is also used with time expressions which refer to long periods or situations which lasted a long or indefinite time in the past. Look for some of these in **Say it in French**.

À cette époque, nous étions plutôt pauvres.	*At that time, we were rather poor.*
Avant la naissance de ma sœur, mes parents pouvaient continuer à jouer au golf.	*Before my sister was born, my parents could still play golf.*
Tout le monde portait des vêtements bizarres **pendant les années 80.**	*Everyone wore weird clothes in the 80s.*

Insight

Other useful expressions:

à cette époque	*at that time*
avant cet événement	*before that event*
pendant cette période	*during that time*

3 USING THE IMPERFECT AND THE PERFECT TOGETHER

Both the perfect and the imperfect are used when talking about past time. Often you will need to make a choice between the two tenses. In the examples in **Getting started 3** and in **The story**, you will find the two tenses used together.

Sometimes the imperfect is used to set the scene in the past, while the perfect is used for a single action or a series of actions (**Say it in French 3, The story**):

Mark:

Oui! Je me souviens! Tu **étais** horrible. Tu **pleurais** tout le temps et Maman s'**occupait** de toi toute la journée. Je te **détestais**. Puis Andrew **est né** et tout **a changé**.	*Yes, I remember! You were awful. You cried all the time and mum looked after you the whole day long. I hated you. Then Andrew was born and everything changed.*

Sandy:

Je n'**étais** pas horrible! Tu ne **voulais** pas jouer avec moi et tu **prenais** tous mes jouets. Quand tu **as commencé** à l'école, tu **as cessé** de m'embêter.	*I was not awful! You didn't want to play with me and you used to take all my toys. When you went to school, you stopped bothering me.*

See also **The next stage 2**.

The story

Make a list of all the verbs in the imperfect and another one of the verbs in the perfect. Can you explain why each one was chosen?

Isabelle parle à Alison de la jeunesse de Stéphanie

Isabelle	Elle était très calme quand elle était petite et elle a appris à parler et à marcher plus tôt que Nicolas. Elle avait trois ans quand elle est allée à l'école maternelle et elle ne l'aimait pas beaucoup. Même très petite, elle chantait toujours juste et je n'ai pas été surprise quand, plus tard, elle a décidé de chanter avec la chorale *Les Quatre Vents*. Avant d'aller en Écosse, elle chantait avec la chorale deux fois par semaine.

Tous les enfants font des dessins à l'école, mais, pour Stéphanie, le dessin était très important. Elle adorait les couleurs vives et pour son anniversaire et à Noël elle demandait toujours des crayons ou des peintures à l'eau. Et elle aimait beaucoup les musées d'art. On allait assez souvent voir des expositions, au moins deux ou trois fois par an. Je me souviens d'une exposition des impressionnistes à Paris, quand elle avait 12 ans. Elle a tant insisté que je suis allée à Paris avec elle, et nous avons vu l'exposition trois fois!

A quick check

1 Using the verbs in the imperfect below, write five or six sentences about your childhood (real or imagined).

Nous habitions …

J'aimais …

Je n'aimais pas …

Mon père était …

Nous n'avions pas de …

Mes frères et mes sœurs étaient …

Ce qui nous amusait, c'était …

2 In the following paragraph, Nicolas is speaking about his memories of childhood. Identify the time expressions which signal the imperfect and the two usually followed by the perfect. Fill in the blanks with the appropriate tense (imperfect or perfect). See **The main points 3**.

Nicolas: Tu te souviens, Stéphanie? Moi, j'(**être**) toujours plus petit que toi et pendant mon enfance, j'(**avoir**) honte, parce que ma sœur (**être**) plus grande que moi. Et puis, un jour, je (**remarquer**) que je (**mesurer**) quelques centimètres de plus que toi. Ce jour-là, je (**faire**) la fête!

The next stage

1 OTHER TIME EXPRESSIONS USED WITH THE IMPERFECT

▶ **de** (date) **à** (date)　　　　　*from* (date) *to* (date)

De 2001 à 2005, Stéphanie　　*From 2001 to 2005, Stéphanie*
allait au collège.　　　　　　*was at college.*

▶ **entre** (date) **et** (date)　　　　*between* (date) *and* (date)

Nicolas était membre d'un　　*Nicolas was a member of a film*
club cinéma **entre février**　　*club between February 2005*
2005 et juin 2006.　　　　　*and June 2006.*

2 MORE ABOUT THE PERFECT AND THE IMPERFECT USED TOGETHER

See above, **The main points 3.**

To say what the situation was, or what was going on, when something else happened, you use the imperfect for the background situation and the perfect for a single event:

Quand Stéphanie **est allée** à　　*When Stephanie went to*
　Aberdeen, elle **avait** 20 ans.　　*Aberdeen, she was 20.*
Je lui **ai offert** de l'argent, parce　*I gave her some money because*
　qu'elle **était** sans le sou.　　　*she didn't have a penny.*

Nous lui **avons ouvert** un compte en banque, car elle ne **savait** pas organiser ses finances.

We opened a bank account for her, because she didn't know how to organize her money.

Un soir, elle a **téléphoné** pendant que j'**étais** absente. Elle **voulait** me raconter ses problèmes. Elle **a rappelé** plus tard.

One evening, she phoned while I was out. She wanted to talk to me about her problems. She phoned back later.

3 *THE IMPERFECT IN DIRECT AND INDIRECT (REPORTED) SPEECH*

Notice how the tenses change when direct speech (the actual words spoken by the person) is reported and becomes indirect speech:

	Direct speech	**Indirect speech**
Georges	J'aime beaucoup le ball-trap mais je déteste l'équitation.	Georges a dit qu'il **aimait** beaucoup le ball-trap mais qu'il **détestait** l'équitation.
	I like clay-pigeon shooting very much but I hate horse-riding.	*Georges said that he liked clay-pigeon shooting very much but (that) he hated horse-riding.*
Nicolas	Tous les soirs je m'amuse avec mon ordinateur. J'ai des amis partout dans le monde et on correspond par courrier électronique.	Nicolas m'a assuré qu'il **s'amusait** avec son ordinateur tous les soirs. Il a expliqué qu'il **avait** des amis partout dans le monde, et qu'ils **correspondaient** par courrier électronique.
	Every evening I play with my computer. I have friends all over the world and we correspond by e-mail	*Nicolas told me that he played with his computer every evening. He explained that he had friends all over the world and that they corresponded by e-mail.*

TEN THINGS TO REMEMBER

1 The past tenses in French are different from English. In English, there is no direct equivalent of the French imperfect. It is used to talk about things you habitually did: **Nous <u>allions</u> tous les jours à la plage.** (*We <u>went</u>/<u>used to go</u>/<u>would go</u> to the beach every day.*)

2 The imperfect is also used to talk about things that were going on when something else happened: **Nous <u>étions</u> sur la plage quand le tsunami est arrivé.** (*We <u>were</u> on the beach when the tsunami came.*)

3 The imperfect is one of the easiest tenses to form: take the **nous** form of the verb, remove the **-ons** and add the following endings: **-ais, -ais, -ait, -ions, -iez, -aient.**

4 The only exception is **être**: add the same endings to the stem **ét-**.

5 There is an economy of effort here – you will also use the imperfect endings for the conditional tense (Unit 18).

6 And once you have learned the imperfect of **avoir** and **être**, you will know all you need to form the pluperfect tense (Unit 15).

7 The time expressions that signal the need to use the imperfect mention frequency (**souvent, toujours, tous les jours, chaque année**) or a state of affairs that lasted for some time (**pendant cette période, quand il était enfant**).

8 Often there will be a series of verbs in the imperfect leading up to an important one-off event in the perfect, which may be signalled by **quand: Nous <u>étions</u> jeunes, nous ne <u>gagnions</u> pas beaucoup d'argent et les enfants n'<u>allaient</u> pas encore à l'école <u>quand</u> nous <u>avons gagné</u> le premier prix à la loterie.**

9 At first, you will need to develop an awareness of the difference between the perfect and the imperfect so that you use the correct tense. With time, this distinction becomes automatic.

10 The imperfect tense is also used, both in speech and in writing, in reported (or indirect) speech: **Elle a dit: « Je ne veux pas aller au cinéma ce soir. » Elle a dit qu'elle ne <u>voulait</u> pas aller au cinéma ce soir.**

15

Going back in the past

In this unit you will learn
- *To relate various past events to one another*
- *To say that something happened before or after something else*
- *To write an account of past actions and events*
- *To say that something was done by someone else*

Topics
- *Travel memories*
- *First World War battle sites*

Grammar
▶ The pluperfect tense
▶ Conjunctions of time
▶ Complex sentences
▶ The perfect passive

The next stage
▶ Other ways of expressing the passive
▶ Saying how long something has been going on
▶ Using the perfect infinitive
▶ The infinitive after **avant de** (*before*)

Getting started

1 If you want to go further back in time than the immediate past, you need to be able to use the pluperfect tense. This works just like the similar tense in English where we use the auxiliary verb *had*:

Before I began to learn French, I **had** already **learned** Spanish.

To form this tense, you will need to use the imperfect of **avoir** (Unit 14 **The main points 1**) and use the appropriate past participles (Unit 13 **The main points 1**).

Mon père m'a offert un téléphone portable pour mon anniversaire. Malheureusement, j'**avais** déjà **vu** un portable que j'aimais et je l'**avais acheté** avant mon anniversaire. Mon père était déçu.	*My father gave me a mobile phone for my birthday. Unfortunately I had already seen a mobile that I liked and I had bought it before my birthday. My father was disappointed.*

2 To use longer sentences explaining when one event happened in relation to another, and if you want to write more formal French, you will find there are a number of useful words which join parts of a sentence together. In Unit 10 (**The main points 4**) you learned some conjunctions expressing cause and effect. Here you will learn some you can use in time sequences.

Il y a quelques années, Nicolas et moi, nous avons décidé de nous connecter à Internet **après que** son professeur en avait parlé. Le soir, Nicolas envoyait des méls **pendant que** moi, je regardais la télé. Il est vite devenu expert et a demandé un nouvel ordinateur.	*Some years ago, Nicolas and I decided to get an Internet connection after his teacher had spoken about it. In the evening Nicolas used to send e-mails while I was watching TV. He quickly became an expert and asked for a new computer.*

3 You have already met the present passive in Unit 10, **The next stage 2**. In this unit, you will learn how to use the passive form when you are speaking about the past, to say that something *was done by someone.*

L'ordinateur **a été acheté** par Georges pour Nicolas, et à Noël beaucoup de jeux informatisés lui **ont été offerts**. Les logiciels de base **ont été développés** par Microsoft.

The computer was bought for Nicolas by Georges, and at Christmas he was given lots of computer games. The basic software was developed by Microsoft.

Say it in French

1 RELATING VARIOUS PAST EVENTS TO ONE ANOTHER

Isabelle:

L'année où nous sommes allés en Belgique – c'était en été 2006? Non, c'était avant. Nicolas **avait gagné** le prix au club cinéma en mars 2005 et c'est cette année-là que nous y sommes allés.

The year we went to Belgium – was that in summer 2006? No, it was before. Nicolas had won the prize at the film club in March 2005 and that's the year we went.

Georges:

Non. C'était l'année après, 2006, qu'il a gagné le prix et il a décidé d'aller à Paris pour visiter les studios de France 2. La Belgique, c'était donc en 2005.

No. It was the year after, 2006, that he won the prize and he decided to go to Paris to visit the France 2 studios. So Belgium was in 2005.

2 SOMETHING HAPPENED BEFORE OR AFTER SOMETHING ELSE

Isabelle:

Je me souviens d'un concert de la chorale de Stéphanie, les

I remember a concert given by Stéphanie's choir, les Quatre

Quatre Vents, à Lille. Nous **avions réservé** une chambre à l'hôtel bien avant la date du concert. **Puis** ils ont changé la date.

Vents, in Lille. We had reserved a hotel room well before the date of the concert. Then they changed the date.

Georges:

Non, tu n'**avais pas réservé** la chambre avant l'annonce de la nouvelle date! Tu **avais fait** la réservation au restaurant **d'abord. Ensuite,** ils ont annoncé le changement de date et nous avons eu du mal à trouver une chambre d'hôtel.

No, you hadn't booked the hotel room before the new date was announced! You had made the restaurant booking first. Then they announced the change of date and we had trouble finding a hotel room.

3 WRITING ABOUT PAST ACTIONS AND EVENTS

Devoir d'Alison pour la classe de français – *Notre visite en France* (*Alison's homework for her French class* – Our trip to France)

En septembre nous **avions décidé** d'aller visiter les Lemaire en France. J'ai donc écrit à Isabelle Lemaire pour lui demander de nous suggérer des dates. Nous **avions commencé** nos cours de français en octobre et au Nouvel An, nous **avions commencé** à préparer le voyage. Au commencement du mois de février j'ai écrit encore une fois à Isabelle Lemaire pour lui confirmer les dates de notre visite.

In September we had decided to visit the Lemaires in France. So I wrote to Isabelle Lemaire to ask her to suggest some dates. We had started our French classes in October and at the New Year, we had started to make preparations for the trip. At the beginning of February I wrote again to Isabelle Lemaire to confirm the dates of our visit.

4 SOMETHING WAS DONE BY SOMEONE ELSE

Les cours de français **ont été organisés** par le conseil de la ville. Une salle a **été réservée** au lycée et les manuels et les dictionnaires français–anglais **ont été achetés** par le professeur.	*The French classes were organized by the town council. A room was booked in the secondary school and the textbooks and the French–English dictionaries were bought by the teacher.*

The main points

1 *THE PLUPERFECT TENSE*

This is the tense of the verb you use to say that something **had** already happened before another event in the past, or to say that you **had** already done one thing before you did something else.

Like the perfect (Unit 13 **The main points 1, 2, 3**), it is made up of two words, an auxiliary verb (**avoir** or **être**) and a past participle:

▶ the auxiliary verb is in the imperfect (Unit 14 **The main points 1**)

avoir	→	**j'avais** (+ past participle)
être	→	**j'étais** (+ past participle)

▶ the past participles are the same as the ones you learned for the perfect (Unit 13 **The main points 1**).

Avant notre voyage en France:

J'	**avais écrit**	à Isabelle Lemaire.
Tu	**avais fait**	des économies.
Il (Georges)	**avait essayé**	d'apprendre l'anglais.
Nous	**avions appris**	le français.
Vous (G & I)	**aviez préparé**	notre itinéraire.
Ils (les enfants)	**avaient promis**	d'être sages.

2 CONJUNCTIONS OF TIME

In order to be able to tell a story, or speak or write about a number of past events, you need to use linking words called conjunctions.

Insight

You will find more time expressions and **conjunctions** in Unit 10 **The main points 1–4**. These words allow you to sequence different happenings in relation to one another.

Some of the most useful conjunctions of time are:

quand	*when*
après que	*after*
pendant que	*when/while*
puis/ensuite	*then*

Quand Mark nous a parlé de Stéphanie, nous avons compris que c'était sérieux.

When Mark spoke to us about Stéphanie, we realized that it was serious.

Après que nous avions décidé de visiter les Lemaire, nous avons commencé à apprendre le français.

After we had decided to visit the Lemaires, we started to learn French.

Mark perfectionnait son français **pendant qu**'il parlait à Stéphanie.

Mark was improving his French when he was talking to Stéphanie.

3 COMPLEX SENTENCES

When you are speaking or, more particularly, if you are writing about a series of events, you will need to be able to link different events and experiences together into longer sentences.

To do this, you use a variety of other conjunctions:

Simple link	Time	Reason/purpose	Opposition
et *and*	**après que** *after*	**parce que** *because*	**mais** *but*
	pendant que *while*	**car** *because/for*	**pourtant** *however/ and yet*
	quand *when*	**donc** *thus*	**cependant** *however*

J'ai commencé à apprendre le français **et** Patrick veut l'apprendre aussi.

I started learning French and Patrick wants to learn too.

Nous avons acheté les cadeaux **après que** Stéphanie nous avait parlé de ses parents.

We bought the presents after Stéphanie had spoken to us about her parents.

La visite en France a été organisée **parce que** notre fils Mark a une partenaire française.

The trip to France was organized because our son Mark has a French partner.

Georges et Isabelle ne parlent pas anglais, **pourtant** nous avons réussi à communiquer avec eux.

Georges and Isabelle don't speak English, nevertheless we managed to communicate with them.

4 THE PERFECT PASSIVE

In Unit 10 **The next stage 2**, you learned how to use the present passive (present tense of **être** + the past participle).

You will also need the passive to talk or write about past events. To do this, you use the perfect of **être**, followed by a past participle:

La visite en France a **été suggérée** par Mark.

The visit to France was suggested by Mark.

Les cours de français **ont été donnés** par un professeur du lycée.

The French classes were taken by a secondary teacher.

Les plans de St Amand et de sa région nous **ont été envoyés** par les Lemaire.

The maps of St Amand and the region were sent to us by the Lemaires.

The story

While you are reading this letter, make a note of the **verbs in the pluperfect tense** and the **conjunctions** or **linking words** Alison uses.

Alison écrit à son professeur de français en Écosse.

Cher Alain,

Vous m'aviez demandé de vous écrire pendant notre séjour en France. J'avais donc commencé une lettre le jour de notre arrivée, mais nous avions trop de choses à faire et tout était si intéressant que je n'ai pas pu écrire plus tôt.

Nous avions prévu de passer quelques jours chez les Lemaire et de visiter ensuite la région de St Amand. Plusieurs suggestions de choses à voir nous ont été offertes par Georges et Isabelle Lemaire, et nous allons maintenant quitter St Amand et visiter les sites des batailles de la Première Guerre mondiale dans le nord de la France. Nous irons ensuite à Paris.

Pendant que Patrick parlait à Georges, Isabelle et moi avons bavardé de nos enfants, de sorte que je comprends mieux Stéphanie maintenant.

Je n'y avais pas pensé, mais ma formation de professeur d'histoire et de géographie est très utile pour un voyage à l'étranger. Je me suis renseignée sur la situation géographique de St Amand et parce que j'ai lu plusieurs livres sur l'histoire de la France et de la Première Guerre mondiale, le nord de la France m'intéresse beaucoup.

Nous vous remercions des excellents cours de français et nous espérons que vous passez des vacances très agréables. À bientôt!

    Avec notre meilleur souvenir,

    Alison Dickson

A quick check

1 In the following paragraph, the verbs are in bold. Rewrite the paragraph one stage further back in the past, putting the verb in the perfect tense into the pluperfect and the verbs in the present tense into the perfect:

Avant la Première Guerre mondiale, les Allemands **ont** bien **préparé** leurs armées, de sorte que les armées des Alliés **perdent** des millions d'hommes dans des batailles dans le nord de la France. À Verdun, des millions de soldats **meurent** et les Allemands **traversent** facilement la ligne Maginot.

2 Using the conjunctions given, connect the sentences below into a single complex sentence:

> **a** Dans le nord de la France la terre est très plate.
> Le paysage est quelquefois monotone.
> Les villages sont agréables à voir.
> *Conjunctions*: donc, mais

> **b** Les coquelicots poussent dans les champs de la Flandre.
> On achète des coquelicots ce jour-là en Grande-Bretagne.
> La guerre a cessé le 11 novembre.
> On célèbre le jour de l'Armistice le 11 novembre.
> *Conjunctions*: car, et, parce que

The next stage

1 OTHER WAYS OF EXPRESSING THE PASSIVE

Insight

In French, the passive form of the verb (**être** + past participle) is used less often than in English.

There are two other ways of expressing the passive (something being done to someone/something by someone/something else) in French:

Using *on* as the subject of the sentence

On nous a priés de ne pas prendre de photos dans le musée.	*We **were asked** not to take photos in the museum.*
Quand nous avons visité les cimetières de guerre, **on** nous a expliqué la construction de la ligne Maginot.	*When we visited the war cemeteries, the construction of the Maginot Line **was explained** to us.*

Using a reflexive verb

Le guide a commencé par nous dire: « **Je m'appelle** Henri. Mon grand-père est mort à Verdun. »	*The guide began by saying: 'I am called Henri. My grandfather died at Verdun.'*
Le nombre de morts dans ces batailles **s'explique** par le manque de préparation des troupes alliées.	*The number killed in these battles **is explained** by the lack of preparation of the allied troops.*
Des livres d'histoire et des plans des sites intéressants **se vendent** en librairie.	*History books and maps of the interesting sites **are sold** in bookshops.*

2 TO SAY HOW LONG SOMETHING HAD BEEN GOING ON

In French you use the word **depuis** (*since, for*), with the imperfect, to say that something *had been going on* for a certain time when something else happened:

J'attendais **depuis** une heure quand Stéphanie a enfin téléphoné.	*I **had been waiting** for an hour when Stéphanie finally phoned.*
Quand Nicolas est né, nous étions à St Amand **depuis** cinq ans.	*When Nicolas was born we **had been** in St Amand **for** five years.*

3 USING THE PERFECT INFINITIVE

To say that you did something after (**après**) something else, you can use **après** with a perfect infinitive. This is made up of the past participle of the main verb, with the infinitive form of **avoir** before it:

Après avoir quitté St Amand, nous avons visité le nord de la France.
After leaving St Amand, we visited the north of France.

Après avoir acheté un ordinateur, Georges a commencé à s'intéresser à l'Internet.
After buying a computer, Georges started to get interested in the Internet.

4 THE INFINITIVE AFTER AVANT DE

You can use an infinitive after **avant de** to say something happened before something else:

Avant de quitter St Amand, nous avons remercié les Lemaire.
Before leaving St Amand, we thanked the Lemaires.

Georges s'est renseigné auprès d'un ami, **avant d'acheter** un ordinateur.
Georges asked a friend for advice before buying a computer.

TEN THINGS TO REMEMBER

1 The pluperfect tense corresponds almost always to the use of the same tense in English: **J'avais** déjà <u>acheté</u> un ordinateur. (*I <u>had</u> already <u>bought</u> a computer.*) It helps you to keep track of when past events happened in relation to one another.

2 Make a list in your notebook of the time conjunctions you will need to use with the pluperfect: **après que, pendant que …**

3 Check that you are comfortable with the present passive and the rules for agreements (Unit 10 **The next stage 2**) before learning how to use the passive in the perfect: <u>La</u> **visite aux champs de bataille a été organisé<u>e</u> par une agence de voyage.**

4 This is a good opportunity to make sure that you can use all the tenses of **avoir** and **être** you have learned so far. They are the main building blocks of the verb system.

5 It is also a good moment to revise the formation of past participles. Remember that the past participles of **avoir** verbs agree with the preceding direct object and that those of **être** verbs agree with the subject. (See Unit 10 **The next stage 2**, Unit 13 **The main points 1–3**, Unit 13 **The next stage 1**.)

6 Practise making longer and longer sentences, using all the conjunctions you know. This will give you the confidence to write and speak in any situation.

7 As with the other past tenses, to use the pluperfect you need to be able to say how long something had been going on when something else happened. Remember that with **depuis**, the use of tenses is different in French and English: **Ils <u>étaient</u> en France depuis une semaine quand ils ont quitté St Amand.** (*They <u>had</u> <u>been</u> in France for a week when they left St Amand.*)

8 Whenever you want to use the present participle (French **-ant**, English *-ing*), remember that it is used much less frequently in French than in English – and in different ways. See points 9 and 10 ...

9 In French, the perfect infinitive (**avoir** + past participle) is used where in English we would use the present participle (*-ing*): **Après <u>avoir quitté</u> St Amand, ils ont visité Lille.** (*After <u>leaving</u> St Amand, they visited Lille.*)

10 In French, **avant de** + infinitive is used for the English expression 'before ...ing': **avant de quitter St Amand** (*before leaving St Amand*), **avant de téléphoner** (*before phoning*).

16

Wishes, probability and possibility

In this unit you will learn
- **To talk about what you want and what you wish for**
- **To say what is probable or possible**
- **To construct longer and more complex sentences**

Topic
- **Visiting Paris**

Grammar
- ▶ Using the subjunctive
- ▶ Forming the present subjunctive: regular verbs
- ▶ The subjunctive of irregular verbs
- ▶ Verb 'signals' for the subjunctive
- ▶ Other verb signals followed by the subjunctive: *wishing,
  wanting, fear, regret*
- ▶ Impersonal expressions followed by the subjunctive: *necessity,
  importance, pity*
- ▶ Relative pronouns **ce qui** and **ce que**

The next stage
- ▶ Probability and the subjunctive
- ▶ Other verbs followed by the subjunctive
- ▶ The subjunctive to express the future
- ▶ **Lequel**, **laquelle** after the preposition **de**

Getting started

Insight

To understand this unit, you will need to have a feel for the difference between events or outcomes that are certain (indicative mood) and things that are doubtful, unlikely or uncertain (subjunctive mood).

1 There is another very useful form of the verb in French called the **subjunctive**. You have to use it in some common contexts. You will soon learn to recognize the most frequent ones:

Ma femme **veut que** nous **allions** à Paris, mais, avant d'y aller, **il faut que** nous **fassions** une réservation à l'hôtel.	*My wife wants us to go to Paris, but before we go, we'll have to reserve a hotel room.*

2 The subjunctive is used after certain expressions to 'signal' that a subjunctive is required. Different signals are used to express wishes, to show doubt or approval and to give orders:

Les Lemaire **veulent que** nous passions la nuit à Arras.	*The Lemaires want us to spend the night in Arras.*
Ils **doutent que** nous trouvions un hôtel à Amiens.	*They doubt we'll find a hotel in Amiens.*
Ils **sont contents que** nous allions ensuite à Paris.	*They are glad that we're going to Paris afterwards.*
Georges **insiste que** Patrick prenne la carte Michelin.	*Georges insists that Patrick takes the Michelin map.*

3 You have already learned a number of impersonal expressions in Unit 10 **The next stage 2**. In this unit you will learn some more, to express probability and possibility:

Patrick n'a pas l'habitude de conduire en France. **Il est possible qu**'il ait des problèmes, mais **il est probable qu**'il s'y habituera facilement.

Patrick is not used to driving in France. It is possible that he will have some problems, but probably he will easily get used to it.

4 In Unit 11 **The main points 5**, you met the relative pronouns **qui** and **que**. In this unit, you will learn how to write more polished sentences using other relative pronouns:

Ce qui attire Alison, c'est surtout l'histoire de la Révolution française.

What interests Alison especially is the history of the French Revolution.

Patrick et Alison visiteront le musée Carnavalet **dont** la section sur la Révolution est très connue.

Patrick and Alison will visit the Carnavalet Museum whose section on the French Revolution is well known.

La Révolution est la période pendant **laquelle** les institutions politiques de la France moderne ont été créées.

The Revolution is the period during which the political institutions of modern France were created.

Say it in French

1 *WHAT YOU WANT OR WISH FOR*

Je veux que nous **visitions** le Musée Carnavalet et **j'aimerais que** nous **allions** aussi au Musée de l'Histoire de France. Patrick **souhaite qu**'on **ait** le temps de voir des stades de sport.

I'd like us to visit the Carnavalet Museum and I'd like us to go to the Musée de l'Histoire de France too. Patrick hopes we have time to visit some sports stadiums.

2 ENVISAGING POSSIBILITIES

Avant d'arriver à Paris,
il est possible qu'on **voie** la
cathédrale à Beauvais.

*Before we get to Paris, we could
see the cathedral at Beauvais.*

Penses-tu que nous **puissions**
nous y arrêter?

*Do you think we could stop
there?*

Je ne crois pas que nous **ayons** le
temps de nous arrêter en route.

*I don't think we'll have time to
stop on the way.*

3 LONGER AND MORE COMPLEX SENTENCES

Les touristes à Paris ont un
grand choix. Les grands
monuments **dont** on parle
dans tous les guides, les musées
dans **lesquels** on trouve des
expositions magnifiques, les
attractions pour **lesquelles** la
ville est connue, voilà ce qu'il
faut voir!

*Tourists in Paris have a great
choice. The big monuments
all the guide books talk about,
the museums in which there
are magnificent exhibitions, the
attractions for which the city is
famous, that's what they have
to see!*

The main points

1 USING THE SUBJUNCTIVE

Most of the verbs you know how to use are in what is called the
indicative mood (all tenses in Units 1-15; see also Unit 12 **The
main points** 1). This is the mood for statements and comments.
There are two other important moods:

▶ To express commands and instructions, you use the **imperative
mood** (Unit 12).
▶ To express some feelings: *wishing, wanting, approval,
disapproval, regret, doubt,* etc., you use the **subjunctive mood**
(Units 16, 17).

The subjunctive **mood** (*If only he were here, Intelligent though she be,* etc.) has virtually disappeared from English but it is very frequently required in French.

Its use is always signalled by a word or expression (the 'signal') coming before it in the sentence. There are two stages in learning to use it:

▶ learning how to form the subjunctive (stem + endings)
▶ learning to recognize the various 'signals' (Units 16, 17 and 18).

Insight

Look back at **Getting started 1** and **2** and **Say it in French 1** and **2**, and see if you can identify some of the 'signals'.

2 FORMING THE PRESENT SUBJUNCTIVE

The present subjunctive of both regular and irregular verbs is formed from the **ils/elles** (third person plural) part of the present tense. You are already familiar with this form (Unit 1).

To get the stem, you remove the **-ent** ending:

ils parlent	→	**parl-**
ils choisissent	→	**choisiss-**
ils mettent	→	**mett-**

To the stem you add the endings (you have met similar endings already in the present and the imperfect): **-e, -es, -e, -ions, -iez, -ent.**

Avant de visiter Paris,

il faut	que	je		**lise**	un livre d'histoire.
	que	tu		**apprennes**	à conduire plus vite.
	qu'	il	nous	**prête**	un plan.
		(*Georges*)			
	que	nous		**trouvions**	un hôtel.
	que	vous	nous	**donniez**	des conseils.
		(*Georges et Isabelle*)			
	qu'	ils		**téléphonent**	à l'hôtel pour nous.
		(*Les Lemaire*)			

Virtually all the 'signals' of the subjunctive end in **que** (**il faut que, je veux que**) so, in grammar books, the forms of the subjunctive are often written with **que** (**que je lise, qu'ils téléphonent**) to remind you that **que** is part of the signal.

Que also has many other functions in French. It is only followed by the subjunctive when it is part of one of the special subjunctive signals.

> **Insight**
>
> Although the subjunctive of **-er** verbs looks very like parts of the present tense (**prête, téléphonent**) or the imperfect tense (**trouvions, donniez**), you can recognize that the subjunctive is being used once you are aware of the signalling expressions.

3 *THE SUBJUNCTIVE OF IRREGULAR VERBS*

The verbs **être, avoir** and **aller** are irregular in the subjunctive:

être	**avoir**	**aller**
que je **sois**	que j'**aie**	que j'**aille**
que tu **sois**	que tu **aies**	que tu **ailles**
qu'il **soit**	qu'il **ait**	qu'il **aille**
que nous **soyons**	que nous **ayons**	que nous **allions**
que vous **soyez**	que vous **ayez**	que vous **alliez**
qu'elles **soient**	qu'elles **aient**	qu'elles **aillent**

Other irregular verbs (**faire, savoir, pouvoir**) have an irregular stem. The same stem is used for all parts of the subjunctive:

infinitive	stem	
faire	**fass-**	fasse, fasses, fasse, fassions, fassiez, fassent
savoir	**sach-**	sache, saches, sache, sachions, sachiez, sachent
pouvoir	**puiss-**	puisse, puisses, puisse, puissions, puissiez, puissent

4 VERB 'SIGNALS' FOR THE SUBJUNCTIVE

The subjunctive *must be used* after a number of easily recognized 'signals'. The most common ones are verbs. The two most frequently used 'signals' are:

il faut que (see **The main points 2** above) and
vouloir que:

Alison **veut que** Patrick l'**accompagne** au musée.	*Alison wants Patrick to go with her to the museum.*
Nous **voulons que** Mark **réfléchisse** avant de se marier.	*We want Mark to think carefully before he gets married.*
Sandy et son frère **veulent que** leurs parents **reviennent**.	*Sandy and her brother want their parents to come home.*

5 OTHER VERB 'SIGNALS' FOR THE SUBJUNCTIVE

There are other groups of French verbs, usually expressing an *emotion* or a *condition*, followed by the subjunctive:

Verbs for saying you wish or want something:
In addition to **vouloir que** (**The main points 4**, above), this group includes:

désirer que
souhaiter que
aimer que (especially in the conditional tense – see Unit 18):

Je **désire**...
Je **souhaite**... ⎫ que tu m'**accompagnes** au musée.
J'**aimerais** ... ⎭

I want you to come to the museum with me.

Verbs expressing fear: **avoir peur que, craindre que**

Patrick a **peur que** les musées (ne) **soient** ennuyeux.	*Patrick is afraid the museums will be boring.*
Il **craint qu'**Alison (ne) **passe** trop de temps dans la section sur l'Occupation.	*He fears Alison will spend too much time in the section on the Occupation.*

Insight

Note that in formal French, **ne** is placed before the subjunctive when it is 'signalled' by verbs expressing fear (**Il craint qu'Alison ne passe ...**). This ne has no negative meaning and in informal French it is sometimes omitted.

Verbs expressing regret: **regretter que, être désolé(e) que**

Patrick **regrette qu'**elle n'**accepte** pas de l'accompagner au Musée de l'Automobile.	*Patrick is sorry that she will not agree to go to the Musée de l'Automobile with him.*
Il est **désolé que** le Musée des Arts et Métiers **soit** fermé.	*He is disappointed that the Musée des Arts et Métiers is closed.*

6 IMPERSONAL EXPRESSIONS AND THE SUBJUNCTIVE

Some impersonal expressions, such as **il** + verb + **que**, are followed by the subjunctive. The main ones are used to say that you feel something is *necessary*, *important*, or that it is *a pity*:

il faut/faudra que (see above, **The main points 2, 4**)	
il vaut mieux que	it will be better if
il est préférable que	it is preferable that
il est important que	it is important that
il est dommage que	it is a pity that

Il vaut mieux qu'Alison **aille** seule au Musée de la Libération à Montparnasse.	*It will be better for Alison to go to the Museum of the Liberation at Montparnasse by herself.*
Il est important qu'elle **encourage** Patrick à aller au Musée du Sport au Parc des Princes.	*It is important that she should encourage Patrick to go to the Museum of Sport at the Parc des Princes.*

Il est dommage qu'ils ne s'intéressent pas aux mêmes musées!	*It is a pity they are not interested in the same museums!*

7 *THE RELATIVE PRONOUNS* CE QUI *AND* CE QUE

> **Insight**
>
> When you are writing an account of events, or giving a formal oral presentation, you will find relative pronouns useful to help you to express yourself in a more structured way. See Unit 11 **The main points 5, The next stage 3.**

In addition to the relative pronouns you met in Unit 11, there are others you can use to give what you say or what you write a denser and more tightly knit structure, or to emphasize a particularly important point.

Ce qui and **ce que** (what/which), referring only to *things*, can be used to emphasize a particular word or expression in the sentence.

▶ **ce qui** is the **subject** of the verb in the clause it is in:

Ce qui intéresse Alison, c'est surtout l'histoire de la France.	*What Alison is specially interested in is the history of France.*

▶ **ce que** is the **object** of the verb:

Ce qu'elle veut voir, c'est les musées historiques.	*What she wants to see is the historical museums.*

The story

In this passage, you should be able to find examples of various **'signals'** with **following subjunctive verbs**. Make a list of them and compare your list with **The main points 1-6.**

Voici une description du quartier du Louvre, qu'Alison et Patrick ont visité à Paris.

Ce qui est remarquable dans ce quartier, c'est le grand nombre de monuments qui s'y trouvent. Il faut que les touristes voient non seulement le musée, mais aussi la Cour carrée, la Colonnade, la Pyramide et l'Arc de Triomphe du Carrousel.

Le Palais du Louvre, dont l'architecture est très variée, a été agrandi par Louis XIV. Il est peut-être dommage que la Pyramide, dont on a terminé la construction dans les années 80, soit si différente du reste du Palais.

C'est le président François Mitterrand qui a ordonné qu'on construise une extension moderne au Louvre. Il a insisté que l'architecte soit de renommée internationale.

Certains Français regrettent qu'il ait choisi un architecte étranger. Ils craignent que le contraste entre les bâtiments historiques et la Pyramide ne soit trop choquant. Il faut cependant que les gens s'habituent à de tels développements, s'ils veulent que les bâtiments historiques continuent à servir dans le monde moderne.

A quick check

1 Identify the 'signals' and the accompanying verbs in the subjunctive in the following sentences:
Patrick est sûr qu'il faut qu'ils soient à l'aéroport à sept heures du matin.

Sandy a peur que ses parents ne manquent l'avion, mais Nicolas insiste qu'elle se calme.

Alison veut que Patrick soit assis à côté d'elle dans l'avion.

2 Complete these sentences, using an appropriate verb in the subjunctive:

Comme je veux apprendre le français, il faut que je …

Pour bien parler français, il est important que tu …

Je voudrais aller au cinéma ce soir, mais mon père insiste que nous …

Ma mère va au supermarché demain. Qu'est-ce que tu veux qu'elle …?

3 Put the words in the groups below in the correct order to form sentences:

▶ Paris, visiter, femme, Tout, ma, musées, que, les, faire, ce, de, est, veut, c'

▶ différence, Louvre, qui, Pyramide, est, Palais, intéressant, et, c', la, Ce, entre, le, la, est, du

▶ qu', faut, voir, il, Musée, c', du, le, Louvre, est, Ce

The next stage

1 *PROBABILITY AND THE SUBJUNCTIVE*

There is a group of expressions used to talk about various degrees of probability.

The expressions telling us that something is likely or almost certain to happen are followed by the **indicative**. See above, **The main points 1**:

il est clair que
      certain que
      sûr que
      probable que
} + verb in the indicative

Il est probable qu'Alison ira au
Musée Carnavalet.

Alison will probably go to the
Musée Carnavalet.

The expressions meaning that an event may not happen, or that it is doubtful, are followed by the **subjunctive**:

il est possible que
    douteux que   } + verb in the subjunctive
    peu probable que
    impossible que

Parce que Patrick n'aime pas
la musique, **il est peu probable**
qu'ils **aillent** au Musée de la
Musique à la Villette.

Since Patrick doesn't like music,
they are unlikely to go to the
Musée de la Musique at La
Villette.

Patrick et Alison ne passent que
trois jours à Paris; **il est** donc
douteux qu'ils **voient** tous les
monuments intéressants.

Patrick and Alison are only
spending three days in Paris,
so it is doubtful if they will see
all the interesting monuments.

2 OTHER VERBS WITH THE SUBJUNCTIVE

There are two other groups of verbs used to 'signal' a subjunctive in the following verb:

Verbs you use to give orders or to make demands:

vouloir que
                                 to wish/want that
                                 (see **The main points 4**)

ordonner que   *to command that*
exiger que   *to demand that*
insister que   *to insist that*

Patrick et Alison **veulent que**
Sandy et Andrew **fassent** le
ménage pendant leur absence.

Patrick and Alison want
Sandy and Andrew to do the
housework while they are away.

| Patrick **a ordonné que** la pelouse **soit** tondue et Alison **a exigé que** les enfants **nettoient** la maison une fois par semaine. | *Patrick instructed them to mow the lawn and Alison demanded that they clean the house once a week.* |
| Sandy et Andrew **ont insisté** qu'Alison leur **prépare** des repas congelés. | *Sandy and Andrew insisted that Alison prepare frozen meals for them.* |

Verbs you use to say that you are pleased about something, or that you are sorry:

être content(e) que	*to be happy that*
être ravi(e) que	*to be delighted that*
regretter que	*to be sorry that*

| Sandy et Andrew **sont contents que** leurs parents **reviennent**. | *Sandy and Andrew are happy that their parents are coming home.* |
| Patrick **regrette qu'**il n'**ait** pas de billet pour le match au Parc des Princes. | *Patrick is sorry that he hasn't got a ticket for the match at the Parc des Princes.* |

3 *THE SUBJUNCTIVE TO EXPRESS THE FUTURE*

In this unit you have learned how to form and use the present tense of the subjunctive.

Insight

Although there is a past tense of the subjunctive (Unit 17), there is no future.

The present tense of the subjunctive can be used to talk about future time:

| Je suis contente que vous **preniez** l'avion du matin. Il est possible que je **vienne** à l'aéroport mais je ne pense pas qu'Andrew **puisse** venir. | *I am glad you'll be taking the morning plane. It is possible that I'll come to the airport, but I don't think Andrew will be able to come.* |

4 LEQUEL/LAQUELLE *AFTER THE PREPOSITION* DE

Although **dont** (Unit 11 **The next stage 3**) is usually used when a relative pronoun follows **de**, there are some circumstances where it is replaced by **de + lequel/laquelle** (Unit 4 **Getting started 4, The main points 4**) to speak about things, or **de + qui** if you are speaking about people.

This happens if the noun the relative pronoun replaces (= the **antecedent**) comes after a preposition:

Nous avons décidé de téléphoner **à** l'hôtel **duquel** les Lemaire nous avaient parlé.	*We decided to phone the hotel the Lemaires had spoken to us about.*
Quand vous serez à Paris, vous pourrez téléphoner **aux** amis **de qui** nous avons parlé.	*When you are in Paris, you can phone the friends we spoke about.*

TEN THINGS TO REMEMBER

1 Sadly, the subjunctive has almost disappeared from English. Learn to enjoy using this richly expressive mood in French.

2 Using the subjunctive is made easier by the way it is signalled in the sentence. You will soon find you can recognize the signals and be ready to understand or use the subjunctive. Look out for **que** which is often part of the signal.

3 Check back in your notes for some useful impersonal expressions: **il faut (que), il est nécessaire (que), il est possible (que)**. They will be handy in learning where to use the subjunctive.

4 In this unit, you have added to the relative pronouns you can use. In your notebook, keep lists of them with examples of how they are used. Use examples that are particularly relevant to you. These pronouns are vital in moving on to a more polished and impressive level of French.

5 Check the formation of the present subjunctive: take the third person plural of the present tense (which you know well), remove the **-ent** and add the following endings: -e, -es, -e, -ions, -iez, -ent.

6 Of course, your old friends the irregular verbs will need some special attention: test yourself on the present subjunctive of **avoir, être** and **aller**. Don't forget **faire, savoir, pouvoir** and **vouloir**.

7 There are two main groups of signals for the subjunctive. The first group are verb signals: **vouloir que, désirer que, aimer** (conditional) **que** …

8 The second group of signals contains impersonal expressions: **il faut que, il vaut mieux que, il est préférable que**.

9 As well as the relative pronouns you can already use (Unit 11), you will find **ce qui** (the subject) and **ce que** (the object) very useful for emphasizing things.

10 Remind yourself of the relative pronoun **dont**. Sometimes it must be replaced by **de** + **lequel** (= **duquel**), **de** + **laquelle**, **de** + **lesquels** (= **desquels**), etc. (referring to things) or by **de** + **qui** (referring to people).

17

How you feel about something

In this unit you will learn
* *To say what you intend to do and why*
* *To restrict what people can do*
* *To express your doubts*
* *To talk about your hopes and fears*

Topic
* *Opinions, hopes and fears*

Grammar
► Conjunctions followed by the subjunctive
► More 'signals' followed by the subjunctive
► The subjunctive or the indicative?
► The subjunctive or an infinitive?
► The present subjunctive and the perfect subjunctive

The next stage
► The subjunctive after superlatives
► The subjunctive after expressions of time
► The past historic
► The imperfect subjunctive

Getting started

1 In Unit 16 (**The main points 2, 3, 4, 5**), you learned some of the 'signals' for the subjunctive.

It is particularly important to be able to use il **faut que** and **vouloir que** (Unit 16 **The main points 4**):

Georges, **il faudra** absolument **que** tu **répondes** aux questions dans ce sondage! Je **voudrais que** tous les membres de la famille y **répondent**. Comme ça, nous nous comprendrons mieux.	*Georges, you'll absolutely have to answer the questions in this questionnaire! I'll want all the members of the family to reply. That way, we'll understand one another better.*

2 The various ways of expressing doubt also involve the use of the subjunctive. You should now revise the present tense of **croire** and **dire** from your list of irregular verbs. These verbs will help you with saying you are doubtful about something:

Je ne crois pas que les réponses **soient** utiles. **Je ne dis pas que** ce **soit** une perte de temps, mais ...	*I don't think the answers are useful. I'm not saying it's a waste of time, but ...*

3 Some aspects of the subjunctive in this unit depend on your having a clear understanding of the difference between the indicative mood (all verbs in Units 1–15) and the subjunctive mood (Units 16 and 17). This is explained in Unit 16 **The main points 1**. You will also need to be quick at identifying the subject of a verb and be able to use the infinitive.

4 Since you will meet the perfect subjunctive in this unit, you should revise the perfect (Unit 13 **The main points 1, 2, 3**) and the present subjunctive of **avoir** and **être** (Unit 16 **The main points 3**):

Georges croit qu'il a déjà répondu à ces questions, mais Isabelle doute qu'il **ait donné** toutes les réponses.

Georges thinks he has already responded to these questions, but Isabelle doubts if he has answered all of them.

Say it in French

1 *WHAT YOU INTEND TO DO AND WHY*

Isabelle:

Je vais demander à tous les membres de la famille de répondre aux questions, **pour que** je **sache** ce qui les trouble et ce qu'ils attendent. Je répondrai moi-même d'abord **de sorte qu'**ils **voient** que ce n'est pas difficile et **afin qu'**ils **puissent** voir que je n'ai rien à cacher.

I'm going to ask all the members of the family to answer the questions, so that I'll know what worries them and what they expect to happen. I'll answer myself first so that they see it's not difficult and that I've got nothing to hide.

2 *RESTRICTING WHAT PEOPLE CAN DO*

J'attendrai d'analyser les réponses **jusqu'à ce que** tout le monde **ait** répondu. **Bien que** les questions **semblent** faciles, il faut du temps pour y répondre. **Pourtant, à moins qu'**il n'y **ait** un problème, tout le monde aura terminé avant la fin de la semaine. Nous analyserons les réponses ensemble – **pourvu que** tout le monde **soit** d'accord.

I'll wait to analyse the answers until everyone has replied. Although the questions seem easy, they'll need time to reply. However, unless there's a problem, everyone will have finished by the end of the week. We'll analyse the answers together – provided everyone agrees.

3 EXPRESSING DOUBT

Tu sais, **je ne suis pas sûr que** ce sondage nous **aide. Je doute que** la personne qui l'a préparé **soit** sérieuse. **Penses-tu** vraiment **qu'on puisse** résoudre nos problèmes de cette façon? **Il est peu probable que** les enfants **répondent** de façon sérieuse et, de toute façon, **je ne trouve pas que** les questions **soient** intéressantes.

You know, I'm not sure that this questionnaire will help us. I doubt that the person who prepared it was serious. Do you really think that we can solve our problems in this way? It is unlikely that the children will answer seriously and, in any case, I don't think the questions are interesting.

4 TALKING ABOUT HOPES AND FEARS

Georges replies to the question about the future of the family:

J'aimerais que les enfants **restent** dans la région et qu'ils ne **quittent** pas St Amand. **Je préfère qu'**ils **soient** près de nous, car, **je suis sûr que, quoi qu'il arrive**, on a toujours besoin de ses parents.

I'd like the children to stay in the area and not to leave St Amand. I prefer them to be close to us because I am sure that, whatever happens, you always need your parents.

Je préférerais que Stéphanie **revienne** en France après avoir terminé son stage, car **je doute qu'**elle **puisse** s'adapter à la vie en Écosse. **Je ne pense pas que** Mark **ait** trop de difficultés à s'habituer à la vie en France.

I'd prefer Stéphanie to return to France when she has finished her work placement, because I doubt that she will be able to adapt to life in Scotland. I don't think Mark would find it too difficult to get used to life in France.

The main points

1 *CONJUNCTIONS FOLLOWED BY THE SUBJUNCTIVE*

Unit 16 gave you examples of some of the verbs and impersonal expressions which are 'signals' for the subjunctive.

There is another important group of 'signals' – certain types of **conjunction**, joining parts of a sentence together. They are all followed by **que**.

Insight

Add the following list to the other lists of conjunctions in your notebook.

Here are some of the most common conjunctions you will need:

bien que	*although*
pourvu que	*provided that*
pour que	*so that*
afin que	*in order that*
sans que	*without*
à moins que	*unless*

Identify the **verb in the subjunctive** that follows the '**signal**' in this passage:

Bien que Stéphanie aime l'Écosse, elle sera contente de revenir en France. Elle aimerait se marier avec Mark, **pourvu qu**'ils puissent vivre en France. Elle a l'intention de chercher un emploi à Paris ou à Lille **pour qu**'ils aient de quoi vivre **sans que** Mark soit obligé

Although Stéphanie likes Scotland, she will be happy to return to France. She would like to marry Mark, provided they can live in France. She intends to look for a job in Paris or Lille so that they have enough to live on, without Mark having to find a job

de trouver un travail immédiatement. **Bien que** son père **veuille qu**'elle revienne à St Amand, elle n'a aucune intention de le faire.

immediately. Although her father wants her to come back to St Amand, she has no intention of doing so.

2 MORE 'SIGNALS' FOLLOWED BY THE SUBJUNCTIVE

Some verbs for expressing opinions are followed by the subjunctive when they are used in the negative: **croire que** *to believe that*, **penser que** *to think that*, **trouver que** *to think that*. See also **Getting started 2** and **Say it in French 3**.

Nicolas répond à la question sur l'avenir:

Je ne crois pas que les matières que j'étudie à l'école **soient** très utiles pour ma carrière dans le cinéma. Mes parents **ne pensent pas** qu'une telle carrière **soit** sérieuse, et mes professeurs **ne trouvent pas** qu'on **puisse** déjà, à mon âge, choisir son métier.

I don't believe that the subjects I am studying at school are very useful for my career in the cinema. My parents don't think that such a career is serious and my teachers don't think you can already, at my age, choose your job.

Another group of expressions can also signal the subjunctive. These involve *time* and *expectation*:

attendre que	*to wait until*
s'attendre à ce que	*to expect that*
jusqu'à ce que/en attendant que	*until*
avant que (ne)	*before*

Identify the **verbs in the subjunctive** in the following sentences:

Isabelle **attendra que** Stéphanie **soit** revenue pour analyser les réponses.

Isabelle will wait until Stéphanie has come home to analyse the answers.

Elle s'**attend à ce que** les réponses de Stéphanie reflètent son indépendance, maintenant qu'elle a fait son stage en Écosse. *She expects that Stéphanie's replies will reflect her independence, now that she has done her work placement in Scotland.*

Stéphanie restera en Écosse **jusqu'à ce qu'**elle ait terminé son rapport de stage. *Stéphanie will stay in Scotland until she has finished the report on her work placement.*

Elle ne reviendra pas à St Amand **avant que** Mark (n')ait promis de passer ses vacances en France. *She will not go back to St Amand before Mark has promised to spend his holidays in France.*

3 THE SUBJUNCTIVE OR THE INDICATIVE?

To help you decide if a verb is followed by the subjunctive or not, look at these two lists:

▶ First, verbs to express *facts*, *certainty* and *probability*. They are followed by the **indicative**:

Isabelle …
  observe que
  remarque que les questions **sont** faciles.
Georges …
  croit que
  pense que les questions **sont** stupides.
Nicolas …
  dit que
  déclare que sa mère l'**ennuie**.

▶ Second, verbs to express *wishes*, *fears*, *commands* and *things which may never happen*. They are followed by the **subjunctive**:

Elle …
  souhaite que
  désire que
  aimerait que les autres **répondent** sérieusement.
Isabelle …
  a peur qu'
  craint qu'il ne **réponde** pas.

Nicolas …
veut que
aimerait que sa mère n'**insiste** pas.

Inversion to form a question

The verbs **croire que, penser que, trouver que** (2, above) are also
followed by the subjunctive if they are **inverted to form a question**:

Georges …
pense que
croit que
trouve que le sondage est stupide.

Pense-t-il que le sondage **soit** sérieux?

Probability and possibility

▶ Expressions of probability (**il est clair/certain que,** i.e. likely to
happen) are followed by the **indicative**:

Il est …
clair que
certain que Georges n'aime pas parler de lui.
Il est **probable** qu'il refusera de répondre.

▶ Expressions of **possibility** (**il est peu probable que,** i.e.
uncertain) are followed by the **subjunctive**:

Il est **peu probable** que Georges **veuille** parler de lui.
Il est **possible** qu'il **réponde** par des mensonges.

Espérer que

Espérer que is *always* followed by the indicative:

Isabelle espère qu'il n'y **aura** pas de conflit entre ses projets et ceux de Georges.	*Isabelle hopes that there will not be a conflict between her plans and Georges'.*

4 THE SUBJUNCTIVE OR AN INFINITIVE?

The subjunctive is usually used in compound sentences – sentences
with at least two verbs. One is the 'signal'; the other is the verb in
the subjunctive.

If the **subjects** of the two verbs are *different*, the **subjunctive** is used:

Georges (subject 1) regrette
  qu'Isabelle (subject 2) lui **ait
  demandé** de répondre aux
  questions du sondage.

*Georges is sorry that Isabelle
  has asked him to reply to the
  questions.*

If the **subject** is the same in each case, you use an infinitive:

Georges ne veut pas **répondre**.
Isabelle a peur de **tomber** malade.
Nicolas préférerait **étudier** le
  cinéma.

Georges doesn't want to reply.
Isabelle is afraid she will fall ill.
*Nicolas would prefer to study
  the cinema.*

5 SUBJUNCTIVE: THE PRESENT AND THE PERFECT

The subjunctive is most often used in its present tense form.
Sometimes, however, if you are talking about a situation in the past,
you need to use a past tense subjunctive – the perfect subjunctive.

Insight

Now is a good time to go over the compound tenses you have
learned so far (the perfect, the passive, the future perfect, the
pluperfect) and to remind yourself how important **avoir** and
être are.

The perfect subjunctive is made up of the present subjunctive of the
auxiliary verb (**avoir, être,** see Unit 16 **The main points** 3) and a
past participle (Unit 13 **The main points** 1):

Isabelle a peur que Stéphanie
  ait décidé de rester en
  Écosse.
Bien qu'elle ne **soit allée** à
  Aberdeen que pour faire un
  stage, il est possible qu'elle
  ait promis à Mark d'y rester.

*Isabelle is afraid that Stéphanie
  may have decided to stay in
  Scotland.*
*Although she only went
  to Aberdeen for a work
  placement, (it is possible that)
  she may have promised Mark
  that she will stay there.*

The story

In this text from the questionnaire published in the magazine, identify the seven verbs in the subjunctive and their 'signals'.

Le sondage du mois!

Vos vœux? Vos craintes? Vos projets?
Répondez à nos questions pour y voir plus clair!
Comparez vos réponses avec celles de vos proches!
Peut-être serez-vous surpris?

Les questions dans notre sondage ont été préparées pour que vous puissiez analyser vous-mêmes les problèmes que vous affrontez. Bien que vous ayez une vie de famille réussie, il est possible que vos projets et ceux de vos proches ne soient pas compatibles.

Vous ne croyez pas qu'un tel conflit puisse se produire? Nous espérons que vous avez raison, et pourtant … N'attendez pas que les problèmes vous accablent!

▶ La première section du sondage concerne vos vœux. Vous voulez voyager? Vous souhaitez changer d'emploi? Vous aimeriez déménager? Qu'en pensent les autres?
▶ Dans la deuxième section, vous allez faire face à vos cauchemars. Avez-vous peur que la pollution nous tue? Craignez-vous de prendre l'avion? Et pour vos amis, vos collègues, votre famille? Pensez-vous que l'avenir leur réserve de mauvaises surprises?
▶ Finalement, nous vous donnons la possibilité de penser sérieusement à vos projets d'avenir. Qu'est-ce que vous pouvez faire afin de surmonter vos craintes et préparer un avenir rose?

Ne dites pas que ce soit trop difficile!

Il est certain que, si vous répondez sérieusement, vous pourrez envisager avec sérénité les petits malheurs que la vie peut vous réserver.

A quick check

1 Write two sentences about your hopes (**espérer que** + the indicative) and two about your fears (**avoir peur que, craindre que** + the subjunctive) for someone else (two different subjects, see **The main points 4**).

Exemples: J'espère que mon collègue sera promu.
J'ai peur que mon ami(e) aille vivre à l'étranger.

2 Write the same sentences, this time about yourself (both subjects the same, **The main points 4**).

Exemples: J'espère être promu(e).
J'ai peur d'aller vivre à l'étranger.

3 Imagine that you are going to change your job. What are the possible problems? Think of three and write three sentences based on the model below, using the conjunction **bien que**:

Bien que le traitement soit modeste, je vais changer d'emploi.

4 After answering the questionnaire, you have decided it would be a good idea to have a big family reunion. What could be a suitable occasion for doing this?

Imagine that you are announcing three of the possible occasions to the rest of the family. Use the expressions **afin que, pour que** and **de sorte que** followed by the subjunctive (see **The main points 1**):

Exemple: J'ai décidé de vous inviter à une grande réunion familiale **afin que** nous **puissions** fêter l'anniversaire de grand-père.

The next stage

1 *THE SUBJUNCTIVE AFTER SUPERLATIVES*

You have learned how to say something is *the most* or *the least* in Unit 6 **The main points 8.** In some situations, you may need to follow a superlative by the subjunctive:

C'est le sondage **le plus stupide** que j'aie jamais **vu**.	*It's the stupidest questionnaire I've ever seen.*
La discussion sur les réponses au sondage est **la plus intéressante** que nous **ayons** jamais **eue**.	*The discussion about the answers to the questionnaire is the most interesting one we've ever had.*

2 *THE SUBJUNCTIVE AFTER EXPRESSIONS OF TIME*

Events that have not yet taken place
Some time expressions are used to speak about events that have not yet taken (or may never take) place. They are followed by the subjunctive:

J'attends que ta sœur **soit** là pour discuter les réponses aux questions.	*I'll wait until your sister is here to discuss the answers to the questions.*
Nous attendrons **jusqu'à ce qu'**elle **soit revenue,** pour lui poser des questions sur ses projets.	*We'll wait until she comes back to ask her questions about her plans.*

S'attendre à ce que ...
The expression **s'attendre à ce que** (*to expect that*) is also followed by the subjunctive:

Georges **s'attend à ce que** Stéphanie **décide** de se marier.	*Georges expects that Stéphanie will decide to get married.*

Avant que, après que

While **avant que** is followed by the **subjunctive** (an event which has not yet happened), **après que** (an event which has happened and is now over) is followed by the **indicative**:

Avant que Stéphanie (ne) **revienne**, il faudra peindre sa chambre.	*Before Stéphanie comes home, we'll have to paint her bedroom.*
Après que Stéphanie **est partie**, je me suis sentie très seule.	*After Stéphanie left, I felt very lonely.*

3 THE PAST HISTORIC TENSE

In formal written texts, you may meet, as well as the perfect and the imperfect, another past tense called the past historic. It is made up of only one word – it is not a compound tense like the perfect.

The past historic is used only in written French, to recount events in the past which do not appear to have an ongoing effect in the present.

Insight

Like the perfect, the past historic is used with (and in contrast to) the imperfect (Unit 14 **The main points 3**).

The stem is usually formed from the infinitive, and endings are added as shown below:

donner → donn-	
je donn-	**ai**
tu donn-	**as**
il/elle donn-	**a**
nous donn-	**âmes**
vous donn-	**âtes**
ils/elles donn-	**èrent**

finir → fin-	
je fin-	**is**
tu fin-	**is**
il/elle fin-	**it**
nous fin-	**îmes**
vous fin-	**îtes**
ils/elles fin-	**irent**

vendre → vend-	
je vend-	**is**
tu vend-	**is**
il/elle vend-	**it**
nous vend-	**îmes**
vous vend-	**îtes**
ils/elles vend-	**irent**

The past historic of irregular verbs may be difficult to recognize, but the endings – apart from the vowel **a**, **i** or **u** – are always the same:

avoir	j'eus	**pouvoir**	je pus
être	je fus	**vouloir**	je voulus

Find the examples of the two tenses in this extract from Stéphanie's **Rapport de stage** (a formal, written report on her work placement):

Je **pris** l'avion avec tous les stagiaires qui allaient en Écosse, et nous **arrivâmes** à Aberdeen à 15 heures 30. Mon directeur de stage, Monsieur Robertson, m'**accueillit** et nous **allâmes** directement à l'entreprise où m'attendait Madame Wilson. Elle m'**expliqua** le travail que j'avais à faire et m'**emmena** ensuite chez Madame Rushton qui a plusieurs chambres qu'elle loue aux étudiants.

I caught the plane with all the other students who were going to Scotland and we arrived in Aberdeen at 3.30 p.m. My supervisor, Mr Robertson, welcomed me and we went straight to the office where Mrs Wilson was waiting for me. She explained the work I had to do and then took me to the home of Mrs Rushton who has several rooms which she lets to students.

4 THE IMPERFECT SUBJUNCTIVE

Another tense you will only need for reading and formal writing is the imperfect subjunctive.

In speaking, you usually use the present subjunctive or, less often, the perfect subjunctive. In formal writing, however, you will sometimes see the imperfect subjunctive.

The stem, and the main vowel, of this increasingly rare tense are found in the second person singular (the **tu** form) of the past historic (above, **The next stage 3**):

donner	→	donnas	→	donn-
finir	→	finis	→	fin-
vendre	→	vendis	→	vend-

Although you are unlikely to meet all the forms of the imperfect subjunctive, you should be able to recognize them if necessary:

donner		**finir**		**vendre**	
que je donn-	**asse**	que je fin-	**isse**	que je vend-	**isse**
que tu donn-	**asses**	que tu fin-	**isses**	que tu vend-	**isses**
qu'il donn-	**ât**	qu'il fin-	**ît**	qu'il vend-	**ît**
que nous donn-	**assions**	que nous fin-	**issions**	que nous vend-	**issions**
que vous donn-	**assiez**	que vous fin-	**issiez**	que vous vend-	**issiez**
qu'ils donn-	**assent**	qu'ils fin-	**issent**	qu'ils vend-	**issent**

Avoir and être, as usual, are very irregular. The past historic will help you:

avoir   que j'e-usse   être   que je f-usse

In formal writing, the imperfect subjunctive must be used after certain tenses: the imperfect, the past historic and the conditional (Unit 18):

Madame Rushton **voulait que** ses locataires **payassent** le loyer au commencement de la semaine.

Mrs Rushton wanted her lodgers to pay the rent at the beginning of the week.

Monsieur Robertson **insista que** je **fusse** dans mon bureau à neuf heures moins le quart.

Mr Robertson insisted that I be (subjunctive in English) in my office at a quarter to nine.

TEN THINGS TO REMEMBER

1 In your notebook, you should have lists of conjunctions to express time and cause and effect. Add another list of conjunctions – the ones used to signal the subjunctive.

2 Copy this list into the section of your notebook on the subjunctive, where you have listed the verbs and impersonal expressions used to signal the subjunctive (Unit 16).

3 Go back to Unit 16 and check that you are clear on the difference between the indicative and the subjunctive.

4 Divide your list of subjunctive conjunctions into two groups: the ones that introduce the result you hope for (**pour que, de sorte que, afin que**) and the ones that put limits on an action (**bien que, à moins que, pourvu que**).

5 It is a good idea to look ahead now to the conditional (Unit 18), since it can also express hopes and fears, or a doubtful or uncertain outcome. In these cases, it is followed by the subjunctive: **J'aimerais** que tu <u>apprennes</u> le français à l'école.

6 Verbs expressing your opinion (**penser que, croire que, trouver que**) are followed by the subjunctive if they are in the negative: **Nous <u>ne croyons</u> pas que les Français <u>soient</u> plus intelligents que les Britanniques.**

7 Other outcomes involving the passage of time or your own expectations can be doubtful and these too need to be expressed in the subjunctive: **Il <u>attendra que</u> j'<u>aie</u> terminé mes études pour rencontrer mes parents. Mon mari restera en Écosse <u>jusqu'à ce qu'il soit</u> libre de voyager.**

8 To use the subjunctive when you are talking about the past, you need to use the present subjunctive of **avoir** or **être: Il**

attendra que j'<u>aie</u> terminé …; Bien que mon fiancé <u>soit</u> déjà venu en France, …

9 Sometimes a comparative or superlative (Unit 6) is followed by a subjunctive: **Le français est la langue <u>la plus facile</u> que j'<u>aie</u> jamais apprise.** Watch out for agreements.

10 If you are going to read or write formal French, you may sometimes need another past tense – the past historic. Knowing how to recognize this tense will open up new possibilities.

18

Imagining what could happen

In this unit you will learn
- *To say what would happen if ...*
- *To say what would need to happen before something else could happen*
- *To imagine how you would react to new or unknown circumstances*
- *To say what you thought would happen*

Topic
- *Wedding plans*

Grammar
▶ The formation of the conditional tense
▶ The conditional with **si**
▶ The polite use of the conditional

The next stage
▶ The conditional to make suggestions
▶ The conditional in reported speech
▶ The conditional perfect
▶ Giving doubtful information

Getting started

Forming the conditional is like forming the future.

Stéphanie: Si mes parents sont *If my parents agree, we'll*
d'accord, nous **pourrons** (future) *be able to get married in the*
nous marier au printemps. *spring.*
Si mes parents étaient d'accord, *If my parents were in*
nous **pourrions** (conditional) *agreement, we could get*
nous marier au printemps. *married in the spring.*

2 You have already met some frequently used parts of the verbs **vouloir** and **aimer** in the conditional. Check back to Unit 4 **Say it in French** 1 (**voudrais**) and Unit 4 **The main points** 1, Unit 16 **The main points** 5 (**aimerais**).

Remember that these verbs are often followed by the subjunctive:

Les Dickson **voudraient** que *The Dicksons would like*
Mark et Stéphanie **puissent** *Mark and Stéphanie to be able*
vivre en Écosse. *to live in Scotland.*
Mark **aimerait** que ses parents *Mark wants his parents to know*
sachent que les Lemaire l'ont *that the Lemaires accepted him*
tout de suite accepté. *straight away.*

Say it in French

1 SAYING WHAT WOULD HAPPEN IF ...

Stéphanie:

Si mes parents pouvaient visiter *If my parents could visit*
l'Écosse, ils **comprendraient** *Scotland, they would soon*
vite pourquoi je l'aime. Mon *understand why I like it.*
père n'aime pas voyager, mais *My father doesn't like*

je suis convaincue que, s'il acceptait de venir en Grande-Bretagne, il **oublierait** qu'il n'aime pas les étrangers. D'ailleurs, il a vite accepté Mark – si seulement il pensait à moi, plutôt qu'à lui-même, il n'y **aurait** pas de problème!

travelling, but I am convinced that, if he agreed to come to Britain, he would forget that he doesn't like foreigners. In any case, he quickly accepted Mark – if only he thought of me, rather than himself, there would be no problem!

2 WHAT WOULD HAVE TO HAPPEN FIRST?

Isabelle:

Pour que le mariage ait lieu au printemps, il **faudrait** vraiment que je commence à m'organiser. Si on n'invitait pas tous les membres de la famille, on **pourrait** envisager une cérémonie intime. On n'**inviterait** pas tous les cousins germains et on **expliquerait** que seulement la famille proche de Mark pourra venir.

So that the wedding can take place in spring, I'll really have to start getting myself organized. If we didn't invite all the members of the family, we could have a small wedding. We wouldn't invite all the second cousins and we would explain that only Mark's close family will be able to come.

3 HOW WOULD YOU REACT IN UNKNOWN CIRCUMSTANCES?

Nicolas:

Si ma copine voulait se marier avec moi, je lui **dirais** tout de suite que je ne me marierai jamais. Je lui **expliquerais** qu'on n'a pas besoin de se marier pour vivre heureux. Je lui **demanderais**: « **Aimerais**-tu passer toute ta vie avec la même personne? Ne t'**ennuierais**-tu

If my girlfriend wanted to marry me, I'd tell her straight away that I'll never get married. I'd explain to her that you don't need to get married to be happy. I'd ask her: 'Would you like to spend your whole life with the same person? Wouldn't

pas? » Je la convaincrais que
la vie d'un couple marié
manque de surprises et nous
continuerions à vivre ensemble,
heureux mais pas mariés.

*you be bored?' I'd convince
her that the life of a married
couple has no surprises and
we'd keep on living together,
happy but not married.*

4 WHAT DID YOU THINK WOULD HAPPEN?

Sandy:

Je croyais que Mark **choisirait**
une fille écossaise. Je n'avais
jamais pensé qu'il **rencontrerait**
une Française et **déciderait** de
se marier avec elle.

*I thought Mark would choose
a Scottish girl. I had never
thought that he would meet
a French girl and decide to
marry her.*

Qui **aurait** cru qu'il **préférerait**
la France à la Grande-Bretagne?
Mes parents pensaient qu'il
continuerait à travailler sur des
plates-formes dans la mer du
Nord.

Who would have thought that
he would prefer France to
Britain? *My parents thought
he would continue working
on oil rigs in the North Sea.*

The main points

1 *THE CONDITIONAL TENSE*

The conditional is a simple (one-word/not compound) tense.

....
Insight
Make a list in your notebook of all the one-word tenses you
have learned.
....

The conditional is made up of the same stem you use for the future
(Unit 11) and the endings you learned for the imperfect (Unit 14):
-ais, -ais, -ait, -ions, -iez, -aient.

For nearly all verbs, the stem is the infinitive (or, for -re verbs, the infinitive with the final -e removed):

se marier	
je me marier-	**AIS**
tu te marier-	**AIS**
il/elle se marier-	**AIT**
nous nous marier-	**IONS**
vous vous marier-	**IEZ**
ils/elles se marier-	**AIENT**

choisir	
je choisir-	**AIS**
tu choisir-	**AIS**
il choisir-	**AIT**
nous choisir-	**IONS**
vous choisir-	**IEZ**
elles choisir-	**AIENT**

attendre	
j'attendr-	**AIS**
tu attendr-	**AIS**
elle attendr-	**AIT**
nous attendr-	**IONS**
vous attendr-	**IEZ**
ils attendr-	**AIENT**

Remember the future stems of the irregular verbs:

aller →	**ir-**	pouvoir →	**pourr-**
avoir →	**aur-**	recevoir →	**recevr-**
devoir →	**devr-**	savoir →	**saur-**
faire →	**fer-**	venir →	**viendr-**
falloir →	**faudr-**	voir →	**verr-**
mourir →	**mourr-**	vouloir →	**voudr-**

2 THE CONDITIONAL WITH SI

This tense is mainly used when in English you use *would* or *could*. It is frequently used in sentences where you imagine something:

Si Stéphanie m'invitait à son mariage, j'**accepterais** avec plaisir.   *If Stéphanie invited me to her wedding, I'd accept with pleasure.*

In sentences like this, where **si** is used, there are strict rules about the tenses you are allowed to use:

The conditional after si + imperfect tense
If the tense used after **si** is the **imperfect** (as in the example above):

Si Stéphanie m'**invitait** à son mariage …

the tense in the main clause must be the **conditional**:

j'**accepterais** avec plaisir.

Si Mark **voulait** vivre en France, il **faudrait** qu'il trouve un emploi.	*If Mark wanted to live in France, he'd have to find a job.*
Si les Lemaire **organisaient** le mariage, ils **voudraient** une cérémonie à l'église, après le mariage civil.	*If the Lemaires were organizing the wedding, they would want a ceremony in the church after the civil marriage.*
Si le repas **avait** lieu dans un restaurant, il y **aurait** plusieurs plats et beaucoup de vins.	*If the wedding breakfast were in a restaurant, there would be several courses and a lot of wines.*

The future after *si* + present tense

If the tense after **si** is in the **present**:

Si Stéphanie m'**invite** à son mariage …

the tense in the main clause must be the **future**:

j'**accepterai** avec plaisir.

Si Mark **veut** vivre en France, il **faudra** qu'il trouve un emploi.	*If Mark wants to live in France, he'll have to find a job.*
Si Stéphanie se **marie**, elle ne **voudra** pas cesser de travailler.	*If Stéphanie gets married, she won't want to stop working.*
Le mariage civil **aura** lieu vendredi, s'ils se **marient** à l'église samedi.	*The civil ceremony will take place on Friday if they are married in the church on Saturday.*

3 THE POLITE USE OF THE CONDITIONAL

The conditional tense is used in French, especially with the verbs **vouloir**, **aimer** (**mieux**) and **préférer**, to make a statement less direct, or less brusque, than it would be if the present tense were used.

Insight

Go back and look at ways that the direct imperative can be made more polite (Unit 12 **Say it in French 1**).

Georges **veut que** Stéphanie reste à St Amand.	*Georges wants Stéphanie to remain in St Amand.*
Georges **voudrait que/aimerait mieux que/préférerait que** Stéphanie reste à St Amand.	*Georges would like Stéphanie to remain in St Amand.*

The verb **devoir** can also be used in the conditional to make what you say more polite:

Tu **dois** inviter Tante Alice au mariage.	*You must invite Aunt Alice to the wedding.*
Tu **devrais** inviter Tante Alice au mariage.	*You ought to invite Aunt Alice to the wedding.*
Selon la tradition britannique, les parents du marié **doivent** payer les boissons.	*According to the British tradition, the groom's parents have to pay for the drinks.*
Selon la tradition britannique, les parents du marié **devraient** payer les boissons.	*According to the British tradition, the groom's parents should pay for the drinks.*

A similar distinction can be made with **falloir:**

Il **faut** célébrer les fiançailles en Écosse et en France.	*The engagement must be celebrated in Scotland and in France.*
Il **faudrait** célébrer les fiançailles en Écosse et en France.	*The engagement should be celebrated in Scotland and in France.*
Tu **dois** te marier dans une robe très simple.	*You must get married in a very simple dress.*
Tu **devrais** te marier dans une robe très simple.	*You should get married in a very simple dress.*

The story

In this letter, Stéphanie uses many **verbs in the conditional**. Identify at least ten of them, with their **subject**.

Lettre de Stéphanie à sa cousine Jeannette:

Ma chère petite Jojo,

Il faudrait que tu t'assoies! Qu'est-ce qui t'étonnerait le plus? Pourrais-tu imaginer ta grande cousine mariée – et avec un étranger? Que dirais-tu d'un mariage au printemps?

Tu serais une des demoiselles d'honneur et l'autre serait … une Écossaise! Car je me marie avec Mark, un Écossais que j'ai rencontré pendant mon stage.

Je sais que tu pensais que je ne me marierais jamais, car je voudrais poursuivre ma carrière. Je commence à penser qu'on pourrait faire les deux. On ne devrait pas accepter de rester à la maison, simplement parce qu'on est mariée. Je compte bien continuer à travailler – à quoi bon avoir fait ce stage en Écosse, si je ne peux pas profiter de tout ce que j'ai appris?

As-tu jamais pensé à faire un stage à l'étranger? Je t'assure que tu profiterais énormément de l'expérience – et peut-être rencontrerais-tu quelqu'un d'aussi merveilleux que Mark. Je pensais que je m'ennuierais et que je trouverais très difficile de me séparer de ma famille, mais je me suis vite habituée à la vie et au travail dans un pays différent …

A quick check

1 Complete the verbs in the following sentences, using the **conditional tense** of the verb given in brackets:

Vous (pouvoir) acheter une grande maison, si vous aviez beaucoup d'argent.
Elle croyait que son frère (se marier) avec une Écossaise.
Nous pensions que le voyage (coûter) moins cher.
Si Mark se mariait en France, nous y (revenir) avec grand plaisir.
J'(aimer) célébrer mes fiançailles à Noël.

2 Following the example given, write two sentences to say what you would do in each of the situations described – see **The main points 2**:

Exemple: Si nous avions un château en Espagne, nous y passerions les vacances d'été.

Si j'avais un oncle très riche, …
Si j'avais perdu les clés de la voiture, …
Si les Martiens envahissaient la terre, …

3 Make the following requests more polite (**The main points 3**) by using the verb in bold in the conditional:

Je **veux** que tu me prêtes ta voiture.
Nicolas, je **préfère** que tu ne sortes pas ce soir.
Chéri, tu sais, **j'aime mieux** que tu rentres sans aller au bar.

The next stage

1 THE CONDITIONAL TO MAKE SUGGESTIONS

The conditional tense of **pouvoir** is used to suggest that something might happen, or that someone might do something:

Le mariage **pourrait** avoir lieu à Noël.

The wedding could take place at Christmas.

Nous **pourrions** réserver des chambres à l'hôtel pour les invités.

We could book rooms at the hotel for the guests.

Ne **pourriez**-vous pas attendre une année avant de vous marier?

Couldn't you wait a year before you get married?

Sometimes the impersonal expression **Il se peut/pourrait que** is used with the subjunctive:

Il se **pourrait** que le mariage **ait** lieu à Noël.

It is possible that the wedding could take place at Christmas.

2 THE CONDITIONAL IN REPORTED SPEECH

Insight

In Unit 14 **The next stage 3**, you saw how the imperfect is used in indirect speech (reporting what other people said).

When you are using indirect speech, a verb the speaker used in the future (**tuerai**) will be changed into the conditional (**tuerais**):

Je **tuerai** Nicolas s'il ne cesse pas de me taquiner.

I'll kill Nicolas if he doesn't stop teasing me.

Stéphanie a dit qu'elle **tuerait** Nicolas s'il ne cessait pas de la taquiner.

Stéphanie said she would kill Nicolas if he didn't stop pestering her.

Nicolas et moi, nous **irons** nous promener parce que nous ne voulons pas vous gêner.

Nicolas and I will go for a walk because we don't want to get in your way.

Georges a dit que lui et Nicolas **iraient** se promener parce qu'ils ne voulaient pas nous gêner.

Georges said he and Nicolas would go for a walk because they didn't want to get in our way.

3 THE CONDITIONAL PERFECT

The conditional tense of **avoir** or **être** + a past participle is used when speaking about conditions in the past – *would/should have* in English:

Je ne l'**aurais** jamais **cru**. On dirait que mes parents sont fous. C'est que ma sœur vient de se fiancer avec un Écossais. Tu te rends compte? Ils **auraient accepté** un Italien, un Allemand **aurait posé** peut-être un petit problème, mais un Écossais! Elle **aurait dû** choisir un Français. Si elle avait pensé à eux, elle se **serait mariée** avec un garçon de St Amand.

I would never have believed it. You'd think my parents were mad. What's happened is that my sister has just got engaged to a Scot. Can you imagine? They would have accepted an Italian, a German would perhaps have caused a slight problem, but a Scot! She should have chosen a Frenchman. If she'd thought about them, she would have married a boy from St Amand.

4 THE CONDITIONAL TO GIVE DOUBTFUL INFORMATION

To suggest that something might not be true, or to cast doubt on a source of information, you can use the conditional in French.

In newspapers and other public accounts of events, it is sometimes necessary to show that one's sources are not absolutely certain to be accurate. In English, expressions such as *alleged* or *suggested* are used. In French the conditional conveys this nuance:

Le marié **aurait** volé l'alliance.

The groom is supposed to have stolen the wedding ring.

Le mariage **aurait** coûté €16 000.

People say the wedding cost 16,000 euros.

TEN THINGS TO REMEMBER

1 You don't need to learn anything new to form the conditional, because (i) the stem is the same as for the future tense, including all the irregular future stems you've learned; ...

2 ... and (ii) the endings that you add to the stem are the same as for the imperfect tense.

3 Remember that you already know two very handy uses of the conditional: (i) to make what you say or write more polite: **Je <u>voudrais</u> une tasse de thé, s'il vous plaît. ...**

4 ... and (ii) to say what someone would like to happen. This is followed by the subjunctive: **Ma fille <u>aimerait</u> que nous <u>assistions</u> tous à son mariage en France.**

5 The conditional in French is very much like the conditional in English and expresses similar things – 'what would happen if ...'.

6 Be careful about choosing the right tense after **si**. If the tense used after **si** is the imperfect, the tense in the main clause must be the conditional: **<u>Si</u> mes parents <u>venaient</u> en France, je serais très contente.** (*If my parents came to France, I'd be very happy.*) If the tense used after **si** is the present, the tense in the main clause must be the future: **<u>Si</u> mes parents <u>viennent</u> en France, je <u>serai</u> très contente.** (*If my parents come to France, I'll be very happy.*)

7 The conditional can be used to make a polite suggestion: **Nous <u>pourrions</u> vous accueillir à la maison.**

8 It is also used when you report what someone said: **La mère de Mark a dit: « Vous serez les bienvenus chez nous. »** → **Elle a dit que nous <u>serions</u> les bienvenus chez eux.**

9 If you want to suggest that some information is doubtful, you can use the French conditional. This is something you can't do so easily in English: **Selon mon professeur de français, je n'aurais rien de plus à apprendre.** (*According to my French teacher, I <u>don't</u> have anything more to learn.*)

10 You know how important **avoir** and **être** are for the formation of the perfect tense (Unit 13), the present passive (Unit 10), the perfect passive (Unit 15), the future perfect (Unit 11), the pluperfect (Unit 15) and the perfect subjunctive (Unit 17). The conditional also has a perfect form, made up of the conditional of **avoir** or **être** and the past participle (with the same rules for agreement): **Mes parents <u>auraient</u> <u>accepté</u> un gendre espagnol ou italien.**

Transcriptions – The story (Units 8–18)

Unit 8

Mark and Stéphanie plan to go horse-riding.

S What do you want to do tomorrow, if it isn't raining? Do you want to go horse-riding or go for walks?

M I don't know how to ride.

S You can learn; it isn't difficult.

M Are there riding schools in St Amand?

S There are several, but I can ride at my friend Monique's; she has several horses. Can you see the pastures over there? They are hers. You can see the horses from here.

M Do you have to wear special clothes?

S Yes and no. You can wear jeans and trainers, but you have to wear a riding hat. My father can lend you his. I'm going to phone Monique to see if we can ride tomorrow. By the way, when do your parents want to come?

M They can come in July. They want to visit the north of France and perhaps go and spend a few days in Paris.

Unit 9

Mark asks Stéphanie if his parents can come in July.

M Stéphanie, my mother has just asked me if she and dad can come to your house on 7 July. Is that all right with your parents?

S I'm going to ask them the question straight away and you can phone her back later to give the answer.

Stéphanie calls her mum and gives her the news.

S Mum, can Mark's parents come and see us on 7 July? They would like to spend three or four days with us, then visit the area and Paris as well.

(Contd)

I	Of course, with pleasure. Your dad can perhaps take a few days' holiday. How are they going to travel?
S	They're going to catch the plane from Glasgow to Paris and hire a car at the airport. Mark is going to give them a road map and a street map of St Amand to help them.

Here are the instructions Mark is going to give his parents.

You arrive at the airport Roissy-Charles de Gaulle and you take the motorway to the north, the A1, up to Péronne.

Then go up the A2 right to the exit Cambrai/Valenciennes. Leave the A2 at Valenciennes and drive on to la Sentinelle. There you have to follow the A23 to the St Amand/Lille exit. Leave the A23 when entering St Amand and take the dual carriageway to the Raismes forest. At the second roundabout, turn left and you are at the Chemin de l'Empire.

Unit 10

The Lemaires are planning how they will entertain the Dicksons.

I	What will happen? First they're going to hire a car at the airport. Then it takes two hours to get to our place. Then we'll have to have dinner, …
G	What do we usually do when we have guests? We show them the town and then we visit some of the local area. The Dicksons will surely be interested in the area around St Amand. So we could drive them to the forest and to Valenciennes. And we could also introduce them to our friends.
I	Yes, of course, but people go on holiday to have a rest! We'll have to give them time to relax and not try to do too many things. In any case, as this is their first time in France, we'll have to show them things that are typically French.
G	It's hard to decide what is interesting for Scottish people since we don't know Scotland.
I	It's better to ask them what they want to see – the countryside, the sea, towns, …
G	And then, it's important to introduce them to Stéphanie's friends because they will certainly want to get to know her better.

Unit 11

'What do you do?' Stéphanie, Mark, Alison and Georges speak about their work and their plans for the future.

S The work I'm doing now doesn't interest me very much, but after my work placement I'll be able to find a job when I go back to France. It's my boss, Mr Williams, who is encouraging me to learn English and to improve my computing skills. 'You'll always use English and computer skills,' he tells me.

M At the moment the job I have means I have to spend a lot of time offshore. But I'll need this experience of drilling at sea. This is the practical experience which I'll need if I want to have a management post later on.

A The work of a teacher is getting harder and harder. During the holidays, which always go too quickly for me, you don't rest. You have to prepare your classes because it's hard to find the time you need during the term. This evening, as usual, I'll be correcting homework and preparing the handouts I'll be using tomorrow.

G A plumber never sleeps peacefully because at any moment the telephone might ring. You always have to help out people who have problems – problems that only happen at night or at the weekend. I hope my son will have a job that will allow him to sleep well and not work at impossible hours.

Unit 12

Nicolas, his mother and father are trying to work out how he can afford to go to Britain next year.

G You ought to completely change your habits. You put money aside, you open a bank account, you deposit at least 150 euros each month and you don't spend anything!

N It's easy for you! Do this! Do that! Don't do this! You give the orders and I obey. But for me it's not easy. Just think! I deprive myself of outings, clothes, books, the cinema. Think of the effect all that will have on me!

(Contd)

I	Yes, listen, Georges! Help him! Don't give him orders. Better give him some advice.
G	That's what I'm trying to do. I want to help him. Don't criticize me for that! In any case I was going to suggest that we give him the money we have put aside for the new car. Let's give it to him! He really needs it.
I	Well really! No! Let's not do anything crazy! He's got a year to find the money. We'll have to think of other solutions because I want a new car!
N	Don't get mad! Let's stay calm. Please don't think I'm completely stupid. I'll find a little job, I'll do some babysitting and soon I'll have the money I need.

Unit 13

Isabelle tells a friend, Chloé, about the Dicksons' arrival at the airport.

I	We tried to learn a bit of English. Fortunately the Dicksons learned French before they came.
C	Did they speak French straight away?
I	No. They started with a few words in English, but afterwards, they remembered their French lessons.
C	But what did you do? Didn't you feel a bit embarrassed?
I	Oh yes. I found the situation very difficult. People you've never met, and foreigners as well. And you must remember that Stéphanie made a great point of this visit! When they got off the plane, I was scared.
C	I really admire you! I've never been able to speak to people I don't know, and as I've never learned English …
I	The beginning wasn't easy. But with good will we managed to communicate. They are perhaps our daughter's future in-laws, after all. And they were so nice to her. They welcomed her into their home and Alison especially helped her a lot. We got on well in the end.

Unit 14
Isabelle tells Alison about when Stéphanie was young.

I She was very calm when she was small and she learned to talk and to walk earlier than Nicolas. She was three when she went to nursery school and she didn't like it much. Even when she was very small, she always sang in tune and I wasn't surprised when, later on, she decided to sing in the Quatre Vents choir. Before she went to Scotland, she sang with the choir twice a week.

All children draw at school, but for Stéphanie drawing was very important. She loved bright colours and for her birthday and at Christmas she always used to ask for colouring pencils or watercolours. And she loved art galleries. We used to go fairly often to see exhibitions, at least two or three times a year. I remember an Impressionist exhibition in Paris, when she was 12. She made such a fuss that I went to Paris with her and we saw the exhibition three times!

Unit 15
Alison writes to her French teacher in Scotland.

Dear Alan,

You asked me to write to you during our time in France. So I had started a letter the day we arrived, but we had too many things to do and everything was so interesting that I couldn't write sooner.

We had planned to spend a few days with the Lemaires and then to visit the area round St Amand. Several suggestions for things to see were given to us by Georges and Isabelle Lemaire and we are now going to leave St Amand and visit the battlegrounds from the First World War in the north of France. Then we'll go to Paris.

While Patrick was speaking to Georges, Isabelle and I chatted about our children, so now I understand Stéphanie better.

(Contd)

I hadn't thought about it, but my training as a history and geography teacher is very useful for a trip abroad. I found out about the geographical situation of St Amand and because I've read several books about French history and the First World War, the north of France interests me very much.

We both thank you for your excellent French classes and we hope you're having a very enjoyable holiday. See you soon!

Best wishes from us both

Alison Dickson

Unit 16
Here is a description of the area round the Louvre which Alison and Patrick visited in Paris.

What is remarkable in this area is the great number of monuments there are here. Tourists have to see not only the museum, but also the Cour carrée, the Colonnade, the Pyramide and the Arc de Triomphe du Carrousel.

The palace of the Louvre, whose architecture is very varied, was enlarged by Louis XIV. It is perhaps a pity that the Pyramide, the construction of which was completed in the 80s, should be so different from the rest of the palace.

It was President François Mitterrand who ordered a modern extension to be constructed at the **Louvre**. He insisted that the architect should have an international reputation.

Some French people find it regrettable that he should have chosen a foreign architect. They are afraid that the contrast between the historic buildings and the Pyramide will be too striking. However, people will have to get used to such developments if they want the historic buildings to continue to be used in the modern world.

Questionnaire of the month!
Your wishes? Your fears? Your plans?
Answer our questions to understand them all better!
Compare your replies with those of your family and friends!
Maybe you'll get a surprise?

The questions in our questionnaire have been prepared so that you can analyse for yourself the problems you are confronted with. Even though you may have a happy family life, it is possible that your plans and those of your nearest and dearest may not be compatible.

You don't believe such a conflict could arise? We hope you're right, however … Don't wait for the problems to overwhelm you!

▶ The first part of the questionnaire is about what you want. You'd like to travel? You want to change your job? You'd like to move house? What do the others think?
▶ In the second section, you will confront your nightmares. Are you afraid that we'll all be killed by pollution? Are you scared to take a plane? And for your friends, your colleagues, your family? Do you think the future may have unpleasant surprises in store for them?
▶ Finally, we give you the chance to think seriously about your future plans. What can you do to overcome your fears and ensure a happy future?

Don't say it's too difficult! It's certain that, if you reply seriously, you will be able to think calmly about the unpleasant things life may have in store for you.

Unit 18

Extract from a letter from Stéphanie to her cousin Jeannette:

My dear little Jojo,

You'd better sit down! What would surprise you the most? Could you imagine your big cousin married – and to a foreigner? How would you feel about a spring wedding?

You'd be one of the bridesmaids and the other one would be … a Scottish girl! because I'm getting married to Mark, a Scots boy I met during my work placement.

I know you thought I'd never get married, because I wanted to pursue my career. I'm starting to think that one could do both. You shouldn't agree to stay at home simply because you're married. I'm really determined to carry on working – what's the use of having done a work placement in Scotland if afterwards I can't take advantage of everything I've learned?

Have you ever thought about doing a work placement abroad? I assure you that you'd benefit enormously from the experience – and maybe you'd meet someone as wonderful as Mark. I thought I'd be bored and that I'd find it hard to leave my family, but I quickly got used to life and work in a different country …

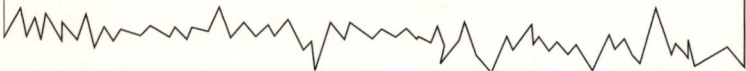

A quick check – Key

Unit 1

1 **a** Je vous présente Alison. Elle a 48 ans.
    b Elle est professeur d'histoire-géographie.
    c Voici Patrick. Il a 54 ans.
    d Il est directeur (de supermarché).
    e Ils ont trois enfants: Mark, Sandy, Andrew.
    f Andrew ne travaille pas. Il est/va à l'école.

2 **a** Comment s'appellent les parents de Mark? Comment vont les parents de Mark?
    b Quel âge a Sandy?
    c Est-ce que Sandy travaille?
    d Les Dickson habitent-ils (à) Aberdeen?
    e Et Stéphanie? Habite-t-elle (à) Dundee?

3 **a** Ils s'appellent Alison et Patrick. Ils vont bien.
    b Sandy a 20 ans.
    c Elle ne travaille pas. Elle est étudiante.
    d Ils n'habitent pas (à) Aberdeen. Ils habitent (à) Dundee.
    e Elle n'habite pas (à) Dundee. Elle habite (à) Aberdeen.

Unit 2

1 **a** Qu'est-ce que votre maman fait comme passe-temps?
    b Elle aime les randonnées en montagne, la photographie et faire du ski.
    c Et votre père? Quels sports fait-il?
    d Il joue au golf.
    e Où est-ce qu'il joue au golf?
    f Qui est sur la photo?
    g C'est mon frère Andrew et ici c'est ma sœur Sandy.
    h Qu'est-ce qu'elle fait dans la vie?
    i Elle est étudiante. Elle fait des études de sciences humaines et de français.

2 Comment t'appelles-tu?/Comment tu t'appelles?/Tu t'appelles comment?

Où est-ce que tu habites?/Où tu habites?/Tu habites où?

Quand joues-tu au rugby?/Quand est-ce que tu joues au rugby?

3 Mon anniversaire est le 26 mai.

Je suis né/e le 26 mai 1993.

Aujourd'hui, la date est/c'est le 25 février 20--.

Aujourd'hui, nous sommes le 25 février 20--. C'est/nous sommes le mercredi 25 février 20--.

Unit 3

1 **a** George est un homme grand. Il mesure 1.92 m.

Il est blond. Il a les cheveux bouclés et les yeux bleus.

Isabelle a les cheveux bruns, mi-longs. Elle est mince et jolie. Elle a les yeux marron.

Ils ont la quarantaine.

   b Stéphanie est jolie. Elle a les yeux bleus. Elle a les cheveux blonds, bouclés. Elle est blonde. Elle a les cheveux bouclés. Elle est mince.

Nicolas est blond. Il a les cheveux blonds. Il est grand et mince. Il mesure 1.90 m. Il a les yeux noisette.

2 231 456: deux cent trente et un mille quatre cent cinquante-six

245 985: deux cent quarante-cinq mille neuf cent quatre-vingt-cinq

3 500 765: trois million cinq cent mille sept cent soixante-cinq

   12-hour system

6.15: Il est six heures et quart.

3.45: Il est quatre heures moins le quart.

3.05: Il est trois heures cinq.

   24-hour system

13.55: Il est treize heures cinquante-cinq.

22.35: Il est vingt-deux heures trente-cinq.

23.45: Il est vingt-trois heures quarante-cinq.

Unit 4

1　**a** Je voudrais un kilo de belles pommes rouges.

　　b Quelle taille vous désirez acheter?/Vous désirez acheter quelle taille? Quelle taille désirez-vous acheter?

　　c Je ne veux plus de viande, merci.

　　d Nous voudrions acheter du parfum pour ma mère.

　　e Laquelle de ces robes voudriez-vous?

2　**a** Isabelle voudrait du pâté, du beurre, du fromage, des pommes de terre, de la limonade, des croissants.

　　b Stéphanie a besoin de/d':
　　une bouteille de bordeaux.
　　un gros poulet.
　　un kilo d'oignons.
　　500 grammes de champignons.
　　une livre/une plaquette de beurre.
　　5 kilos de pommes de terre.

3　Je voudrais:

un pantalon	Lequel préfères-tu?
des bonbons	Lesquels préfères-tu?
des cerises	Lesquelles préfères-tu?
du whisky	Lequel préfères-tu?

Unit 5

1　**a** Je choisis une fleur. Je prends celle-ci.

　　b Tu choisis un pot de confiture. Tu prends celui-ci.

　　c Il/Elle/On choisit un stylo-plume. Il/Elle/On prend celui-ci.

　　d Nous choisissons un livre. Nous prenons celui-ci.

　　e Vous choisissez des brochures. Vous prenez celles-ci.

　　f Ils/Elles choisissent des biscuits. Ils/Elles prennent ceux-ci.

2　**a** À St Amand nous entendons les cloches de l'Abbaye sonner tous les jours.
　　Ils entendent leurs voisins partir très tôt.
　　Quand Mark joue au rugby il salit son maillot.
　　Mark réfléchit et choisit l'assiette en porcelaine pour sa voisine.

b À St Amand nous les entendons sonner tous les jours.

Ils les entendent partir très tôt.

Quand Mark joue au rugby il le salit.

Mark réfléchit et la choisit pour sa voisine.

3 Un hôtel quatre étoiles est plus luxueux qu'un hôtel deux étoiles.

Un hôtel deux étoiles est moins luxueux qu'un hôtel quatre étoiles.

La Tour Eiffel est plus haute que la Tour de Blackpool.

La Tour de Blackpool est moins haute que la Tour Eiffel.

Mark est plus âgé que Stéphanie.

Stéphanie est moins âgée que Mark. Elle est plus jeune que Mark.

Unit 6

1 **a** Je vais visiter l'Abbaye de St Amand.

  b Est-ce que tu vas acheter des cartes postales?

  c J'aimerais aller voir les sangliers dans le bois de St Amand.

2 **a** Mark écrit des cartes postales de St Amand et les envoie à sa famille à Dundee et à ses amis.

  b Les parents de Mark vivent dans un quartier résidentiel de/à Dundee.

  c Mr Dickson prend le bus pour/afin de se rendre au travail le matin.

  d Il est directeur d'un supermarché à quelques kilomètres du centre ville près de/au bord de la rivière Tay.

  e Il part à 8 heures le matin et revient à 18 heures, sauf le jeudi soir car il travaille jusqu'à 21 heures.

3 Dundee occupe une position très/vraiment privilégiée sur la côte est de l'Écosse. Les deux collines, Balgay et Law, offrent une vue vraiment superbe de la Tay et de la campagne. Dundee est une ville très/principalement/bien connue pour le bateau Discovery et l'observatoire de Balgay avec ses vues féeriques. Dundee est une ville toujours/très/vraiment accueillante pas très loin de St Andrews, mondialement/très célèbre pour le golf.

Unit 7

1 Où se trouve votre maison? Où se trouve la vôtre?
Andrew ne trouve pas ses disques compacts. Andrew ne trouve pas les siens.
Il prend mes CD. Il prend les miens.
J'oublie souvent de rendre tes DVD. J'oublie souvent de rendre les tiens.

2 C'est le dictionnaire de Sandy.
Ce magazine appartient à Sandy.
Ce livre n'est pas à toi. C'est le mien.
Leurs voisins sont plus aimables que les nôtres.
Ce catalogue La Redoute appartient à Sandy.
« Est-ce qu'il y a des photos de toi dans ce catalogue? », demande Andrew.
La voiture garée en face de la maison des Dickson est à eux.
La nouvelle Peugeot 405 n'est pas la leur. C'est celle de leurs voisins.

Unit 8

1
S Je vais demander à mes parents s'ils veulent rester chez nous à ce moment-là. Je crois que Papa ne doit pas travailler le 14 juillet car c'est férié. Est-ce que tu sais combien de temps ils peuvent/veulent rester?

M Je ne sais pas exactement. Une quinzaine de jours. Ils veulent/ont envie d'inviter tes parents à venir en Écosse l'année prochaine. Est-ce que tu crois que tes parents ont envie de/veulent venir à Dundee?

S Oui, j'en suis sûre. Cette année ils ne peuvent pas partir en vacances.

2 Est-ce que vous savez parler français?
Est-ce que tu veux aller au cinéma?
Est-ce qu'il peut rentrer tard?
Est-ce que nous devons ranger nos affaires?

Unit 9

1 Tu arrives à l'aéroport Roissy-Charles de Gaulle et tu prends l'autoroute du nord, la A1, jusqu'à Péronne.
Ensuite, prends la A2 jusqu'à la sortie Cambrai/Valenciennes.
Quitte la A2 à Valenciennes et continue jusqu'à la Sentinelle. Là, tu dois prendre la A23 jusqu'à la sortie St Amand/Lille.
Quitte la A23 à l'entrée de St Amand et prends la voie rapide jusqu'à la forêt de Raismes. Au deuxième rond-point, tourne à gauche et tu es au chemin de l'Empire.

2 Prenez la première à droite/à gauche.
Continuez tout droit jusqu'au coin.
Descendez la rue de Lille.
Tournez à gauche/à droite.

3 **a** Tu leur dis que c'est d'accord.
   b Tu lui téléphones pour dire quand tu vas revenir.
   c Tu leur donnes les directions.
   d Patrick lui demande les directions exactes.

Unit 10

1 (model answer): Pendant les vacances, nous voulons nous reposer, mais nos parents préfèrent être très actifs.
C'est pour cette raison que nous essayons de nous lever le plus tard possible.
D'abord nous mangeons un petit déjeuner copieux.
Puis nous prenons une douche et nous nous habillons très lentement.
Alors nous discutons interminablement le programme du jour.
Il est donc midi et nous n'avons pas pris une décision.
Après avoir mangé, il faut accepter de sortir car nos parents commencent à se fâcher.
Finalement, tout le monde est prêt, et nous pouvons enfin partir.

Unit 11

Stéphanie: Aujourd'hui je travaillerai au bureau. Je taperai des lettres pour mon chef et j'assisterai à une réunion des membres du département de ressources humaines. Est-ce que tu viendras me chercher à 17 heures 30?
On achètera de quoi manger à Marks et Spencer.

Mark: Ce soir je mangerai avec Stéphanie. Mardi je ne serai pas ici car je prendrai l'hélicoptère et je recommencerai à travailler sur une plate-forme BP. Je règlerai l'appareil de forage et je le contrôlerai par ordinateur. Nous serons sur plate-forme pour trois semaines. Je ne verrai pas Stéphanie et elle me manquera beaucoup.

Alison: Aujourd'hui à 4 heures nous aurons une réunion de tous les enseignants. Elle durera au moins deux heures et demie et je ne rentrerai pas avant 19 heures 30. Vous préparerez vous-mêmes le dîner – et il ne faudra pas oublier de faire la vaisselle!

Georges: Est-ce que nous pourrons manger à 21 heures ce soir? La réparation de la tuyauterie chez Madame Vincent ne sera pas terminée et je devrai aussi remplacer les robinets dans sa salle de bains.

Unit 12

1 (model answer)
Utilise ta carte bancaire à la banque.
Utilise ta carte Visa dans les restaurants.
Utilise tes euros dans les magasins.
Change des devises à la banque.
Achète une ceinture porte-monnaie dans un grand magasin.

2 (model answer)
N'ouvrez pas votre porte-monnaie dans le métro!
Ne changez pas votre argent à l'hôtel!
Ne laissez pas votre carte de crédit et votre passeport dans votre chambre!
Ne laissez pas votre porte-monnaie dans le métro!

3 (model answer)
Tu nous donnes ton numéro de téléphone.

Il apporte la rose à Stéphanie.

Nous offrons les cadeaux à toi, Maman!

4 Oui, je le lui donne. Non, je ne le lui donne pas.

Oui, je les leur apporte. Non, je ne les leur apporte pas.

Oui, nous le leur recommandons. Non, nous ne le leur recommandons pas.

Unit 13

1 Par exemple:

Nous avons laissé la voiture dans le parking. Ma femme a tout de suite reconnu les Dickson. Ils ont appris à parler français, et ma femme leur a parlé lentement.

2 Quel voyage! D'abord le taxi n'est pas arrivé à l'heure. Nous avons téléphoné à la compagnie et ils ont envoyé un autre taxi, mais nous sommes arrivés à la gare deux minutes avant le départ du train. Nous avons couru et nous avons attrapé le train de justesse. Avec des valises très lourdes et tous les paquets des enfants, nous avons eu du mal à trouver des places. Finalement, nous nous sommes assis dans un wagon fumeurs. Naturellement ça m'a donné la migraine!

3 (model answer)

Oui, nous sommes parti(e)s en vacances en été.

Nous sommes allé(e)s à St Omer.

Nous avons vu la mer et beaucoup de gens sur la plage.

Non, je n'ai pas acheté de souvenirs parce que je n'ai pas d'argent.

Bien sûr que oui! Elle a acheté des choses stupides – des animaux en peluche et une assiette horrible.

Unit 14

1 (model answer)

Nous habitions San Francisco aux États-Unis.

J'aimais le pont qui s'appelle le Pont d'or.

Je n'aimais pas la brume.

Mon père était ingénieur et il travaillait souvent dans d'autres villes.

Nous n'avions pas de famille à San Francisco, car mes parents sont français.

Mes frères et mes sœurs étaient très contents de se trouver aux
États-Unis.
Ce qui nous amusait, c'était de cacher le chat dans la corbeille à
linge.

2 imparfait – pendant mon enfance
passé composé – un jour; ce jour-là
Tu te souviens, Stéphanie? Moi, j'étais toujours plus petit que
toi et pendant mon enfance, j'avais honte, parce que ma sœur
était plus grande que moi. Et puis, un jour, j'ai remarqué que je
mesurais quelques centimètres de plus que toi. Ce jour-là, j'ai fait
la fête!

Unit 15

1 Avant la Première Guerre mondiale, les Allemands avaient bien
préparé leurs armées, de sorte que les armées des Alliés ont perdu
des millions d'hommes dans des batailles dans le nord de la France.
À Verdun, des millions de soldats sont morts et les Allemands ont
traversé facilement la ligne Maginot.

2   **a**   Dans le nord de la France la terre est très plate, donc le
paysage est quelquefois monotone, mais les villages sont
agréables à voir.

  b   On célèbre le jour de l'Armistice le 11 novembre parce
que/car la guerre a cessé le 11 novembre et on achète des
coquelicots ce jour-là en Grande-Bretagne, car/parce que les
coquelicots poussent dans les champs de la Flandre.

Unit 16

1

'Signals'	Verbs
il faut que	soient
a peur que	ne manquent
insiste que	se calme
veut que	soit

2 (model answers)
Comme je veux apprendre le français, il faut que je travaille
beaucoup.

Pour bien parler français, il est important que tu assistes à toutes les classes.

Je voudrais aller au cinéma ce soir, mais mon père insiste que nous restions à la maison.

Ma mère va au supermarché demain. Qu'est-ce que tu veux qu'elle achète?

3 ▸ Tout ce que ma femme veut faire c'est visiter les musées de Paris.

▸ Ce qui est intéressant c'est la différence entre le Palais du Louvre et la Pyramide.

▸ Ce qu'il faut voir, c'est le Musée du Louvre.

Unit 17

1 (model answer)

J'espère que mes parents aimeront les Lemaire.

J'ai peur qu'ils aient du mal à comprendre le français.

J'espère que mon père m'achètera un nouvel ordinateur.

Je crains qu'il n'ait pas suffisamment d'argent.

2 (model answer)

J'espère aimer les Lemaire.

J'ai peur d'avoir du mal à parler français.

J'espère acheter un nouvel ordinateur.

Je crains de ne pas avoir suffisamment d'argent.

3 (model answer)

Bien que j'aime bien mes collègues, je vais changer d'emploi.

Bien que mes enfants veuillent rester ici, je vais changer d'emploi.

Bien que ma femme soit contente ici, je vais changer d'emploi.

4 (model answer)

J'ai décidé d'inviter tous mes cousins britanniques à la réunion afin que nous puissions les rencontrer.

J'ai décidé de louer plusieurs chambres à l'hôtel pour que tout le monde soit ensemble.

J'ai décidé de faire une grande réunion familiale en été de sorte que tous nos parents soient libres au même moment.

Unit 18

1 Vous pourriez acheter une grande maison, si vous aviez beaucoup d'argent.

Elle croyait que son frère se marierait avec une Écossaise.

Nous pensions que le voyage coûterait moins cher.

Si Mark se mariait en France, nous y reviendrions avec grand plaisir.

J'aimerais célébrer mes fiançailles à Noël.

2 (model answers)

Si j'avais un oncle très riche, je lui demanderais de m'acheter une voiture.

Si j'avais un oncle très riche, il me donnerait des cadeaux merveilleux.

Si j'avais perdu les clés de la voiture, j'irais à la police.

Si j'avais perdu les clés de la voiture, je serais affolé(e).

Si les Martiens envahissaient la terre, nous verrions qu'ils ne sont pas verts.

Si les Martiens envahissaient la terre, tout le monde aurait peur.

3 Je voudrais que tu me prêtes ta voiture.

Nicolas, je préférerais que tu ne sortes pas ce soir.

Chéri, tu sais, j'aimerais mieux que tu rentres sans aller au bar.

Key irregular verbs in different tenses

.. = past participle repeated

— = part in bold repeated

Present (Imperative)	Future	Conditional	Imperfect	Perfect (Past Historic)	Pluperfect	Present Subjunctive (Perfect Subjunctive)

avoir *to have* Present participle: **ayant** Past participle: **eu/e/s**

Present (Imperative)	Future	Conditional	Imperfect	Perfect (Past Historic)	Pluperfect	Present Subjunctive (Perfect Subjunctive)
j'ai	aurai	aurais	avais	ai eu	avais eu	aie
tu as	auras	aurais	avais	as eu	avais eu	aies
il/elle/on a	aura	aurait	avait	a eu	avait eu	ait
nous avons	aurons	aurions	avions	avons eu	avions eu	ayons
vous avez	aurez	auriez	aviez	avez eu	aviez eu	ayez
ils/elles ont	auront	auraient	avaient	ont eu	avaient eu	aient
(aie, ayons, ayez)				(eus, eus, eut, eûmes, eûtes, eurent)		(aie eu, aies eu, etc.)

| Present (Imperative) | Future | Conditional | Imperfect | Perfect (Past Historic) | Pluperfect | Present Subjunctive (Perfect Subjunctive) |

être *to be* Present participle: **étant** Past participle: **été**

Present (Imperative)	Future	Conditional	Imperfect	Perfect (Past Historic)	Pluperfect	Present Subjunctive (Perfect Subjunctive)
je suis	serai	serais	étais	ai été	avais été	sois
tu es	seras	serais	étais	as été	avais été	sois
il/elle/on est	sera	serait	était	a été	avait été	soit
nous sommes	serons	serions	étions	avons été	avions été	soyons
vous êtes	serez	seriez	étiez	avez été	aviez été	soyez
ils/elles sont	seront	seraient	étaient	ont été	avaient été	soient
(sois, soyons, soyez)				(fus, fus, fut, fûmes, fûtes, furent)		(aie été, aies été, etc.)

s'asseoir *to sit down* Present participle: **s'asseyant** Past participle: **assis/e/s**

Present (Imperative)	Future	Conditional	Imperfect	Perfect (Past Historic)	Pluperfect	Present Subjunctive (Perfect Subjunctive)
je m'assieds	– assiérai	– assiérais	– asseyais	– suis assis(e)	–étais assis(e)	– asseye
tu t'assieds	– assiéras	– assiérais	– asseyais	– es assis(e)	–étais ..	– asseyes
il/elle s'assied	– assiéra	– assiérait	– asseyait	– est assis(e)	–était ..	– asseye
nous nous asseyons	– assiérons	– assiérions	– asseyions	– sommes assis(e)s	–étions ..	– asseyions
vous vous asseyez	– assiérez	– assiériez	– asseyiez	–êtes assis(e)(s)	–étiez ..	– asseyiez
ils/elles s'asseyent	– assiéront	– assiéraient	– asseyaient	– sont assis(e)s	–étaient ..	– asseyent
(assieds-toi, asseyons-nous, asseyez-vous)				(– assis, – assis, – assit, – assîmes, – assîtes, assirent)		(– sois assis(e), – sois assis(e), etc.)

Present (Imperative)	Future	Conditional	Imperfect	Perfect (Past Historic)	Pluperfect	Present Subjunctive (Perfect Subjunctive)

aller *to go* Present participle: **allant** Past participle: **allé/e/s**

Present (Imperative)	Future	Conditional	Imperfect	Perfect (Past Historic)	Pluperfect	Present Subjunctive (Perfect Subjunctive)
je vais	irai	irais	allais	suis allé(e)	étais allé(e)	aille
tu vas	iras	irais	allais	es allé(e)	étais ..	ailles
il/elle va	ira	irait	allait	est allé(e)	était ..	aille
nous allons	irons	irions	allions	sommes allé(e)s	étions ..	allions
vous allez	irez	iriez	alliez	êtes allé(e)(s)	étiez ..	alliez
ils/elles vont	iront	iraient	allaient	sont allé(e)s	étaient ..	aillent
(va, allons, allez)				(allai, allas, alla, allâmes, allâtes, allèrent)		(sois allé(e), sois allé(e), etc.)

boire *to drink* Present participle: **buvant** Past participle: **bu/e/s**

Present (Imperative)	Future	Conditional	Imperfect	Perfect (Past Historic)	Pluperfect	Present Subjunctive (Perfect Subjunctive)
je bois	boirai	boirais	buvais	ai bu	avais bu	boive
tu bois	boiras	boirais	buvais	as bu	avais ..	boives
il boit	boira	boirait	buvait	a bu	avait ..	boive
nous buvons	boirons	boirions	buvions	avons bu	avions ..	buvions
vous buvez	boirez	boiriez	buviez	avez bu	aviez ..	buviez
ils boivent	boiront	boiraient	buvaient	ont bu	avaient ..	boivent
(bois, buvons, buvez)				(bus, bus, but, bûmes, bûtes, burent)		(aie bu, aies bu, etc.)

	Present (Imperative)	Future	Conditional	Imperfect	Perfect (Past Historic)	Pluperfect	Present Subjunctive (Perfect Subjunctive)

croire *to believe* Present participle: **croyant** Past participle: **cru/e/s**

Present (Imperative)	Future	Conditional	Imperfect	Perfect (Past Historic)	Pluperfect	Present Subjunctive (Perfect Subjunctive)
je crois	croirai	croirais	croyais	ai cru	avais cru	croie
tu crois	croiras	croirais	croyais	as cru	avais ..	croies
il croit	croira	croirait	croyait	a cru	avait ..	croie
nous croyons	croirons	croirions	croyions	avons cru	avions ..	croyions
vous croyez	croirez	croiriez	croyiez	avez cru	aviez ..	croyiez
ils croient	croiront	croiraient	croyaient	ont cru	avaient ..	croient
(crois, croyons, croyez)				(crus, crus, crut, crûmes, crûtes, crurent)		(aie cru, aies cru, etc.)

devoir *to have to/to owe* Present participle: **devant** Past participle: **dû** (for *owed* only: **dû/s/due/s**)

Present (Imperative)	Future	Conditional	Imperfect	Perfect (Past Historic)	Pluperfect	Present Subjunctive (Perfect Subjunctive)
je dois	devrai	devrais	devais	ai dû	avais dû	doive
tu dois	devras	devrais	devais	as dû	avais ..	doives
il doit	devra	devrait	devait	a dû	avait ..	doive
nous devons	devrons	devrions	devions	avons dû	avions ..	devions
vous devez	devrez	devriez	deviez	avez dû	aviez ..	deviez
ils doivent	devront	devraient	devaient	ont dû	avaient ..	doivent
				(dus, dus, dut, dûmes, dûtes, durent)		(aie dû, aies dû, etc.)

Present (Imperative)	Future	Conditional	Imperfect	Perfect (Past Historic)	Pluperfect	Present Subjunctive (Perfect Subjunctive)

dire *to say* Present participle: **disant** Past participle: **dit/e/s**

Present (Imperative)	Future	Conditional	Imperfect	Perfect (Past Historic)	Pluperfect	Present Subjunctive (Perfect Subjunctive)
je dis	dirai	dirais	disais	ai dit	avais dit	dise
tu dis	diras	dirais	disais	as dit	avais ..	dises
il dit	dira	dirait	disait	a dit	avait ..	dise
nous disons	dirons	dirions	disions	avons dit	avions ..	disions
vous dites	direz	diriez	disiez	avez dit	aviez ..	disiez
ils disent	diront	diraient	disaient	ont dit	avaient ..	disent
(dis, disons, dites)				(dis, dis, dit, dîmes, dîtes, dirent)		(aie dit, aies dit, etc.)

dormir *to sleep* Present participle: **dormant** Past participle: **dormi**

Present (Imperative)	Future	Conditional	Imperfect	Perfect (Past Historic)	Pluperfect	Present Subjunctive (Perfect Subjunctive)
je dors	dormirai	dormirais	dormais	ai dormi	avais dormi	dorme
tu dors	dormiras	dormirais	dormais	as dormi	avais ..	dormes
il dort	dormira	dormirait	dormait	a dormi	avait ..	dorme
nous dormons	dormirons	dormirions	dormions	avons dormi	avions ..	dormions
vous dormez	dormirez	dormiriez	dormiez	avez dormi	aviez ..	dormiez
ils dorment	dormiront	dormiraient	dormaient	ont dormi	avaient ..	dorment
(dors, dormons, dormez)				(dormis, –is, –it, –îmes, –îtes, –irent)		(aie dormi, aies dormi, etc.)

envoyer *to send* Present participle: **envoyant** Past participle: **envoyé/e/s**

Present (Imperative)	Future	Conditional	Imperfect	Perfect (Past Historic)	Pluperfect	Present Subjunctive (Perfect Subjunctive)
j'envoie	enverrai	enverrais	envoyais	ai envoyé	avais envoyé	envoie
tu envoies	enverras	enverrais	envoyais	as envoyé	avais ..	envoies
il envoie	enverra	enverrait	envoyait	a envoyé	avait ..	envoie
nous envoyons	enverrons	enverrions	envoyions	avons envoyé	avions ..	envoyions
vous envoyez	enverrez	enverriez	envoyiez	avez envoyé	aviez ..	envoyiez
ils envoient	enverront	enverraient	envoyaient	ont envoyé	avaient ..	envoient
(envoie, envoyons, envoyez)				(envoyai, –as, –a, –âmes, –âtes, –èrent)		(aie envoyé, aies envoyé, etc.)

faire *to do* Present participle: **faisant** Past participle: **fait/e/s**

Present (Imperative)	Future	Conditional	Imperfect	Perfect (Past Historic)	Pluperfect	Present Subjunctive (Perfect Subjunctive)
je fais	ferai	ferais	faisais	ai fait	avais fait	fasse
tu fais	feras	ferais	faisais	as fait	avais ..	fasses
il fait	fera	ferait	faisait	a fait	avait ..	fasse
nous faisons	ferons	ferions	faisions	avons fait	avions ..	fassions
vous faites	ferez	feriez	faisiez	avez fait	aviez ..	fassiez
ils font	feront	feraient	faisaient	ont fait	avaient ..	fassent
(fais, faisons, faites)				(fis, fis, fit, fîmes, fîtes, firent)		(aie fait, aies fait, etc.)

Present (Imperative)	Future	Conditional	Imperfect	Perfect (Past Historic)	Pluperfect	Present Subjunctive (Perfect Subjunctive)

falloir *to be necessary* Present participle: **fallant** Past participle: **fallu/e/s**

Present (Imperative)	Future	Conditional	Imperfect	Perfect (Past Historic)	Pluperfect	Present Subjunctive (Perfect Subjunctive)
il faut	il faudra	il faudrait	il fallait	il a fallu (il fallut)	il avait fallu	il faille (il ait fallu)

offrir *to offer* Present participle: **offrant** Past participle: **offert/e/s**

Present (Imperative)	Future	Conditional	Imperfect	Perfect (Past Historic)	Pluperfect	Present Subjunctive (Perfect Subjunctive)
j'offre	offrirai	offrirais	offrais	ai offert	avais offert	offre
tu offres	offriras	offrirais	offrais	as offert	avais ..	offres
il offre	offrira	offrirait	offrait	a offert	avait ..	offre
nous offrons	offrirons	offririons	offrions	avons offert	avions ..	offrions
vous offrez	offrirez	offririez	offriez	avez offert	aviez ..	offriez
ils offrent	offriront	offriraient	offraient	ont offert	avaient ..	offrent
(offre, offrons, offrez)				(offris, –is, –it, –îmes, –îtes, –irent)		(aie offert, aies offert, etc.)

Present (Imperative)	Future	Conditional	Imperfect	Perfect (Past Historic)	Pluperfect	Present Subjunctive (Perfect Subjunctive)

ouvrir *to open* Present participle: **ouvrant** Past participle: **ouvert/e/s**

Present (Imperative)	Future	Conditional	Imperfect	Perfect (Past Historic)	Pluperfect	Present Subjunctive (Perfect Subjunctive)
j'ouvre	ouvrirai	ouvrirais	ouvrais	ai ouvert	avais ouvert	ouvre
tu ouvres	ouvriras	ouvrirais	ouvrais	as ouvert	avais ..	ouvres
il ouvre	ouvrira	ouvrirait	ouvrait	a ouvert	avait ..	ouvre
nous ouvrons	ouvrirons	ouvririons	ouvrions	avons ouvert	avions ..	ouvrions
vous ouvrez	ouvrirez	ouvririez	ouvriez	avez ouvert	aviez ..	ouvriez
ils ouvrent	ouvriront	ouvriraient	ouvraient	ont ouvert	avaient ..	ouvrent
(ouvre, ouvrons, ouvrez)				(ouvris, –is, –it, –îmes, –îtes, –irent)		(aie ouvert, aies ouvert, etc.)

partir *to leave* Present participle: **partant** Past participle: **parti/e/s**

Present (Imperative)	Future	Conditional	Imperfect	Perfect (Past Historic)	Pluperfect	Present Subjunctive (Perfect Subjunctive)
je pars	partirai	partirais	partais	suis parti(e)	étais parti(e)	parte
tu pars	partiras	partirais	partais	es parti(e)	étais ..	partes
il/elle part	partira	partirait	partait	est parti(e)	était ..	parte
nous partons	partirons	partirions	partions	sommes parti(e)s	étions ..	partions
vous partez	partirez	partiriez	partiez	êtes parti(e)(s)	étiez ..	partiez
ils/elles partent	partiront	partiraient	partaient	sont parti(e)s	étaient ..	partent
(pars, partons, partez)				(partis, –is, –it, –îmes, –îtes, –irent)		(sois parti(e), sois parti(e), etc.)

Present (Imperative)	Future	Conditional	Imperfect	Perfect (Past Historic)	Pluperfect	Present Subjunctive (Perfect Subjunctive)

pouvoir *to be able to* Present participle: **pouvant** Past participle: **pu**

Present (Imperative)	Future	Conditional	Imperfect	Perfect (Past Historic)	Pluperfect	Present Subjunctive (Perfect Subjunctive)
je peux	pourrai	pourrais	pouvais	ai pu	avais pu	puisse
tu peux	pourras	pourrais	pouvais	as pu	avais pu	puisses
il peut	pourra	pourrait	pouvait	a pu	avait pu	puisse
nous pouvons	pourrons	pourrions	pouvions	avons pu	avions pu	puissions
vous pouvez	pourrez	pourriez	pouviez	avez pu	aviez pu	puissiez
ils peuvent	pourront	pourraient	pouvaient	ont pu	avaient pu	puissent
				(pus, pus, put, pûmes, pûtes, purent)		(aie pu, aies pu, etc.)

prendre *to take* Present participle: **prenant** Past participle: **pris/e/s**

Present (Imperative)	Future	Conditional	Imperfect	Perfect (Past Historic)	Pluperfect	Present Subjunctive (Perfect Subjunctive)
je prends	prendrai	prendrais	prenais	ai pris	avais pris	prenne
tu prends	prendras	prendrais	prenais	as pris	avais ..	prennes
il prend	prendra	prendrait	prenait	a pris	avait ..	prenne
nous prenons	prendrons	prendrions	prenions	avons pris	avions ..	prenions
vous prenez	prendrez	prendriez	preniez	avez pris	aviez ..	preniez
ils prennent	prendront	prendraient	prenaient	ont pris	avaient ..	prennent
(prends, prenons, prenez)				(pris, pris, prit, prîmes, prîtes, prirent)		(aie pris, aies pris, etc.)

Present (Imperative)	Future	Conditional	Imperfect	Perfect (Past Historic)	Pluperfect	Present Subjunctive (Perfect Subjunctive)

recevoir *to receive* Present participle: **recevant** Past participle: **reçu/e/s**

je reçois	recevrai	recevrais	recevais	ai reçu	avais reçu	reçoive
tu reçois	recevras	recevrais	recevais	as reçu	avais ..	reçoives
il reçoit	recevra	recevrait	recevait	a reçu	avait ..	reçoive
nous recevons	recevrons	recevrions	recevions	avons reçu	avions ..	recevions
vous recevez	recevrez	recevriez	receviez	avez reçu	aviez ..	receviez
ils reçoivent	recevront	recevraient	recevaient	ont reçu	avaient ..	reçoivent
(reçois, recevons, recevez)				(reçus, –us, –ut, –ûmes, –ûtes, –urent)		(aie reçu, aies reçu, etc.)

savoir *to know* Present participle: **sachant** Past participle: **su/e/s**

je sais	saurai	saurais	savais	ai su	avais su	sache
tu sais	sauras	saurais	savais	as su	avais ..	saches
il sait	saura	saurait	savait	a su	avait ..	sache
nous savons	saurons	saurions	savions	avons su	avions ..	sachions
vous savez	saurez	sauriez	saviez	avez su	aviez ..	sachiez
ils savent	sauront	sauraient	savaient	ont su	avaient ..	sachent
(sache, sachons, sachez)				(sus, sus, sut, sûmes, sûtes, surent)		(aie su, aies su, etc.)

Present (Imperative)	Future	Conditional	Imperfect	Perfect (Past Historic)	Pluperfect	Present Subjunctive (Perfect Subjunctive)

sortir *to go out* Present participle: **sortant** Past participle: **sorti/e/s**

Present (Imperative)	Future	Conditional	Imperfect	Perfect (Past Historic)	Pluperfect	Present Subjunctive (Perfect Subjunctive)
je sors	sortirai	sortirais	sortais	suis sorti(e)	étais sorti(e)	sorte
tu sors	sortiras	sortirais	sortais	es sorti(e)	étais ..	sortes
il/elle sort	sortira	sortirait	sortait	est sorti(e)	était ..	sorte
nous sortons	sortirons	sortirions	sortions	sommes sorti(e)s	étions ..	sortions
vous sortez	sortirez	sortiriez	sortiez	êtes sorti(e)(s)	étiez ..	sortiez
ils/elles sortent	sortiront	sortiraient	sortaient	sont sorti(e)s	étaient ..	sortent
(sors, sortons, sortez)				(**sortis**, –is, –is, –îmes, –îtes, –irent)		(sois sorti(e), sois sorti(e), etc.)

tenir *to hold* Present participle: **tenant** Past participle: **tenu/e/s**

Present (Imperative)	Future	Conditional	Imperfect	Perfect (Past Historic)	Pluperfect	Present Subjunctive (Perfect Subjunctive)
je tiens	tiendrai	tiendrais	tenais	ai tenu	avais tenu	tienne
tu tiens	tiendras	tiendrais	tenais	as tenu	avais ..	tiennes
il tient	tiendra	tiendrait	tenait	a tenu	avait ..	tienne
nous tenons	tiendrons	tiendrions	tenions	avons tenu	avions ..	tenions
vous tenez	tiendrez	tiendriez	teniez	avez tenu	aviez ..	teniez
ils tiennent	tiendront	tiendraient	tenaient	ont tenu	avaient ..	tiennent
(tiens, tenons, tenez)				(tins, tins, tint, tînmes, tîntes, tinrent)		(aie tenu, aies tenu, etc.)

Present (Imperative)	Future	Conditional	Imperfect	Perfect (Past Historic)	Pluperfect	Present Subjunctive (Perfect Subjunctive)

voir *to see* Present participle: **voyant** Past participle: **vu/e/s**

Present (Imperative)	Future	Conditional	Imperfect	Perfect (Past Historic)	Pluperfect	Present Subjunctive (Perfect Subjunctive)
je vois	verrai	verrais	voyais	ai vu	avais vu	voie
tu vois	verras	verrais	voyais	as vu	avais ..	voies
il voit	verra	verrait	voyait	a vu	avait ..	voie
nous voyons	verrons	verrions	voyions	avons vu	avions ..	voyions
vous voyez	verrez	verriez	voyiez	avez vu	aviez ..	voyez
ils voient	verront	verraient	voyaient	ont vu	avaient ..	voient
(vois, voyons, voyez)				(vis, vis, vit, vîmes, vîtes, virent)		(aie vu, aies vu, etc.)

vouloir *to want* Present participle: **voulant** Past participle: **voulu/e/s**

Present (Imperative)	Future	Conditional	Imperfect	Perfect (Past Historic)	Pluperfect	Present Subjunctive (Perfect Subjunctive)
je veux	voudrai	voudrais	voulais	ai voulu	avais voulu	veuille
tu veux	voudras	voudrais	voulais	as voulu	avais ..	veuilles
il veut	voudra	voudrait	voulait	a voulu	avait ..	veuille
nous voulons	voudrons	voudrions	voulions	avons voulu	avions ..	voulions
vous voulez	voudrez	voudriez	vouliez	avez voulu	aviez ..	vouliez
ils veulent	voudront	voudraient	voulaient	ont voulu	avaient ..	veuillent
(veuille, veuillons, veuillez)				(voulus, –us, –ut, –ûmes, –ûtes, –urent)		(aie voulu, aies voulu, etc.)

Other irregular verbs

The forms given here are for the first persons singular and plural.

Verb *meaning* *present participle* *past participle*	*Present	Future/ Conditional	Imperfect
CONDUIRE *to drive* conduisant conduit/e/s	conduis conduisons	**conduir**ai/–ais **conduir**ons/–ions	conduisais conduisions
CONNAÎTRE *to know* connaissant connu/e/s	connais connaissons	**connaîtr**ai/–ais **connaîtr**ons/– ions	connaissais connaissions
COURIR *to run* courant couru/e/s	cours courons	**courr**ai/–ais **courr**ons/–ions	courais courions
CRAINDRE *to fear* craignant craint/e/s	crains craignons	**craindr**ai/–ais **craindr**ons/–ions	craignais craignions
CUEILLIR *to pick* cueillant cueilli/e/s	cueille cueillons	**cueiller**ai/–ais **cueiller**ons/–ions	cueillais cueillions
ÉCRIRE *to write* écrivant écrit/e/s	écris écrivons	**écrir**ai/–ais **écrir**ons/–ions	écrivais écrivions

* These forms are also the **tu** and **nous** forms of the imperative. For the **vous** form, just add –**ez** to the stem: e.g. **condui**sez.

Perfect/ Pluperfect	Past historic	Present subjunctive	Perfect subjunctive
ai/avais conduit	conduisis	conduise	aie conduit
avons/avions conduit	conduisîmes	conduisions	ayons conduit
ai/avais connu	connus	connaisse	aie connu
avons/avions connu	connûmes	connaissions	ayons connu
ai/avais couru	courus	coure	aie couru
avons/avions couru	courûmes	courions	ayons couru
ai/avais craint	craignis	craigne	aie craint
avons/avions craint	craignîmes	craignions	ayons craint
ai/avais cueilli	cueillis	cueille	aie cueilli
avons/avions cueilli	cueillîmes	cueillions	ayons cueilli
ai/avais écrit	écrivis	écrive	aie écrit
avons/avions écrit	écrivîmes	écrivions	ayons écrit

(Contd)

Verb *meaning* *present participle* *past participle*	*Present	Future/ Conditional	Imperfect
LIRE *to read* lisant lu/e/s	lis lisons	**lir**ai/–ais **lir**ons/–ions	lisais lisions
METTRE *to put* mettant mis/e/s	mets mettons	**mettr**ai/–ais **mettr**ons/–ions	mettais mettions
MOURIR *to die* mourant mort/e/s	meurs mourons	**mourr**ai/–ais **mourr**ons/–ions	mourais mourions
PARTIR *to leave* partant parti/e/s	pars partons	**partir**ai/–ais **partir**ons/–ions	partais partions
PLAIRE *to please* plaisant plu	plais plaisons	**plair**ai/–ais **plair**ons/–ions	plaisais plaisions
PLEUVOIR *to rain* pleuvant plu/e/s	il pleut	il pleuvra/il pleuvrait	il pleuvait
RIRE *to laugh* riant ri	ris rions	**rir**ai/–ais **rir**ons/–ions	riais riions
SOUFFRIR *to suffer* souffrant souffert/e/s	souffre souffrons	**souffrir**ai/–ais **souffrir**ons/–ions	souffrais souffrions

Perfect/ Pluperfect	Past historic	Present subjunctive	Perfect subjunctive
ai/avais lu	lus	lise	aie lu
avons/avions lu	lûmes	lisions	ayons lu
ai/avais mis	mis	mette	aie mis
avons/avions mis	mîmes	mettions	ayons mis
suis/étais mort(e)	mourus	meure	sois mort(e)
sommes/étions mort(e)s	mourûmes	mourions	soyons mort(e)s
suis/étais parti(e)	partis	parte	sois parti(e)
sommes/étions parti(e)s	partîmes	partions	soyons parti(e)s
ai/avais plu	plus	plaise	aie plu
avons/avions plu	plûmes	plaisions	ayons plu
Il a plu/avait plu	il plut	il pleuve	il ait plu
ai/avais ri	ris	rie	aie ri
avons/avions ri	rîmes	riions	ayons ri
ai/avais souffert	souffris	souffre	aie souffert
avons/avions souffert	souffrîmes	souffrions	ayons souffert

(Contd)

Verb *meaning* *present participle* *past participle*	*Present	Future/ Conditional	Imperfect
SUIVRE *to follow* suivant suivi/e/s	suis suivons	**suivr**ai/–ais **suivr**ons/–ions	suivais suivior
VALOIR *to be worth* valant valu/e/s	il vaut	il vaudra il vaudrait	il valait
VENIR *to know* venant venu/e/s	viens venons	**viendr**ai/–ais **viendr**ons/–ions	venais venions
VIVRE *to live* vivant vécu/e/s	vis vivons	**vivr**ai/–ais **vivr**ons/–ions	vivais vivions

Some –er verbs which have spelling changes in the present and future tenses:

Present tense
acheter *to buy* j'achète, tu achètes, il achète, nous achetons, vous achetez, ils achètent

appeler *to call* j'appelle, tu appelles, il appelle, nous appelons, vous appelez, ils appellent

commencer *to begin* je commence, tu commences, il commence, nous commençons, vous commencez, ils commencent

enlever *to take off/out* j'enlève, tu enlèves, il enlève, nous enlevons, vous enlevez, ils enlèvent

Perfect/ Pluperfect	Past historic	Present subjunctive	Perfect subjunctive
ai/avais suivi avons/avions suivi	suivis suivîmes	suive suivions	aie suivi ayons suivi
il a/avait valu	il valut	il vaille	il ait valu
suis/étais venu(e) sommes/étions venu(e)s	vins vînmes	vienne venions	sois venu(e) soyons venu(e)s
ai/avais vécu avons/avions vécu	vécus vécûmes	vive vivions	aie vécu ayons vécu

envoyer *to send* j'envoie, tu envoies, il envoie, nous envoyons, vous envoyez, ils envoient

jeter *to throw* je jette, tu jettes, il jette, nous jetons, vous jetez, ils jettent

placer *to place* je place, tu places, il place, nous plaçons, vous placez, ils placent

préférer *to prefer* je préfère, tu préfères, nous préférons, vous préférez, ils préfèrent

promener *to take for a walk* je promène, tu promènes, il promène, nous promenons, vous promenez, ils promènent

Future tense

acheter j'achèterai, tu achèteras, il achètera, nous achèterons, vous achèterez, ils achèteront

appeler j'appellerai, tu appelleras, il appellera, nous appellerons, vous appellerez, ils appelleront

Verbs following the same pattern: **épeler, rappeler.**

enlever j'enlèverai, tu enlèveras, il enlèvera, nous enlèverons, vous enlèverez, ils enlèveront

Verb following the same pattern: **relever.**

jeter je jetterai, tu jetteras, il jettera, nous jetterons, vous jetterez, ils jetteront

promener je promènerai, tu promèneras, il promènera, nous promènerons, vous promènerez, ils promèneront

Glossary

This glossary is here to help you with some of the technical grammatical terms in *Essential French grammar*. Words which have their own entry in the glossary are in bold (**noun**) so that you can check them easily. The unit where you will find fuller explanations and examples is shown in square brackets [Unit 1]. You will get the best results if you use the glossary in conjunction with the Index.

active voice *(la voix active)* See **voice**.

adjective *(adjectif)* A word which qualifies a **noun**. In French, adjectives agree (see **agreement**) in **gender** and number with the noun they qualify, i.e. their **ending** changes according to whether the noun is masculine or feminine, singular or plural. French adjectives usually come after **nouns**, although there are a few important short ones (*petit, grand*, etc.) that can come before [Unit 3].

demonstrative adjective *(un adjectif démonstratif)* ce, cet, cette, ces *(this, that, these, those)* + **noun** [Unit 2].

interrogative adjective *(un adjectif interrogatif)* quel, quelle, quels, quelles *(which, what)* + **noun** [Unit 4].

possessive adjective *(un adjectif possessif)* mon, ton, son, mes, tes, ses, etc. *(my, your, his, her)* + **noun** [Unit 2]. See **possessives**.

adverb *(un adverbe)* A word (or group of words) which modifies the meaning of a **verb**, an **adjective** or another adverb. Adverbs never change their form. They describe *how, when* or *where* something happens. In English they usually end in *-ly*, in French usually in *-ment*. Their **stem** is normally an adjective (*__principalement__ mainly*; __heureuse__ment *happily*). Their usual position is after the **verb** or before the **adjective** or adverb they modify [Unit 6].

. . . .

agreement (*un accord*) The matching of a **verb** with its **subject** [Unit 1] or an **adjective** with a **noun** [Unit 3]. In French, words agree in number (singular/plural) and in **gender**.

. . . .

article (*un article*) A short word which goes with a **noun**.

definite article (*un article défini*) *le, la, l', les* the [Unit 1].

indefinite article (*un article indéfini*) *un, une* a/an, *des* some [Unit 1].

partitive article (*un article partitif*) *du, de la, de', des* some/any [Unit 4].

. . . .

auxiliary verb (*le verbe auxiliaire*) A **verb** used with other verbs to construct different **tenses**: *être to be*; *avoir to have* [Unit 13].

. . . .

clause (*la proposition*) A group of words including a **verb** and its subject (**main clause, relative clause, subordinate clause**).

. . . .

comparative (*le comparatif*) Used to compare or contrast two ideas: *plus/moins ... que more/less ... than; aussi ... que as ... as* [Unit 5].

. . . .

compound sentence (*la phrase complexe*) A sentence which has more than one **clause**, a **main** or principal clause and a **subordinate clause** or clauses [Units 10, 15].

. . . .

compound tense (*le temps composé*) A **tense** made up of more than one word: an **auxiliary verb** + the **past participle**, e.g. the **perfect, pluperfect** or **future perfect**.

conditional tense (*le conditionnel*) The **tense** that tells you what <u>*could/would/should happen*</u>: a single word in French, **infinitive stem + imperfect** endings [Unit 18].

conditional perfect tense (*le passé du conditionnel*) A **compound** tense made from the **conditional** tense of the auxiliary *être* or *avoir* + **past participle**. It tells you what <u>*could/would have*</u> happened [Unit 18].

conjunction (*la conjonction*) Words which join two **clauses**, either coordinating conjunctions *et, mais and, but* or subordinating conjunctions *parce que, bien que, quand because, although, when* [Unit 10].

direct object (*un objet direct*) The person or thing acted on directly by the **verb** [Units 5, 12]. See also **indirect object**.

ending (*la terminaison*) Added to a verb **stem** to form **tenses** (*dis – <u>ais</u>*), **adjectives** (*intéress – <u>ante</u>*) or **adverbs** (*vrai – <u>ment</u>*).

future tense (*le futur*) This tense tells you what <u>*will happen*</u> (a single word in French). The **endings** *-ai, -as, -a, -ons, -ez, -ont* are added to the **infinitive** of *-er, -ir* regular verbs (minus *-e* for *-re* verbs) [Unit 11].

future perfect tense (*le futur antérieur*) The future of the auxiliary **verb** + the **past participle** [Unit 11].

immediate future (*le futur immédiat*) To speak about something that <u>*is going to happen*</u> soon: the present tense of *aller to go* + the **infinitive** [Unit 6].

gender (*le genre*) All French **nouns** have a **gender** (masculine or feminine). This is indicated by the **article**: <u>*le*</u> *voyage*; <u>*la*</u> *rencontre* [Unit 1].

imperative (*un impératif*) Used to give an **order**, an **instruction** or to make a **suggestion**. The imperative has no **subject pronoun** [Units 9, 12].

....

imperfect (*un imparfait*) A one-word **tense** describing ongoing past situations and actions or events which happened often in the past. The **endings -ais, -ais, -ait, -ions, -iez, -aient** are added to the **stem** of the first person plural (*nous*) form of the present **tense** of the **verb**: *allais, parlions* (equivalent of *was doing, used to do, would do*) [Unit 14].

....

impersonal verb (*le verbe impersonnel*) A **verb** without a personal **subject**: *il faut*, *il s'agit de*, *il y a*: *It is necessary*, *It concerns*, *There is* ... These expressions cannot be used with another subject [Units 8, 10, 16].

....

indicative mood (*le mode indicatif*) All French **verbs** except those in the **subjunctive** and **imperative** belong to the indicative [Unit 12].

....

indirect object (*un objet indirect*) A **noun**, a group of words or a **pronoun** which goes with a **verb**. It is usually introduced by the **preposition** *to* in English [Units 9, 12]. See also **direct object**.

....

infinitive (*un infinitif*) The main form of the **verb**. It is a single word in French: *habiter, appeler, faire* to live, to call, to do. Infinitives have these **endings** in French: *-er, -ir, -re, -oir, -oire.*

....

interrogative (*un interrogatif*) Used for asking **questions** [Units 1, 2, 4, 6].

interrogative adjective See **adjective**.

interrogative pronoun See **pronoun**.

inversion (*une inversion*) The **verb** and the **subject** change position, usually to ask a **question** [Units 1, 13].

main clause (*la proposition principale*) The main part of a **sentence**. It has a **subject** and a **verb** and may have **objects**. It may be extended by a **subordinate** or a **relative clause**.

modal verbs (*le verbe modal*) **Verbs** which are used to express possibilities: *vouloir, pouvoir, devoir should, might, would, could* [Units 8, 9].

mood of a **verb** (*le mode*): See **indicative, subjunctive, imperative**.

negative (*la négation*) This is often expressed by two words in French: *ne ... pas; ne ... jamais; ne ... plus not, never, no longer*, etc. [Units 1, 4, 11, 12, 13].

noun (*le nom*) Nouns can be **concrete** (things, people, animals, anything tangible), abstract (concepts, ideas or feelings) or proper (names). All French nouns have a **gender**, i.e. they are either masculine or feminine [Unit 1].

passive voice (*la voix passive*) A form of the **verb** which tells us that the **subject** has something done to it by someone/ something else. It is formed from the verb *être* in the appropriate **tense + past participle** [Unit 10]. In French, only the **direct object** of an **active voice verb** can become the **subject** of a passive verb. For English forms such as *He has been given ...* use *on*.

past historic tense (*le passé simple*) A past **tense** only used in writing, never orally, to replace the **perfect** [Unit 17].

past participle (*le participe passé*) Used with **auxiliary verbs** to form **compound tenses**. The commonest **ending** for an

English past participle is -_ed_. In French the past participles of regular -_er_ verbs end in -_é_, -_ir_ verbs in -_i_, -_re_ and -_oir_ verbs in -_u_. The past participle of verbs which take _être_ usually **agrees** in number and **gender** with the **subject** [Units 10, 13]. Past participles can also be used as **adjectives**.

....

perfect tense (_le passé composé_) The usual past **tense** in French. It is a **compound tense**, made up of the **auxiliary verb** _avoir_ or _être_ + the **past participle**. It is used both for the English _have done_ and _did_ (_j'ai fait_). It describes actions that are already completed or finished or which happened at a specific time in the past [Unit 13].

....

phrase (_la locution_) A group of words which does not contain a **verb**. Phrases often begin with a **preposition**: _près de la source_; _au centre_.

....

pluperfect tense (_le plus-que-parfait_) A compound tense formed from the **imperfect** of _avoir_ or _être_ + **past participle** [Unit 15].

....

possessives (_les possessifs_)

possessive adjective (_un adjectif possessif_) Agrees in **gender** and number with the thing possessed, **not with the possessor**: _mon, ma, mes, ton, son, notre, vos, leur_ my, your, his/her, etc. [Unit 2].

possessive pronouns (_le pronom possessif_) A pronoun which replaces the thing possessed: _le mien, le tien, la nôtre, les leurs_, etc. _mine, yours, his/hers_, etc. [Unit 7].

....

preposition (_la préposition_) A word (or group of words) closely connected to a **noun, pronoun** or **verb**. Like **adverbs**, they often indicate _where, when, how_ or _why_: _dans, à, sur, avant, après, avec, pour, de, par_ in, at, on, before, after, with, for, from, of, by [Unit 6].

present participle (*le participe présent*) This part of a **verb** ends in *-ing* in English and *-ant* in French. The present participle can also be used as an **adjective** [Units 3, 6].

present tense (*le présent*) French only has one **present** tense but English has two: *does* and *is doing*. For regular *-er* **verbs** the **endings** are *-e, -es, -e, -ons, -ez, -ent* (according to the *subject: je, tu, il/elle/on, nous, vous, ils/elles*) [Unit 1]. For regular *-ir* verbs the endings are *-is, -is, -it, -issons, -issez, -issent* [Unit 5]. For regular *-re* verbs the **endings** are *-s, -s, -, -ons, -ez, -ent* [Unit 5]. The present tense in French is sometimes also used when talking about **future** actions [Unit 11].

pronoun (*le pronom*) A word that stands in place of a **noun**. It agrees in **gender** and number with the **noun** it replaces.

demonstrative pronouns (*le pronom démonstratif*) *celui(-ci), ceux(-là), celle(-là), celles(-ci)* this, that, these, those; this one, that one, etc. [Unit 5].

emphatic/stressed pronouns (*le pronom fort*) are used after **prepositions** and for emphasis [Units 1, 7].

interrogative pronouns (*le pronom interrogatif*) such as *qui? who?* are used to ask a question [Unit 4].

object pronouns (*pronoms compléments d'objet direct*) Object pronouns can be **direct** and **indirect**. They come before the verb in French. If there is more than one object pronoun, there are strict rules in French about word order [Unit 12].

direct the person(s)/thing(s) acted on by a **verb** [Unit 5].

indirect the person(s)/thing(s) to/for whom/which the action is done [Unit 9].

possessive pronouns (*le pronom possessif*) See **possessives**.

reflexive pronouns (*le pronom réfléchi/réciproque*) are used with **reflexive verbs** showing that people do something to themselves or to one another. The same words are used as for **direct object pronouns**: *me, te, se, nous, vous, se* and they have the same position before the verb [Units 3, 6, 13].

relative pronouns (*le pronom relatif*) link the **main clause** to a **clause** related to a noun in the main clause: *qui, que, dont, lequel,* etc. [Units 11, 16].

compound relative pronouns (*le pronom relatif composé*) are formed when the relative **pronoun** *lequel, laquelle,* etc. comes after the **prepositions** *à* or *de* [Units 11, 16].

subject pronouns (*le pronom sujet*) are the subjects of **verbs** and the verbs agree with them in number and sometimes in gender: *je, tu, il, elle, on, nous, vous, ils, elles* [Unit 1].

....

question (*la question*) There are several ways of asking a question in French [Units 1, 2]. Some of the words which are used to ask questions are **interrogative adjectives** and **interrogative pronouns**. Other question words are *Quand? Où? Comment? Pourquoi?* [Unit 2].

....

reflexive pronouns See under **pronouns**.

....

reflexive verbs (*le verbe pronominal/réciproque*) Verbs where the **subject** and the **object** are the same person, showing that the subject does something to himself/herself (*pronominal*) or that the subject and another person do something to one another (*réciproque*) [Units 3, 6, 13]. See **pronouns**.

....

relative clause (*la proposition relative*) A group of words including a **verb** and its **subject**, related to the **main clause** by a relative **pronoun**.

sentence (*la phrase*) A group of words containing at least one clause, the **main clause**. It usually also has a **subject** and often an **object**.

stem (*la racine*) Part of the **verb** to which the **endings** are added to indicate the **subject**, the **tense** and the **mood**.

subject (*le sujet*) The person or thing that performs the action expressed by the **verb**. See also **subject pronouns**, under **pronouns**.

subjunctive mood (*le mode subjonctif*) A **mood** of the **verb** which only survives in English in a few set expressions, e.g. '*If I <u>were</u> you*', '*Peace <u>be</u> with you*'. In French, the subjunctive **must** be used after the structure *il faut que* and after verbs of necessity, possibility, will, strong desire, emotion, doubt [Units 16, 17].

subordinate clause (*la proposition subordonnée*) A part of a compound sentence which has its own **verb**. It is joined to the **main clause** by a **conjunction** or a **relative pronoun**.

superlative (*le superlatif*) Used to say that something or someone is *the most ...*: *le plus **intelligent**; la plus intéressante; les plus délicieuses*. Often shown in English by adjectives ending in *-est* [Unit 6].

tense (*le temps*) The form of the **verb** that shows when an action was done: **present** [Unit 1], past (**perfect** [Unit 13], **imperfect** [Unit 14], **pluperfect** [Unit 15]), **future** [Unit 11], **conditional** [Unit 18].

transitive verb (*le verbe transitif*) A **verb** which takes a **direct object** is transitive. **Verbs** which cannot take a **direct object** are intransitive. **Verbs** which are transitive in English may be intransitive in French [Units 9, 12].

verb (*le verbe*) A verb is the main word in a sentence. It expresses an action, a state or an event. Verbs change their form according to who or what did the action (**subject**), when the action was done (**tense**) and the purpose of the action (**voice**).

voice (*la voix*) A form of the **verb**. A verb can be in the active or **passive voice**.

active The usual form of the verb showing that the **subject** does something.

passive See passive voice.

Index

References are to units, followed by sections or tasks (e.g. 7:SiiF2):

MP – The Main Points
SiiF – Say it in French
NS – The Next Stage
GS – Getting Started
QC – A Quick Check